The Eurosceptical Reader 2

LEEDS BECKETT UNIVERSITY

Leeds Metropolitan University

17 0364420 X

Also by Martin Holmes

BEYOND EUROPE

THATCHERISM: Scope and Limits, 1983–7

THE EUROSCEPTICAL READER (*editor*)

THE FAILURE OF THE HEATH GOVERNMENT

THE FIRST THATCHER GOVERNMENT: Contemporary Conservatism and Economic Change

THE LABOUR GOVERNMENT, 1974–9: Political Aims and Economic Reality

EUROPEAN INTEGRATION: Scope and Limits

The Eurosceptical Reader 2

Edited by

Martin Holmes
St Hugh's College, Oxford

palgrave

Editorial matter, selection and Introduction © Martin Holmes 2002
For other chapters see Acknowledgements

All rights reserved. No reproduction, copy or transmission of
this publication may be made without written permission.

No paragraph of this publication may be reproduced, copied or
transmitted save with written permission or in accordance with
the provisions of the Copyright, Designs and Patents Act 1988,
or under the terms of any licence permitting limited copying
issued by the Copyright Licensing Agency, 90 Tottenham Court
Road, London W1T 4LP.

Any person who does any unauthorised act in relation to this
publication may be liable to criminal prosecution and civil
claims for damages.

The authors have asserted their rights to be identified
as the authors of this work in accordance with the
Copyright, Designs and Patents Act 1988.

First published 2002 by
PALGRAVE
Houndmills, Basingstoke, Hampshire RG21 6XS and
175 Fifth Avenue, New York, N.Y. 10010
Companies and representatives throughout the world

PALGRAVE is the new global academic imprint of
St. Martin's Press LLC Scholarly and Reference Division and
Palgrave Publishers Ltd (formerly Macmillan Press Ltd).

ISBN 0–333–97375–5 hardback
ISBN 0–333–97376–3 paperback

This book is printed on paper suitable for recycling and
made from fully managed and sustained forest sources.

A catalogue record for this book is available
from the British Library.

Library of Congress Cataloging-in-Publication Data
Eurosceptical reader 2 / edited by Martin Holmes.
        p. cm.
    Includes bibliographical references and index.
    Contents: British influence and the Euro / John Coles — The
Euro and regional divergence in Europe / Tony Thirlwall — British
trade and Europe since the 1960's / Martin Holmes — The UK and
Euroland / Graeme Leach — Euroland and NAFTA compared / Keith
Marsden — The bank that rules Europe / M. Baimbridge, B. Burkitt &
P. Whyman — Has the Euro lived up to expectations? / Wilhelm
Nölling — The myth of Europe / Russell Lewis — Britain, Europe,
and the United States / Oliver Wright — Can self-government
survive? / Nevil Johnson — Separate ways / Lord Shore of Stepney –
– Nice and beyond / Christopher Booker — Aiming for the heart of
Europe / John Bercow.
    ISBN 0–333–97375–5
    1. Great Britain—Relations—Europe. 2. Europe—Relations—
Great Britain. 3. Europe—Politics and government—1989- 4.
European Economic Community. 5. Europe—Economic conditions–
–1945– I. Title: Eurosceptical reader two. II. Holmes, Martin, 1954
Apr. 26–

D1065.G7 E87 2001
940.55—dc21
                                                    2001051019

10   9   8   7   6   5   4   3   2   1
11   10 09 08 07 06 05 04 03 02
Printed in Great Britain by Antony Rowe Ltd, Chippenham, Wiltshire

LEEDS METROPOLITAN
UNIVERSITY
LEARNING CENTRE
1703694420X
97-
CC-3859
317.03
EUR

Contents

v

List of Tables, Figures and Illustrations

Tables

Figures

Illustrations

List of Abbreviations and Acronyms

APEC	Asia Pacific Economic Community
ASEAN	Association of South East Asian Nations
BoE	Bank of England
CAP	Common Agricultural Policy
CBI	Confederation of British Industry
CEPR	Centre for Economic Policy Research
CFP	Common Fisheries Policy
CFSP	Common Foreign and Security Policy
COMECON	Council for Mutual Economic Assistance
CRCE	Centre for Research into Communist Economies
EAGGF	European Agricultural Guidance and Guarantee Fund
EC	European Community
ECB	European Central Bank
ECE	Economic Commission for Europe
ECJ	European Court of Justice
EEA	European Economic Area
EEC	European Economic Community
EERU	European Economies Research Unit
EFTA	European Free Trade Area/Association
EMS	European Monetary System
EMU	Economic and Monetary Union/European Monetary Union
ERDF	European Regional Development Fund
ERM	Exchange Rate Mechanism
ESCB	European System of Central Banks
ESF	European Social Fund
EU	European Union
FCO	Foreign and Commonwealth Office
FDI	foreign direct investment
FEER	fundamental equilibrium exchange rate
FET	five economic tests
FO	Foreign Office
FSA	Financial Services Authority
GATT	General Agreement on Tariffs and Trade
GDP	gross domestic product
GNP	gross national product

HICP	harmonised index of consumer prices
HDI	Human Development Index
HMG	Her Majesty's Government
HMT	Her Majesty's Treasury
IGC	Inter-Governmental Conference
IMF	International Monetary Fund
IoD	Institute of Directors
ILO	International Labour Organisation
IT	information technology
MEP	Member of the European Parliament
MP	Member of Parliament
MPC	Monetary Policy Committee (Bank of England)
NAFTA	North American Free Trade Area
NAIRU	non-accelerating inflation rate of unemployment
NATO	North Atlantic Treaty Organisation
NIC	newly industrialised country
NIESR	National Institute for Economic and Social Research
NUTS	Nomenclature of Statistical Territorial Units (France)
OECD	Organisation for Economic Co-operation and Development
PCY	per capita income
ppp	purchasing power parity
PPS	purchasing power standard
PSE	producer subsidy equivalent
QMV	qualified majority voting
R&D	research and development
TUC	Trades Union Congress
UKIP	United Kingdom Independence Party
UNCTAD	United Nations Conference on Trade and Development
UNDP	United Nations Development Programme
VAR	variable
VAT	value added tax
WTO	World Trade Organisation

Acknowledgements

I wish to thank all the contributors to this book for permission to reprint articles or speeches which had already entered the public domain. I am particularly indebted to those contributors who reduced in length previously published longer articles which could not appear in full in this voulme because of necessary space constraints.

I would also like to thank the Principal and Fellows of St Hugh's College for providing an atmosphere conducive to scholarship and appreciative of research.

Alison Howson at the publishers handled the manuscript with customary courtesy and efficiency and I am grateful to her.

Needless to say, any errors in the following pages are my responsibility alone.

MARTIN HOLMES

St Hugh's College, Oxford
June 2001

Notes on Contributors

Dr Mark Baimbridge is Lecturer in Economics at the University of Bradford and European Economies Research Unit's Director of Research. He co-authored *What 1992 Really Means: Single Market or double cross?* (1989), *From Rome to Maastricht* (1992), *There is an Alternative* (1996) and *A Price Not Worth Paying: The economic cost of EMU* (1997) for the Campaign for an Independent Britain. He has published over 100 articles, primarily concerning Britain's relationship with the EU, in learned and current affairs journals in economics, politics and social policy. He is a frequent contributor and commentator on economic issues to radio and in newspapers, including the *Sunday Times*, the *Sunday Telegraph*, the *Financial Times* and the *Guardian*.

John Bercow was elected MP for Buckingham on 1 May 1999 with a majority of 12,386. He was educated at Finchley Manorhill School and the University of Essex where he graduated in 1985 with First Class Honours in Government. From 1986–7, he served as National Chairman of the Federation of Conservative Students and subsequently as student head of the Conservative Collegiate Forum. After a spell of merchant banking, he joined Rowland Sallingbury Casey, the public affairs arm of the Saatchi and Saatchi group, in 1988. There he rose from a junior executive to a board director in five years. Meanwhile he became a Conservative Councillor in the London Borough of Lambeth in 1986 (until 1990) and served from 1987 to 1989 as Deputy Leader of the 21-strong Conservative Opposition group. He contested Motherwell South in the 1987 General Election and Bristol South in 1992.

Christopher Booker, through his weekly column in the *Sunday Telegraph*, is one of the most trenchant and well-informed critics of the European Union system of government and its growing impact on British life. He has been particularly identified with his campaign to highlight the regulatory excesses of Brussels and Whitehall bureaucracy, as exemplified in the contradictions of the EU's single market or the social and ecological disaster created by the Common Fisheries Policy. He has extended this analysis in two books, co-written with Dr Richard North: *The Mad Officials* (1994) and *The Castle of Lies* (1996), a unique picture of how the EU system of government operates in practice. Educated at Shrewsbury and Cambridge University, he was founding editor of the satirical magazine *Private Eye*. He has also written various works of contemporary history, including *The Neophiliacs* (1969), *The Seventies* (1980), *The Games War* (1981) on the Moscow Olympics, and *A Looking Glass Tragedy* (1997).

Dr Brian Burkitt is Senior Lecturer in Economics at the University of Bradford and Director of EERU. He wrote two widely quoted reports, *Britain and the European Economic Community: An economic re-appraisal*, and *Britain and the European Economic Community: A political re-appraisal* at the time of the 1975 referendum on EEC membership. He is also author of *Trade Unions and Wages* (1975 and 1980), *Trade Unions and the Economy* (1979), *Radical Political Economy* (1984) and over 150 articles in learned journals. He has previously co-authored *What 1992 Really Means: Single market or double cross?* (1989), *From Rome to Maastricht* (1992), *There is an Alternative* (1996) and *A Price Not Worth Paying: The economic cost of EMU* (1997). He is a frequent contributor, and commentator on economic issues, to television and radio programmes, including *Newsnight* and *A Week In Politics*.

Sir John Coles was, until late 1997, Head of the British Diplomatic Service and Permanent Under-Secretary of the Foreign office. In a career spanning 37 years, he held posts in the Foreign office, the Cabinet office, Cairo, Dubai and Khartoum, and served as British High Commissioner in Australia and British Ambassador in Jordan. From 1977 to 1980, he worked in the United Kingdom mission to the European Communities in Brussels and, from 1981 to 1984, he was private secretary to the Prime Minister, Margaret Thatcher.

Dr Martin Holmes is Lecturer in politics at St Hugh's College, Oxford, and Director of the College of Business Administration (UNL), Oxford. He is the author of *Beyond Europe* (1993) and *European Integration: Scope and limits* (2001). He was Co-Chairman of the Bruges Group 1993–2001, and edited the first publication of *The Eurosceptical Reader* in 1996.

Nevil Johnson is an Emeritus Fellow of Nuffield College, Oxford, where he held a professorial fellowship from 1965 to 1996. He has specialised in the study of political institutions, especially in Western Europe, and has written extensively on government and politics in both Britain and Germany. Amongst his books are *In Search of the Constitution: Reflections on state and society in Britain* (1997) and *State and Government in the Federal Republic of Germany* (1982). He was a member of the Economic and Social Research Council from 1981 to 1987 and a part-time Civil Service Commissioner from 1982 to 1985.

Graeme Leach joined the Institute of Directors (IoD), as their Chief Economist, in 1998. Graeme has written widely on the euro and EU-related economic issues. His publications include 'The UK and the euro – better out than in' and 'EU membership – what's the bottom line?' He is also a frequent speaker and media commentator arguing against UK participation in the euro. Prior to joining the IoD, he was Associate Director at the Henley Centre, analysing all aspects of future economic and social change. In 1998 he was awarded the WWP Atticus Award for original published thinking. He has also worked as an economic adviser to the Scottish Provident Investment group.

Russell Lewis was formerly Director of the European Foundation. He has been a prominent and distinguished commentator on European affairs for over 20 years, serving as a leader writer on the *Daily Mail*, Director of the Bow Group, and General Director of the Institute of Economic Affairs. His much acclaimed *Master Eurocrat: The making of Jaques Delors* was published by the Bruges Group in 1991. He also authored the Bruges Group Occasional Paper No. 21, *Delors, Germany and the Future of Europe*.

Keith Marsden is an economic consultant to several UN agencies, based in Geneva. He was previously an operations adviser at the World Bank, an expert and senior economist in the International Labour Office, and an economist in British industry. He has undertaken studies and advisory missions in over 50 countries, and has written numerous articles on economic policy for the *International Labour Review, Finance and Development* and the *Wall Street Journal*. Other recent publications include *Miracle or Mirage?: Britain's economy seen from abroad* (Centre for Policy Studies, 1997), *Is Tax Competition Harmful?* (European Policy Forum, 1998), *Handicap not Trump Card* (Centre for Policy Studies, 1999) and *The Five Per Cent Solution* (Centre for Policy Studies, 2000).

Professor Dr Wilhelm Nölling teaches in the economics department at the University of Hamburg and is a consultant to government and business. He is a former member of the Bundesbank Council.

Peter Shore was elected Labour MP for Stepney in 1964 before Ministerial appointments as Secretary of State for Economic Affairs and Secretary of State for Trade and Industry. In opposition he served as Front Bench spokesman for Europe and later Foreign Affairs. Created a Life Peer in 1997 as Lord Shore of Stepney, he died in September 2001.

Professor Anthony Thirlwall has been Professor of Applied Economics at the University of Kent at Canterbury since 1976. He was educated at the University of Leeds and Clark University, USA, and from 1963 to 1964 was a research student at Christ's College, Cambridge. He has published extensively in the fields of regional economics and the theory of economic growth and development. His major books on these topics include *Regional Growth and Unemployment in the United Kingdom* (with R. Dixon), *Industrialisation and Deindustrialisation in the UK* (with S. Bazen), *Economic Growth and the Balance of Payments Constraint* (with J. McCombie), and *Growth and Development with Special Reference to Developing Economies* (6th edition).

Dr Philip Whyman is Lecturer in Economics at the University of Central Lancashire and Honorary Research Fellow of EERU. He co-authored *There is an Alternative* (1996) and *A Price Not Worth Paying: The economic cost of EMU* (1997). He has published widely in learned journals and a number of policy papers, including submissions to the House of Lords Select Committee on the European Communities (1996) and the House of Commons Treasury Select Committee (1998). His research interests include the impact of European integration upon labour markets, fiscal federalism, international monetary developments and the UK's future relationship with the EU. In addition, he has written extensively on the economic development of Sweden.

Sir Oliver Wright GCMG, GCVO, DSC was educated at Christ's College, Cambridge, and served with the Royal Navy in World War II. He joined HM Diplomatic Service in 1945. He served in New York, Bucharest, Singapore, Berlin and Pretoria. Sir Oliver was Private Secretary to Prime Ministers the Rt Hon Sir Alec Douglas-Home and the Rt Hon Harold Wilson. He was appointed Ambassador to Denmark, 1966–9; seconded to the Home Office as UK Representative to the Northern Ireland Government 1969–70; Chief Clerk, HM Diplomatic Service, 1970–2; Deputy Under-Secretary of State, FCO, 1972–5; Ambassador to the Federal Republic of Germany, 1975–81; retired, then reappointed, Ambassador to Washington, 1982–6. Sir Oliver has served on the boards of directors of many blue-chip companies and has been appointed Distinguished Visiting Professor at the Universities of South Carolina and at Washington University, St Louis. From 1988 to 1992 he was chairman of the Advisory Board of the Institute of United States Studies. He was knighted in 1974.

Introduction

It is axiomatic to state that Europe is the biggest political issue in contemporary Britain. The 'great debate' of the 1970s was seemingly ended with the decisive two-to-one majority in the 1975 referendum; indeed Euroscepticism was dormant, subdued or outside the political mainstream for the next decade. Its rebirth was a slow process until Mrs Thatcher's Bruges speech in 1988 which transformed the issue from sideshow to centre stage. The short-term political consequences led directly to the overthrow of Mrs Thatcher who found herself outmanoeuvred by her cabinet which favoured greater European integration. But the long-term consequences have been positive for Eurosceptics. Euroscepticism has become a permanent feature of the political landscape and opposition to a European single currency – which helped to precipitate Mrs Thatcher's removal – has restricted the integrationist impulses of the Blair government. Even the 2001 General Election landslide majority of 167 is no guarantee that Mr Blair will be able to transform public opinion to favour the abolition of the pound.

Well over a decade on from Bruges, 'Europe' is the most contentious domestic political issue. It now transcends party politics so that cross-party coalitions have emerged. Both the major parties have been split over the issue. The initial hostile reaction to the speech in 1988 has been replaced by an intensive and wide-ranging debate concerning the future of Europe. The former diplomat Sir Roy Denman revealed the devastating effect the speech had upon the British Establishment when he admitted on 'The Poisoned Chalice' (a BBC documentary on the history of Britain's relationship with Europe) that the speech had made Euroscepticism respectable and had unleashed a torrent of opposition against the federal process.

The Eurosceptical Reader 2, like its predecessor published in 1996, is part of that torrent. The contributions which follow all express disapproval and doubt about the integration process. Some favour EU membership while rejecting the single currency; others favour renegotiation of Britain's relationship with the EU; others besides recommend withdrawal. But different preferred solutions do not obscure a commonality of belief that the status quo of EU membership, leading inexorably to a monetary and fiscal Euroland, is undesirable and should be democratically resisted. Similarly, Tony Blair's advocacy of a 'superpower' Europe is conceptually repudiated.

The outcome of the 2001 General Election was an undoubted setback for euroscepticism, given the heavy defeat of the one major party which enthusiastically opposed the euro. Nor was the impressive performance of UKIP in the 1999 European Parliamentary elections sustained in June 2001. With the prospect of New Labour in power for another decade after its 2001 victory the likelihood of withdrawal from the EU is currently remote. Nor is renegotiation on Mr Blair's agenda. But there is no need to panic. The eurosceptic cause had already become disconnected from party politics in previous general elections, as was reflected by public opinion polls which rejected the euro by 70 per cent to 30 per cent, while also rejecting the Conservatives as a governmental alternative to New Labour. Indeed as Dominic Cumming of Business for Sterling has rightly argued (*The Times*, 31 May 2001), 'if the No campaign were to be right wing and based on sovereignty and the Union Jack, while the other side focus on jobs and living standards, we will lose'. Similarly Professor Patrick Minford has advocated (*Daily Telegraph*, 11 June 2001) a backseat role for the Conservatives in any forthcoming referendum as an all-party 'No' campaign would be better able to maximise the vote to preserve the pound. This approach reflects the strategy of newspapers such as *The Times* and the *Sun* which favoured both Blair re-election and the rejection of economic and monetary union.

Thus the crucial lesson for eurosceptics from the 2001 election is that millions of Labour voters, and some Liberal Democrats no doubt, must not be dissuaded from a referendum 'No' vote by the Conservative Party being too closely associated with the campaign to save the pound. The 'No' campaign must be cross-party, reflecting the way that the issue transcends rather than reinforces party political affiliation. Any 'No' campaign must be a broad church embracing both the Conservatives, who stress sovereignty and political opposition to the euro, and Labour voters fearful of the economic and social consequences for employment, public spending priorities, and mortgages. The unpopularity of the Conservatives in 2001 cannot be allowed to obstruct the maintenance of the strong opinion poll lead to retain the pound. Public opinion, including Labour voters, which manacled Mr Blair's first administration so that no referendum was held, can do the same to the second administration. Or should Mr Blair take the plunge, the 'No' campaign must win the argument, and the vote, by broadening rather than narrowing its appeal. The referendum cannot become the surrogate general election that New Labour will seek to contrive.

With this long-term perspective in mind, the following contributions tackle both the economic and the political objections to Britain's ever closer union with the EU. Sir John Coles argues that while British influence in Europe may be diminished by the retention of the pound, around the world British influence is enhanced. In the age of globalisation it would be folly to sacrifice this wider economic reach and political clout for a seat around the ECB table where Britain's voice may rarely prevail. The fatal flaws in the ECB's mandate, structure and lack of accountability also feature in Drs Baimbridge, Burkitt and Whyman's dissection of the Euroland experiment. Professor Tony Thirlwall critically examines the regional dimension of the single currency with its explicit threat to employment and growth, which advocates of the euro have unconvincingly denied or strenuously avoided. The underperformance of the euro since 1999 is explained by Professor Wilholm Nölling, whose monetary policy credentials include membership of the Bundesbank Council, as well as academic economic research at Hamburg University. To Professor Nölling the euro's external weakness reflects its structural deficiencies.

Graeme Leach, the Chief Economist of the Institute of Directors, tackles the complexities of the 'convergence criteria' for euro membership, concluding that any future cyclical economic convergence is likely to be very temporary – as well as irrelevant to the main argument that structural economic divergence between the UK and euroland should preclude the abolition of the pound. Keith Marsden evaluates the lack of economic flexibility and dynamism in the EU compared to the private-sector-driven economic success of North America; that Britain's economy now conforms more to the North American model should recommend extreme caution about further economic integration with the EU's 'Social Model'. Finally, in the economics section, the editor of this volume traces the debate about Britain's trading and commercial relationship with Europe since the 1960s, arguing that prosperity depends on global – rather than European regional – trading and investment opportunities.

In recent years the pace of EU political integration has been remorseless. Treaty after treaty has tilted the balance of power away from the parliaments of the member states and towards the institutions of the EU. Nor is this process completed as the build-up to the 2004 Inter-Governmental Conference gathers pace. Russell Lewis analyses the historic context of European integration and how Europe's commercial and cultural success has been based on diversity and originality rather than on conformity and union.

As far as the UK is concerned, John Bercow questions the wisdom of recent British governments who have sought the 'heart of Europe' by making concessions to the EU in the hope of future favourable treatment or immediate political approval. Such a strategy has signally failed, as John Major's government discovered. Additionally the ratchet of federal integration associated with the Nice Treaty is chronicled by Christopher Booker, who discerns an ultimate parting of the ways if Britain is to maintain self-government and if the EU is to become a fully-fledged federation. This theme is also critically discussed by Nevil Johnson who focuses on the ideological dimensions of European integration including its increasingly strident anti-Americanism. Indeed, it may be argued that 'Europeanism' is an ideology – with supranational integration an end in itself – as the EU acquires superpower status. The same theme concerns Sir Oliver Wright who reviews the damage that Britain's immersion into a federal Europe would do to our wider interests both in the Americas and beyond. Lord Shore of Stepney provides what the April 2001 edition of *Eurofacts* described as the 'best presentation ever of the eurosceptical case'; ranging over the last 40 years, Lord Shore catalogues the erosion of democracy at the hands of British governments intent on forging a European destiny.

Looking ahead eurosceptics must overcome the setback of the landslide 2001 General Election victory by New Labour. Whatever the future of British politics in strictly party political terms, the eurosceptical case can only grow stronger as long as the pound is retained and, as a consequence, democratic self-government is valued. For the time being at least, such a strategy may be one of damage limitation, but it is no less valuable for that.

Martin Holmes
Oxford

Part I
Economic Euroscepticism

1
British Influence and the Euro

John Coles

If we want to avoid Britain losing influence, it is better to stay out of the single currency. We shall forgo the influence that joining would give us over the economies of the countries that have adopted the euro but avoid the much greater influence that they would acquire over ours. On the vast amount of European Union business that is unconnected with the euro, we shall be just as influential as before. In the world at large, we shall be much more influential if we keep our distinctive currency, assets and policies. By staying out, we avoid a major surrender of national decision-making powers, preserve the functions of the national institutions such as government and parliament that we know and understand and thus sustain our senses of belonging to Britain.

The sound bite debate

If this chapter stopped with these assertions, it would be typical of much of the debate about the euro. Propositions are asserted rather than analysed. The debate is riddled with sound bites. Unless Britain adopts the single European currency 'we shall lose influence'. So argue many of the advocates of entry. British entry, we are told, will be 'good for jobs', 'good for growth', 'good for consumers'. Not to enter would be a 'dereliction of national responsibility'. To think that we could stay out and still make a major contribution to other European Union business is 'to live in cloud-cuckoo land'. Those who advocate non-entry are dismissed as 'Little Englanders'.

The air is full of assertions but these will not win the debate. It is already too deeply rooted for that. By the time a referendum is held (if it is held), the arguments will have been analysed too thoroughly for sound bites and truth-doctors (why not give spin-doctors their proper name?) to carry the day.

The New Europe group, which is pro-European and in favour of constructive British membership of the EU but believes we shall be better off outside the single currency, aims to ensure that all the issues involved in this complex problem are fully presented and fully debated. Despite the government's claims (on which more below), the matter cannot be settled by economic tests alone. The majority of people opposed to entry probably base their opposition on political grounds – on the belief that, by entering, we would surrender so much national decision-making power that even if there would be some economic benefits – which is by no means certain – they should not be bought at so high a price. They sense, correctly, that the issues are bigger than the convenience for individuals of not having to change money when travelling in Europe and the convenience for firms of reducing foreign exchange transactions. They note, too, the divided views among economists about the other claimed economic benefits. They feel that the character of our political system and, to an extent, of our country, is involved.

This chapter is concerned with the question of British influence: whether it will be reduced or not by a decision to adopt or not adopt the euro. The answer to that question cannot by itself settle whether we should join. It is only one of the factors but it is important. Through influence, we defend and promote the interests of the citizen and try to make the world a better and a safer place. So we need to assess carefully both the immediate impact of entry on our influence and how it would be affected in the longer term. It is worth noting at the outset that, even if it could be demonstrated that Britain would lose influence, this could still be a price worth paying if it meant that worse things were thereby avoided.

It is not a straightforward matter. Our influence might indeed be weakened in some areas but it is the overall impact that counts. There are three questions:

- How will our influence in the EU itself be affected?
- What will the impact be on our influence in the world more generally?
- What of our influence over our domestic affairs?

Britain in Europe

Nowadays the EU covers a wide of range of domestic and international policy. The impact of the British decision on the euro will not be the same in all areas.

Clearly, if we stay out, we shall not be a member of the so-called Euro-11, the group of Finance Ministers from the countries that have adopted the single currency. This now holds meetings, from which non-signatories like Britain are excluded, before each full meeting of EU Finance Ministers. It is a new body. It is early days to say how much impact it will have on EU business. On issues that relate purely to the single currency, it will certainly have, together with the European Central Bank, the decisive voice. It could, as time goes on, acquire broader economic power if, as many believe, the single currency arrangements are, in due course, buttressed by central control of taxation and other areas of economic policy. The French Finance Minister has already referred to the Euro-11 as the 'economic government of Europe'. His description is interesting further evidence of the trend towards a central government but as it stands it is greatly exaggerated. The Euro-11 has no power whatsoever over the economies of the majority of European countries.

But it is reasonable to think of the Euro-11 as the putative economic government of those countries which operate a single currency. Does it matter if we are not in it? If we joined the single currency we would be able to cast one weighted vote in the then Euro-12 to help determine the economic policies of France, Germany, Italy and others, which we cannot do today. But note well: we should then have only one weighted vote out of 12 in the determination of the economic policies of Britain. We would thus have acquired marginally more influence over the economic policies of others at the price of a major transfer of influence over our own economic affairs. Bear in mind, too, that by joining the club we would risk impairing the success of our 'Anglo-Saxon' economy by providing fresh openings for pressure on us to adopt features of the much less successful 'Continental' model.

Some advocates of British membership of the euro argue that, unless we join, we cannot expect to have significant influence over other areas of EU activity, those areas that are outside the reach of the Euro-11. There is a hint of blackmail in this argument. And it is rather familiar. In the last couple of decades, we have often heard the more or less muted threat that, unless we sign up to a particular EU project, we shall be made to pay a price elsewhere. Experience shows that such threats are part of the diplomatic game and need not be taken seriously. In the real world, when our partners wish to take advantage of British assets, they will seek to do so whether or not we give up the pound. They will always need us – as a major economy and a major trading power, as a country with a serious defence capability, special international experience, acknowledged diplomatic skills and so on. These assets will remain whether we join the euro or not.

Moreover; the EU is not a free-for-all. It is regulated by treaty. Respect for the British opt-out on the single currency is a treaty obligation for all the signatories of Maastricht. The Single Market, trade policy, foreign and defence policy and many other EU policies are determined by treaty. The suggestion that we shall be in some way debarred from playing a full role in these areas because we have not adopted the euro is one of the less serious (and more desperate) arguments of the euro-advocates. Most EU business unconnected with the single currency will continue to be determined by the familiar process of hard-nosed negotiation and bargaining to which we are well accustomed and where it is economic and political weight and diplomatic skills that determine the outcome, not whether we have signed up to some unconnected project at present in fashion.

Foreign and defence policy in the EU

One specific version of the threat theory described above is that, unless we agree to join the euro, we shall be increasingly sidelined in such matters as the expansion of EU membership and the formation of EU foreign and defence policy. But these are all matters which are handled in their own right by the EU, not the Euro-11, and in accordance with established procedures, not least those of the European Council in which Britain has a full voice. Nor is it imaginable that our European partners would want to exclude us from these activities. They need us to help solve the complex and weighty problems involved in the EU's eastern expansion and to help pay for it. They need British foreign policy and defence assets more generally if the EU is to pursue credible international activity.

These areas – foreign policy and defence – may present an increasingly difficult dilemma for Britain in the future. It depends on how they develop. The tension between the majority of member states who wish them to become matters of sole EU responsibility and those who believe that the ultimate decision-making power should rest with national governments is of long standing and is unlikely to disappear.

Foreign policy in the EU

Few would argue that the Common Foreign and Security Policy has been a conspicuous success so far. Since the initiation of 'European political cooperation', the 1970s forerunner of the CFSP, the EU has managed to do some useful common work in areas such as observance of elections. However, on the major foreign policy issues it has rarely done much more than publish laboriously negotiated joint statements setting out the Union's position. The statements have usually represented the lowest common denominator of EU opinion (since consensus was required) and were rarely followed by meaningful action. There was no capacity for sustained and creative diplomacy as opposed to public position taking, and no power-projection capability, without which diplomacy is often hamstrung.

But the fundamental problem has been more serious: the interests of the member states have often not been sufficiently common to make viable the pursuit of a genuinely common foreign policy. Examples are legion. It suffices to recall European disarray in 1986 when President Reagan asked for support for US air-strikes on Libya, the deeply divided EU response to Iraq's invasion of Kuwait in 1990 (and to subsequent developments in the Gulf) and the unfortunate decision in 1991 to recognise the independence of Croatia and Slovenia, with the grudging acquiescence but against the better judgement of some member states. To date, the CFSP has been largely directed at situations on the (broadly conceived) borders of the EU – in Eastern Europe and Russia, the Balkans and the Mediterranean. This reflects the reality that there is more likely to be a convergence of member states' interests close to home than elsewhere in the world where those interests often diverge widely. But even on our borders there has been plenty of evidence of disagreement.

The response of many in the EU to these difficulties is to argue for the increased centralisation of foreign policy, the creation of new machinery and procedures at the centre, the provision of new resources for EU diplomacy and further limitation of the power of individual member states to pursue independent foreign policies. They have made a good deal of headway. (In describing this, some of the jargon is unavoidable. Readers who have no appetite for it could skip the rest of this paragraph and the next two.) The 1991 Maastricht Treaty provided for 'common positions' of the Union to be adopted on a particular area or issue. Unanimity was to be required for the adoption of a common position but thereafter 'implementation' of that position could be by Qualified Majority Voting: i.e. it could proceed against the wishes of a minority of member states. Of course, the means to be adopted to achieve an agreed aim are often highly controversial.

The 1997 Amsterdam Treaty went further and introduced mechanisms which make it harder for a country, when it is in a minority, to block a particular foreign and security policy acceptable to the majority. The treaty gave the European Council the power to define, by consensus, 'common strategies' in areas where member states had interests in common. But Qualified Majority Voting would then apply when adopting or implementing joint actions, common positions or the taking of any other decisions on the basis of a common strategy. Recognising that, for the time being at any rate, a minority of member states cannot be persuaded to give up entirely their independent power of decision-making on foreign policy, Amsterdam also introduced the concept of a qualified abstention whereby a member state can make a formal declaration which allows it not to apply the decision itself, even though it is binding on the other states in the EU.

If a member state declares that for important and stated reasons of national policy it intends to oppose the adoption of a decision to be taken by Qualified Majority Voting, then a vote shall not be taken but the Council (i.e. foreign ministers) may, by a qualified majority vote, request that the matter be referred to the European Council (i.e. heads of state and government) for a decision which then has to be taken by unanimity.

In practice, this means that Britain could, if it wished, block the adoption of a policy, provided it was prepared to stand out in isolation at all stages of the proceedings and resist all the pressure that would be applied by the other member states and, perhaps, sections of the public and the media, to conform with the majority view.

Amsterdam also provided for the appointment of a High Representative of the CFSP. Xavier Solana, the former NATO Secretary-General, has now taken up this post where he will be assisted by a new Policy Planning and Early Warning Unit.

That is what the CFSP has come to. For the time being, it falls short of a single European foreign policy but only just. The Union has given itself the power to 'define and implement a common foreign and security policy covering all areas of foreign and security policy' and member states are required 'to support that policy actively and unreservedly'. It is only because unanimity is required for common strategies and because there is a right of abstention in specified circumstances that individual countries retain a measure of independence in their foreign policy.

Whether it all stops there, or whether at some point in the future member states will lose their independence in foreign policy entirely, is an open question. Much will depend on the experience of operating the Amsterdam provisions, whether Mr Solana operates by consensus or is more ambitious, whether he tries to take on part of the role of national foreign ministers (he will be 'taking the bread off their plates', according to Sir David Hannay in a recent issue of *Prospect* magazine), whether member states are prepared to use the implied veto which Amsterdam gives them, and so on. Partly, too, it will depend on the way the EU handles real-life situations. Past experience suggests that, where serious national interests are at stake, no member state is likely to allow itself to be over-handicapped by arcane procedures.

If Britain decides not to join the single currency, there are no direct implications for its influence on the CFSP. It will have every right to take part in the treaty procedures. The interests of the other member states will require British participation. No other country can bring to the table Britain's combination of permanent membership of the UN Security Council, membership of the Group of Eight, significant influence in Washington, a leading role in NATO and the Commonwealth, serious armed forces and world-wide interests and experience.

In that sense, British influence on the EU's external policies will be unaffected by the decision on the euro. But the introduction of the single currency is the biggest step so far towards a central government of Europe. If the centralising tendencies of the EU continue unchecked in the coming years and indeed if the CFSP moves any closer to a single European foreign policy, then the independent British voice will be increasingly muffled, with consequences for our influence in the rest of the world (see below).

The CFSP is an area where successive British governments have wished to play an active and constructive role. It obviously makes sense for member states to cooperate to the maximum possible extent to achieve a common approach to international issues. The weight of the EU, thus applied, is likely to be more effective than the actions of individual member states. In situations close to its borders, for example in Russia or Turkey, the Union should usually be able to pursue agreed policies for it is hard to see how the interests of member states can diverge significantly in such cases (though Bosnia is a constant reminder that serious problems can still arise).

Most of the difficulties that have arisen in the past have been due to an unwillingness to recognise that where interests are not common, or at least similar, there is little to be gained by attempts to pressurise countries into adopting a common stance. As others have pointed out, the most successful organisations, like NATO and the World Trade Organisation, operate by consensus. They are more decisive than the

EU. The Amsterdam arrangements are likely to put considerable strain on internal consensus. Perhaps they already diverge too far from that principle. Certainly any British government that agreed to concede yet further foreign policy powers to the centre would be surrendering a good part of the influence which comes from having an independent foreign policy.

Defence policy in the EU

The moves in recent years to give the Union a defence policy also have significance for British influence. The Maastricht Treaty referred to 'the eventual framing of a common defence policy, which might in time lead to a common defence'. This wording was so unspecific that it attracted little controversy at the time. Yet it contained the seeds of a departure from the traditional policy of relying on NATO in defence matters. Unsurprisingly, because each new intergovernmental conference sees further attempts to promote integration, the Amsterdam Treaty a few years later provided for 'the progressive framing of a common defence policy', thus making actual what at Maastricht had been futuristic. It gave the EU the power to 'avail itself' of Western European Union assets to implement EU decisions and actions that had defence implications. It further provided that, in humanitarian and rescue tasks, peacekeeping tasks and tasks of combat forces in crisis management, including peace-making, there should be a European structure of decision-making that could act when the United States and Canada (our NATO partners) did not wish to become involved militarily.

In 1998 the British and French governments took things further by agreeing that the EU must have the capacity for autonomous action, backed up by credible military force. Thus, we have moved a consider-able distance from the earlier British policy that insisted that only NATO should have responsibility for collective defence. However, the two governments did stipulate that any new defence arrangement for Europe should be entirely intergovernmental and that there should be no involvement of the European Commission, European Parliament or European Court. It remains to be seen how widely that view is shared in the EU and whether it can be sustained over time.

The ability to deploy sizeable, highly professional and well-equipped armed forces is a crucial element in British influence abroad. Should that ability ever become limited by the creation of European armed forces, subsuming national forces and subject to central EU direction, then British influence overseas would be sharply reduced. Romano Prodi, the new President of the Commission, has expressed his belief in the need for a European Army and he is by no means alone in his approach. But it seems unlikely that there will be serious moves in this direction for some years yet. We can be certain, in view of the quality, experience and reputation of the armed forces of Britain, that a decision not to join the single currency will in no way impair the ability of British governments to influence defence activity in the EU. The EU countries are not likely to embark on military activity except for the weightiest reasons. To deprive themselves of the British contribution in such circumstances would be unthinkable folly.

It thus seems reasonably clear that, if we remain outside the single currency, we shall forego the influence that could be obtained by being a member of the Euro-11 but shall avoid that body gaining influence over our own economy. Our ability to influence other areas of the EU's policies, especially its external policies, is unlikely to be affected.

Britain and the world

A curious feature of the discussion about British influence and the euro is that it is usually confined to the impact of the eventual decision on our influence within and upon the EU itself. Such eurocentrism is misleading. Much British influence in the world has little or no connection with the Union. Unlike all other member states except France, Britain's assets, interests and influence are spread worldwide. There is no region of the world from which we could withdraw without material damage to our interests or a feeling that we were abandoning people whom we had an obligation to help (or both). We are, of course, no longer a global power but we have global interests and responsibilities, the latter deriving from our permanent seat on the UN Security Council, our membership of the G8 and our possession of dependent territories.

We have a worldwide network of diplomatic posts, the British Council with its extensive spread of overseas offices, the BBC World Service and BBC World television with their audiences of millions, and a large aid programme. British firms and the City of London are active across the globe, as are British non-governmental organisations. The British armed forces have a greater reach and capability than most. We are more active in conflict prevention and international problem-solving than most other countries. It is these assets, coupled with less tangible ones such as the English language and respect for our international experience, that enable us to exert an influence on world affairs which, though not as great as it was, is still substantial and is frequently underestimated, not least by the British themselves.

Very little, if any, of this influence stems from our EU membership. There are, of course, cases where we act together with our European partners to carry out a particular piece of business in a third country. That can be useful. But the further you get from Europe, the less likely it is that the EU itself will be exerting significant influence. In most of Asia, Africa and Latin America, our influence stems from our national assets, not from our EU membership. The Middle East is sometimes cited as a case where collective EU action has had a significant impact. But the truth is that that impact has been very limited. The main players continue to be the US, Israel, the Palestinians and a few of the Arab countries. In most of the Middle East, Britain's influence owes almost nothing to the EU.

Outside the EU, the UK's key relationship is, of course, with the United States. Our interest in sustaining that relationship is huge because of the very significant two-way trade and investment, because of the benefits we derive in the defence and intelligence fields and because it makes obvious sense to be as close as possible to the one country with the resources, the assets and the will to make an impact across the globe.

It is sometimes suggested that British influence in Washington is linked to our readiness to participate constructively in the political and economic integration of Europe. Reality suggests that there is no such link. It is perfectly true that for some years US administrations have favoured the further integration of Europe, usually without defining what they mean by that phrase, and State Department comment sometimes reflects that policy. But, in nearly four decades of diplomatic work, I have never heard an American official make the conditional link described above and, on practical issues, I saw no evidence of such a link. It barely needs saying that Margaret Thatcher's influence in Washington, when Prime Minister, owed nothing to her contribution to the integration of the EU. The same probably goes for any other British Prime Minister. To those who observed meetings at President/Prime Minister level at first hand, it was obvious that British influence depended on our readiness to give America practical support where it mattered, our international experience, the familiarity and ease of the relationship and our shared values, not on our EU role.

Some assert that, unless we join the single currency, our world influence will be reduced. By cutting ourselves off from a major European project, it is claimed, we shall cause other countries to doubt our commitment to the EU which, in turn, will limit our standing in the eyes of the world and make Britain less credible as an international actor and less attractive as a place for foreign investment. Yet there is no sign so far that our failure to join the euro has reduced foreign investment. It is most unlikely that it will do so since investors are influenced by the state of our economy, the conditions for doing business here and their capacity to export from Britain rather (usually) than the currency in which they conduct their business. For the majority of investors it is important that we remain a member of the Single Market but our membership will be unaffected by our decision on the euro.

As to our international standing, a decision not to enter the single currency is most unlikely to affect it adversely. We can make that decision and remain a permanent member of the Security Council, a member of the G8, a leading member of NATO, a leading country of the Commonwealth, a country with worldwide assets and influence.

The obverse is more likely. If we do enter the euro, our global influence is likely to be reduced. Surprising as it may seem to those who have watched the fluctuating fortunes of sterling over the years, the pound still has symbolic, and more than symbolic, importance for our overseas position. A very senior Australian politician once said to me: 'The day you people abandon sterling we lose all interest in you.' He had no sentimental attachment to the pound but he sensed that, from the abandonment of sterling, much else would follow and that Britain's political weight would be so much reduced that it would be a much less valuable partner. Such sentiments could be more widely spread in the Commonwealth, still a significant area of British influence.

But there is a larger probable effect. The more centralised the EU becomes, the less distinctive will be the policies and activities of the individual member states. There can be little doubt that the single currency is the most important act of political centralisation in the EU's history. Indeed, that is its principal value in the eyes of many European politicians and officials. We are on the way to a single economic government of Europe. And since government is largely about economic policy, the ultimate prospect, unless the process is checked, is one of little power being left in national capitals. If we entered the single currency, we would give considerable impetus to this process of centralisation. How far the process will go is a matter for speculation but it seems entirely likely that, if foreign countries saw that the key decisions affecting the British economy were no longer being taken in London, that British foreign policy was being increasingly subsumed in a European foreign policy and that the British armed forces were more and more likely to be subject to European control, they would display markedly less interest in Britain as a country whose assets and experience could be useful to them.

With that waning of foreign interest, British influence in the world would inevitably wane too. It may be objected that that prospect is not real. It is not imminent, but given the pace of European integration and the statements of European leaders, it is not unreal.

As stated above, Britain's position in world organisations would not be threatened by a decision to stay out of the euro. We would, for example, retain our permanent seat in New York and remain a member of the G8. But the closer we get to a central EU government, the more those things are threatened. For just as that government will wish to run its own foreign and defence policy, so it will wish to have its own seat in the Security Council and in the G8. The Euro-11 is already making arrangements to be represented in discussion with other members of the G8 by only one finance minister and one central banker.

An increasingly integrated EU might be harmful to our interests in other ways too. Its possible impact on the Atlantic Alliance is one area of concern. For some, the attraction of a single European foreign and defence policy is precisely that it would, in their minds, be a countervailing force to the United States, that it would give Europe the capacity to pursue policies independent of America. Not surprisingly, some Americans see this and draw certain conclusions. In a much-quoted article in *Foreign Affairs,* Marty Feldstein, who could turn out to be a key adviser to the next US President, said: 'A politically unified Europe with an independent military and foreign policy would accelerate the reduction of the US military presence in Europe, weaken the role of NATO and, to that extent, make Europe more vulnerable to attack.' Dr Kissinger has been quoted as believing that an integrated Europe would almost certainly intensify disagreement with the US in many policy areas and imperil the Atlantic Alliance. While some EU members may believe they could live with such a prospect – and even enjoy it – it is a distinctly uncomfortable prospect for Britain, given the importance to us of the American relationship. In November 1997, Tony Blair proclaimed as one of the guiding lights of British foreign policy: 'We should be strong in Europe and strong with the United States. There is no choice between the two.' That is clearly the approach which best suits British interests but a choice could be forced on us by the process of EU centralisation.

Britain needs to retain independence in its foreign and defence policies if it is to maximise its influence in the world. At the same time we should help to maximise intergovernmental cooperation in the EU and thus the impact of the Union's external policies. There is nothing of the 'Little Englander' in this approach. It is founded on the belief that Britain can best serve its interests and those of the Union by retaining its worldwide influence and role. It is those who are willing to submerge policy in the Union who would diminish the British role.

'It's sovereignty, stupid!'
British domestic influence and the euro

The proposition that Britain will lose influence if it does not join the euro is usually argued in relation to influence outside our borders and usually just in relation to our position inside the EU rather than the wider world. But if it can be shown that, as a result of joining, we either gain or lose influence over our domestic affairs, then this is an important element in the overall equation.

So far the least satisfactory aspect of the debate about the euro has been the implications for our national powers of decision-taking. The government has tended to sideline the consequences of entry for sovereignty and national identity.

On 27 October 1997, the Chancellor of the Exchequer set out the Government's basic policy in a parliamentary statement under the title 'UK membership of the single currency: an assessment of the five economic tests'. He argued that the potential benefits for Britain of a successful single currency were obvious, in terms of trade, transparency of costs and currency stability. He said: 'If it works economically, it is, in our view, worth doing.' He recognised that to share a common monetary policy with other states does represent a major 'pooling' (he avoided words such as 'transfer' or 'loss') of economic sovereignty. He did not explain in his statement which elements of our economic sovereignty would be 'pooled' but argued that this change should not be a 'constitutional bar' to British participation. Again, the choice of language was odd since it is hard to recall anyone arguing that a decision to enter would be unconstitutional. Clearly, Parliament can take any decision it likes. He reiterated the government view baldly: 'If a single currency would be good for British jobs, business and future prosperity, it is right, in principle to join.' Regardless, it would appear, of other considerations. The bulk of the statement was devoted to the five economic tests on which the government's decision would be based. Possibly detecting that this well-nigh exclusive emphasis on the economic case for joining was causing unease, the Prime Minister told the Commons on 23 February 1999, when he described the National Changeover Plan, that he did not 'dismiss the constitutional or political issues. They are real. Monetary union is a big step of integration.' But, he said, 'if joining a single currency is good for British jobs and British industry, if it enhances British influence and power, I believe it is right to overcome these constitutional and political arguments and the fears behind them'.

The debate about the effect of joining on the economy continues and divides economists and businessmen. This chapter has sought to show that entry is unlikely to enhance British influence and power and is more likely to diminish them. On the constitutional and political issues, Mr Blair had little more to say. He argued only that 'this is a world moving together. Sovereignty pooled can be sovereignty or at least power and influence renewed.' He explained that these sensitive matters would be for the people to decide in a referendum.

On 13 May 1999, the Chancellor told a TUC conference that the decisive test was 'clear and unambiguous economic benefit to the country'. He conceded that the single currency raises 'important constitutional questions about the sharing of economic sovereignty – questions which this government has not run from' but then simply reiterated that the decision would be taken on economic grounds. He did not describe the 'important constitutional questions' from which the government had not run nor suggest how they should be answered.

The next day, the Prime Minister told a continental audience: 'We treasure our national identity, as you do. But in creating the European Union we have the chance not to suppress our national interest but to advance it in a new way for a New World by working together.' Leaving aside the apparent and odd equating of national identity and interest – two entirely different things – there would seem to be little difficulty about working together for the stated goal without Britain entering the euro.

In sum, it appears that the sovereignty issue is not being faced squarely. There is a long tradition of this. In his book *This Blessed Plot*, Hugo Young recalls how, in the period leading up to British entry into the EEC, the issues were sometimes not presented to the British public in the most open way. He noted: 'That was especially true of the deepest, most inchoate question: what membership of 'Europe' truly meant for national sovereignty.' Thus the Heath White Paper of 1971 stated: 'There is no question of any erosion of essential national sovereignty ... What is proposed is a sharing and an enlargement of individual national sovereignties in the general interest.' Perhaps this was the origin of the 'pooling' concept. Now, as then, it is difficult to see how you share one's sovereignty without reducing it, much less enhancing it.

It seems essential to a mature decision on the single currency that, before any referendum is held, there is the clearest possible appreciation of how the United Kingdom's powers of national decision-making will change if we enter, both as an immediate consequence and in future, say over the next ten years. Earlier this year a well-supported all-party motion in Parliament called for a White Paper on the constitutional, economic and political consequences of the UK joining the euro but there has been no substantive response. It is surely the duty of government to provide such an assessment.

Meanwhile, it seems inevitable that, if Britain did join the single currency, we should indeed lose a good deal of influence over our domestic affairs. At a stroke, we would lose control over interest rates and exchange rates. As the Euro-12 became more and more the economic government of Euroland, the British government would lose an increasing amount of power over the British economy. So would the Westminster Parliament, the Scottish Parliament and the Welsh Assembly. How much and how quickly it is impossible to say. But if, as seems likely, the EU does come to exercise powers over macro-economic policy, taxation and other economic matters, the nature of our political system would be radically altered. The government would no longer be answerable to the electorate on key economic questions, or at least nothing like so answerable as it is now. Parliament would lose an important part of its *raison d'être*. So would the Bank of England. Britain would lose much influence domestically.

Belonging to Britain

But the issue goes beyond influence. The matter of national identity is complex and beyond the expertise of most of us. Yet many people in Britain evidently feel that their sense of belonging to a country called Britain is threatened by the remorseless drive towards political and economic union in the EU. Nobody now seriously contests that the single currency is a political project, designed to promote political integration. Just take two from the long list of available quotations from European figures:

> We must now face the task of moving towards a single economy, a single political unity ... Amsterdam and Maastricht need to be followed by a treaty which will give us our defence capabilities. (Romano Prodi, President of the Commission)

> A European currency will lead to member nations transferring sovereignty over financial and wages policy as well as monetary affairs. It is an illusion to think that states can hold on to their autonomy over taxation policies. (Hans Tietmeyer, President of the Bundesbank)

The constantly repeated mantra that 'nobody in Europe wants a superstate' is designed to soothe our fears. But it brings no comfort since it is perfectly possible to have a single political entity that falls short of an undefined superstate, and since the ambition within the EU to create a single political entity is clear.

It is not surprising that these concerns are at the root of many people's opposition to the single currency, for something very fundamental is at issue. History teaches that there are dangers in forcing people into a single political unit unless they already feel a common sense of belonging. The late Sir Isaiah Berlin said: 'To be human you must be able to feel at home somewhere with your own kind. People ... need to belong to a group where communication is instinctive and effortless.' That implies shared institutions, tried over time and more or less trusted. But as Melanie Phillips wrote in the *New Statesman* on 9 May 1997: '... the centre-left apparently wants to deny these expressions of national identity through the erosion of Britain's distinctive constitution, law and economy. Institutions which bind British people to each other are to be subsumed into a meaningless European political identity.' And she added: 'The idea that national identity will remain untouched by the federal state envisaged under the Single European Act can be sustained only by those who fail to understand national identity or wish to erode it. National identity is impotent if it cannot control the principal levers of its expression in law or economic policy.'

If we join the euro, the relationship of the British voter to the British government of the day and to Parliament will change. Two of our most important national institutions will be deprived of much of their meaning. Criticism of British politicians and the institutions they staff may be fashionable. But those of us who have travelled the world and seen others often count our blessings. Like them or not, what matters for our system of democracy is that we know these institutions, we can change their incumbents through the ballot-box, we can get at them between elections and that they deal with issues that matter to every British citizen. People must feel that their votes count, that they can influence the decisions that affect them. They expect national governments to be accountable to them for the state of the economy. Issues of this kind must be fully ventilated in the debate on the single currency. A decision on the euro, taken solely or even largely on economic grounds, would be highly defective.

There is an alternative

To summarise, if we join the single currency, Britain will have less influence in the world, not more, and less influence over our own affairs. If we stay out, we can perfectly well make a major contribution to EU policies, excepting only those matters directly connected with the single currency. We shall retain our current global status and roles undiminished unless the centralising process in the EU reaches the point where an EU government presses for its own seat on the UN Security Council and G8 or takes over foreign and defence policy from national governments. We shall keep our present influence over our domestic economy. We shall not weaken further our national identity, our sense of belonging or our national institutions.

The opt-out provided by the Maastricht Treaty was not meant to be merely a delaying device. It was designed to give the British people a genuine chance to decide whether it wished to join the euro or not and in its own good time. We now have the advantage of being able to test some of the assertions that are made about the consequences of staying out. The single currency has been in existence for many months. As Bagehot argued in *The Economist* on 10 July 1999, the Government's 'hesitation' on the issue has not visibly damaged Britain's influence in wider European affairs. It did not appear to restrict in any way the leadership of Mr Blair over Kosovo nor his initiative on creating an autonomous EU defence capacity. His influence in Washington seems as strong as ever. There is no sign of foreign investment faltering. All this comes as no surprise to those of us who believe that staying out will have little effect on British influence.

Admittedly, we need a longer period of time to test fully this proposition and others like it. But that time is available. We can take a further period of years to see whether Britain's influence diminishes, whether genuine economic convergence with our European partners is really likely, whether jobs, prices and growth are affected. Better that than to take the plunge before these things can be properly assessed. There is simply no need to incur the manifest disadvantages of entry unless and until it is overwhelmingly clear that the disadvantages of non-participation are real and decisive.

The truth is that the disadvantages of entry are unlikely to change over time. The fundamental issue in any referendum that may be held is likely to remain that of Britain's national decision-making powers and our sense of belonging in an EU that is moving remorselessly towards a central government. It is better to face this issue now than attempt to bury it. We should work hard for an EU that recognises that many, perhaps most, Europeans identify primarily with the country in which they live rather than with a single state of Europe, and which fully respects that sense of belonging. We should develop an EU where foreign and defence policy are irreversibly intergovernmental and not subject to Qualified Majority Voting, where economic structures are flexible and competitive, an EU which rises properly to the challenge of incorporating new members from the East, and which works vigorously with all like-minded countries, especially the United States, to uphold western values, maintain peace, safeguard western interests and help solve the world's problems.

The difficulty is that much current EU thinking and activity run counter to these goals. The process of centralisation overshadows everything. In the end, if it continues unchecked, it will indeed reduce British influence. By staying out of the euro, we shall help to slow, and hopefully stop, the process. At the same time we can devote our energies to creating a new and better Europe, designed to deal with today's problems, not yesterday's. If the British decision is clear and well supported in a referendum, this will become a fact of life in Europe, a reality to which our partners will adapt.

2

The Euro and Regional Divergence in Europe

Tony Thirlwall

A personal manifesto

In a toast to the Royal Economic Society just before he died in 1946, the great English economist John Maynard Keynes assigned to economists the role of the trustees of the possibility of civilisation. He wanted to emphasise economics as a moral science, concerned with understanding how the functioning of economies affects the everyday lives of people and how economic policies can be designed and implemented to improve their economic and social welfare. In this respect, he believed that the study of economics, and the art of policy-making, has enormous potential for good. In thinking about the euro and regional disparities in Europe, it is the economic wellbeing of the people of Europe that I have in mind.

As far as welfare is concerned, I attach great importance to the right to work and the goal of full employment, which in recent years has largely been lost sight of in Britain and the rest of the European Union. Unemployment represents a vast waste of resources and potential output, and is a major cause of poverty and social deprivation. Crime, divorce, mental illness and alcoholism are also all closely associated with the lack of work. The economies of Europe could – and should – do better.

I would also like to see a more equal distribution of income and wealth across countries (including the countries of the EU) and between regions and people within countries. Inequalities, especially those based on privilege and exploitation, are not only unjust but are also not conducive to social harmony and the smooth functioning of economies.

I believe in the democratic process, and that as far as possible people should be involved in the decisions that affect their own lives. Political power should be decentralised as much as possible and, at the very least, decision-makers should be democratically accountable.

I mention these three points because two of the great worries I have about the experiment of monetary union which 11 countries[1] of the EU embarked on from 1 January 1999, are that:

- It is profoundly undemocratic in the sense that key economic decisions that affect people's lives will be taken by members of an unelected European Central Bank, not accountable or responsible to any democratically elected body. Decisions on interest rates and the exchange rate, previously under the control of national governments, are now the preserve of unelected central bankers. Democratic power has been removed from people in those countries that have so far signed up for monetary union. If citizens do not like the interest rate they have to pay for borrowing, or the mortgage rate to buy a house, too bad! If workers are thrown out of work because the industries in which they work have become (temporarily) uncompetitive, too bad! Workers and borrowers can protest to their national governments, but to no avail.
- Economic policy will be guided not by what is happening to the real economies of Europe – that is, by what is happening to jobs and the growth of output – but by what is happening to prices. The function of the ECB is to conduct monetary policy, and to set interest rates, to keep the rate of inflation below 2 per cent per annum, not to achieve a particular target growth rate or level of unemployment. If price stability, fast growth and full employment are incompatible, the economic remit of the ECB is a recipe for stagnation and high unemployment. People might prefer to trade off some price stability for more employment and a faster growth of output, but they are deprived of the choice.

I should also mention in this brief introduction that I am not an orthodox neo-classical economist in the sense that I believe that, if markets are allowed to function freely without impediments, the price mechanism will work in such a way as to secure full employment and the optimal allocation of resources. Specifically, I don't believe that flexible labour markets, and wage rate reductions, are sufficient to secure full employment. No amount of flexibility will be sufficient if there is not enough demand for labour in the economic system as a whole. The best that more flexible labour markets can do is to reduce frictional unemployment, and perhaps increase employment in particular sectors, but frictional unemployment is only a small fraction of the nearly 20 million unemployed that exist in the EU today.

Structural unemployment requires investment in education and training. Then, jobs need to be available for the retrained to work in through the normal process of physical investment in plant and machinery. The major part of unemployment in the EU today is involuntary in the sense that workers would be willing to work in their existing occupations at the current money wage, but there is no demand for their labour. Demand has been squeezed in most of the EU countries over the last five years or so, in their attempt to meet the Maastricht convergence criteria for entry into the single currency.

I also don't subscribe to the orthodox view that the migration of labour and capital between countries, and between regions within countries, will necessarily lead to the convergence of per capita incomes and living standards across all areas, and to the elimination of unemployment rate differences. The idea that, if unemployed labour migrates from a depressed region to a prosperous region, this will necessarily cause unemployment to fall in the depressed region and rise in the prosperous one, is a very static one. So, too, is the idea that capital will necessarily locate where labour is most abundant and wages are lower. Migration has dynamic effects, and the buoyancy of markets is an equally, if not more, important determinant of location. The migration of the factors of production, made easier by the process of economic and monetary integration, can be potentially disequilibrating. How else can the continued north–south divide in the UK be explained, or the even greater divide between the north and south of Italy?

Should Britain join Euroland?

I am opposed to Britain joining Euroland, and adopting the euro as its currency, for four main reasons:

- Firstly, it is not necessary for the promotion of trade and the completion of the Single Market. There are more important determinants of trade than a single trading currency and the absence of exchange rate risk.
- Secondly, I believe it is important for Britain to maintain monetary, fiscal and exchange rate flexibility, if it is to achieve its full economic potential.

- Thirdly, the euro, as currently managed and operated by the ECB, is highly undemocratic, as I have already mentioned.
- Fourthly, and paradoxically, the euro could become a threat to European integration and stability if it exacerbates regional differences within the EU which I believe it is likely to do. Shocks to countries and to regions within countries are rarely symmetric. Without the instruments to cope, asymmetric shocks will exacerbate regional differences, with the prospect of civil strife, political unrest and disaffection with the whole EU project in the affected regions. Regional policies in the EU are a poor substitute for the ability of individual countries to cope with shocks in their own way.

To steal a phrase from Professor Jim Ball's recent pamphlet,[2] the euro is 'a bad idea', not only for Britain but for Europe as a whole. If, as promised, a referendum is offered in the future on whether Britain should join the euro, I would vote against, even if it was deemed by the government of the day that the 'time is right' (the favourite expression used). In fact, it makes no economic sense to say the 'time is right', or that Britain will join 'when the time is right', because countries can never know what economic conditions may prevail in the future, or what shocks may hit them, which require the use of the very weapons of economic policy that countries joining a single currency surrender: namely the exchange rate, monetary policy and fiscal discretion.

In this chapter, I want to focus on regional differences within the EU, and to consider whether the euro is likely to reduce or exacerbate differences in unemployment and living standards between the peoples of Europe. Before doing so, however, let me briefly elaborate on some of the serious issues mentioned above.

Trade and the Single Market

One of the foremost arguments put forward by supporters of the euro is that a single currency will promote trade by reducing transaction costs and avoiding exchange rate fluctuations. No one disputes that trade is an important engine of growth, and can be of mutual benefit to countries provided it leads to the *balanced* growth of exports and imports, but I think the argument is exaggerated for two reasons. Firstly, there is no firm evidence that multiple currencies and fluctuating exchange rates discourage trade. This is hardly surprising, since where financial markets are well developed, traders hedge against currency fluctuations. Secondly, in the 50 years since World War II, and particularly since the Treaty of Rome was signed in 1957, trade in Europe has grown and flourished with multiple currencies, and would undoubtedly continue to do so without the euro. Indeed, now that barriers to trade have been virtually eliminated, the major determinants of trade will be the increased specialisation of countries and the buoyancy of markets. There is a very real danger that trade may be discouraged or slowed down by the euro if the euro area remains a deflationary zone because the ECB continues to set interest rates to achieve monetary stability as if this is the only goal of economic policy. In the last decade, the EU has been one of the most stagnant regions of the world economy and, as yet, there is still no sign from the ECB that it wants to pursue a growth-orientated strategy. Of course, with a single currency, there is some saving of transaction costs, but they will be small beer compared with the potential costs to countries of the loss of economic sovereignty.

Another argument put forward in favour of the euro is that a single currency is necessary for completion of the Single Market programme initiated in 1986. This is disingenuous. It is true that a single currency leads to greater price transparency, but there is no reason why the dismantling of non-tariff barriers to trade, such as technical specifications and national procurement policies, should depend on the existence of a single currency. Nor is there any reason why the lack of a single currency should impede the free mobility of the factors of production, labour and capital, if such mobility is thought desirable. Labour mobility depends on job opportunities, transport costs, housing availability and language barriers, not on whether currencies have to be changed across national frontiers. Capital already moves very freely – some would argue too freely.

The euro could pose further problems for economic management in this regard. Without speculative opportunities in currency markets and interest rate differentials to take advantage of within Euroland, there is likely to be a switch of capital from intra-European flows to increased flows between Europe and other regions of the world. This will pose problems for the stability of the euro and, by implication, for interest rate policy to secure external equilibrium if the ECB were to pursue an exchange rate target. The euro has been allowed to depreciate against the dollar and sterling since its inception on 1 January 1999, and probably rightly so, given the depressed economic conditions of Euroland, but serious depreciation could become inflationary by raising import prices, and jeopardise the ECB's inflation target.

Loss of economic sovereignty

Adoption of the euro means the abandonment of all the traditional weapons of economic policy that in the past have served countries reasonably well. It is hard to imagine how the countries of Europe would have fared in the post-war years without the active use of monetary, fiscal and exchange rate policy. Relinquishing these instruments of policy could spell disaster for individual countries in the future.

The euro implies one rate of interest for all participating countries regardless of their individual economic circumstances. This can only be described as the economics of the madhouse. The interest rate is a powerful weapon for regulating the level of economic activity, and for influencing the division of output between consumption and investment. There is no reason to suppose that the economic cycles of countries will ever be synchronised sufficiently that all countries require the same interest rate at the same time to influence the level of output or the rate of inflation. Also, for real convergence, some countries need to grow faster than others, which means encouraging investment at the expense of consumption. This, in turn, requires lower interest rates in some countries than others. The interest rate decided by the ECB will always be some compromise rate, which suits no one country in particular, designed primarily to target a Europe-wide inflation rate when the trade-off between inflation and unemployment also differs between countries. The ensuing cost of price stability in one country may be two or three times higher than in another in terms of unemployment.

Eddie George, Governor of the Bank of England, once declared that 'the Bank's job is to maintain macro stability for the whole country, and discrepancies between regions and industries were regrettable but inevitable'. This was a frank statement, but true. Wim Duisenberg, President of the ECB, could equally say the same for the countries of Euroland, but it is hardly an attractive prospect. If regions in the UK already feel dissatisfied and neglected, there would be good reason to be doubly so if Britain signs up to the euro and becomes a region of Europe. The fact is that the people within the nation states of Euroland will no longer be able to decide for themselves whether they would like their economies to expand or contract. Their livelihoods, the prices of their goods, their house prices and mortgage rates will all be decided by a committee of bankers over which they have no democratic control. Then there is the issue of fiscal policy. The ability to vary taxes and government expenditure, and to run budget deficits, are also powerful weapons of economic policy. At the Dublin Summit in 1996, however, a 'stability pact' was agreed that countries joining the single currency should not run deficits of more than 3 per cent of gross domestic product, without incurring a fine of 0.2 per cent of GDP, and 0.1 per cent of GDP for every 1 percentage point of deficit over the 3 per cent limit. Apart from the fact that the 3 per cent limit is arbitrary and rigid, such a pact and its fining mechanism makes no economic sense, particularly if the budget deficit is caused by recession through loss of tax revenue and increased government expenditure on social security. Attempting to meet the 3 per cent limit will compound the deflation, and the fining mechanism will make the deficit even worse. At the very least, cyclical deficits need to be separated from structural deficits in the implementation of such rules.

Finally, let us turn to the exchange rate. A single currency clearly eliminates exchange rates between member countries. The exchange rate as an instrument of economic policy has now disappeared, therefore, among the countries of Euroland (although not, of course, between Euroland and the rest of the world). One currency, and no exchange rate to defend, does not mean, however, that balance of payments problems between countries in a single currency area disappear. Imbalances between exports and imports are just as likely. What it means is that when plans to import exceed plans to export, the exchange rate is no longer there to take the strain, and balance of payments problems manifest themselves not in the form of a depreciating currency which encourages exports and discourages imports, but as falling output and rising unemployment. Regional problems within countries of slow growth and high unemployment are essentially balance of payments problems which, by definition, cannot be alleviated by exchange rate movements because regions within a country are already part of a single currency area. The euro has turned the countries of Euroland into regions as defenceless as regions within countries, with the added disadvantage that the European Structural Funds to cope with Europe-wide pockets of unemployment and deprivation are far smaller in relation to the size of the areas likely to be affected than the size of national regional funds in relation to the regional problems of individual countries. There is no built-in mechanism in

Euroland for the automatic transfer and redistribution of resources between countries, as there is, for example, between states in the United States of America.

Does the loss of exchange rate flexibility within Euroland matter, and would such a loss matter for Britain if it adopted the euro? I would concede that the exchange rate is of limited use in permanently raising the growth rate of a country, unless it can engineer a continuing depreciation of the *real* exchange rate (which is unlikely). However, it remains an invaluable weapon to combat internal and external shocks, or to counter gradually deteriorating competitiveness. Who knows where the shocks will come from in the future, and how they will affect countries differently, as they surely will? The consequences of a single currency in the face of a deterioration in competitiveness could be serious damage to the real economy, which means a loss of output and jobs.

Nowhere in the pacts and conditions governing Economic and Monetary Union and the single currency are there any safeguards against deflationary policies and deflationary conditions such as rising unemployment, falling prices or even governments running budget surpluses. The 'rules of the game' are asymmetrical, biased against inflation, as indeed they are at the international level whereby the International Monetary Fund penalises countries in balance of payments deficit, but not those in surplus, which therefore imparts deflationary bias in the world economy. Most of those sceptical of the euro are not Keynesian economists, but they would, I am sure, concur with Keynes's famous remark that 'it is worse in an impoverished world to provoke unemployment than to disappoint the rentier'. In the conditions now prevailing in Euroland, it would be hard to disagree.

Economic and political integration

For many who support the euro, and Britain joining, the motive is political: to promote a federal European superstate that would put Europe on a more equal footing with the USA, and to avoid once and for all the internecine conflict that for centuries has plagued the countries of Europe. This was the vision of the founding fathers of the European Community, and was undoubtedly the game plan of Chancellor Kohl and the other political heavyweights in Europe who were the driving force behind the various stages of EMU leading ultimately to the euro. We can all unite behind the desire for peace and cooperation in Europe, as we can behind the virtues of motherhood and apple pie, but the euro as the route to political union, even if that is desirable, is fraught with danger, and could just as well lead to the economic and political disintegration of Europe. The dangers are manifold.

As I have repeatedly stressed already, the policy design of the single currency is profoundly undemocratic and does not chime with the mood of the people of Europe at the present time. The citizens of Europe are looking for greater democratic control over their own economic destiny, not less, and understandably so. Regional political groupings in Europe continue to attract strong support, and the Scots and Welsh have recently voted for their own assemblies within the United Kingdom. The euro has been launched despite considerable popular opposition in many of the countries involved.

The regional disaffection that will be caused by deteriorating economic circumstances in countries that lack the policy instruments to deal with economic crisis can too easily become the breeding ground for nationalism and fascism, and political resentment, as witnessed in Europe in the 1920s and 1930s. By all means, let there be more coordination of economic policies in Europe and let the countries of Europe strive for greater political cooperation in areas such as defence, human rights and relations with other countries, but not by luring them into an economic straitjacket over which there is no democratic control and from which there is no easy escape. This is a recipe for political turmoil and the fragmentation of Europe that Britain would be wise to steer clear of.

'Regional' disparities in Europe

Let us now consider the extent of 'regional' disparities in Europe, both between countries and between regions across countries. We shall then examine the case for regional policies and the implementation of regional policy within the EU. Finally we shall consider the difficult question of what is likely to happen to regional disparities in Europe now that 11 countries have adopted a single currency. This is a controversial issue, the answer to which depends to a large extent on whether the countries of Euroland can be regarded as constituting an optimum currency area. My judgement is that they do not, and that regional disparities in Europe are likely to persist and even worsen in the future.

But even if they did not, this would not weaken the case for Britain to say 'no' to the single currency.

The two most common measures taken of 'regional' welfare are the level of per capita income (PCY) as a measure of living standards, and the rate of unemployment. Table 2.1 gives data on these variables for the countries of the EU in 1997 and for some non-EU countries as well. Wide differences in living standards and unemployment are immediately apparent. Denmark is more than three times richer than Portugal, measured in terms of the purchasing power of currencies. In Spain, unemployment is more than 20 per cent of the workforce, over five times higher than in Luxembourg and over twice the EU average of 10 per cent. Notice also that the average unemployment rate in the EU is nearly treble that in Japan and nearly double that in the US.

Table 2.1 Unemployment rates and living standards in Europe, 1997

EU Countries	% Unemployment[a]	Per capita national income ($) measured at purchasing power parity[b]
Austria	6.6	27, 980
Belgium	9.7	26,420
Denmark	6.4	32,500
Finland	15.3	24,080
France	12.6	24,050
Germany	9.5	28,260
Greece	10.0	12,010
Ireland	10.8	18,280
Italy	12.2	20,120
Luxembourg	3.7	
Netherlands	5.6	25,820
Portugal	6.2	10,450
Spain	20.9	14,510
Sweden	10.7	26,220
UK	7.4	20,710
Non-EU Countries		
Australia	8.7	20,540
Canada	9.5	19,290
Japan	3.4	37,850
Norway	4.2	36,090
USA	5.6	28,740

Source: [a] OECD Economic Outlook.
[b] World Bank database.

When we turn to regions across the EU, the disparities are naturally even wider. Maps I and II tell the story.

Map I shows the regional breakdown of Gross Domestic Product per head relative to the average of the 15 member countries of the EU for approximately 200 regions at the NUTS 2 level.[3] Map II shows the rate of unemployment for the same regions. There are basically three types of regions in the EU:

- firstly, large urban service centres where GDP per head is high and unemployment is low
- secondly, industrial regions where GDP per head is slightly above average, with unemployment also above average (and with some very bad black spots)
- thirdly, rural regions where GDP per head is way below average, and unemployment 50 per cent higher than average.

GDP per head in the richest cities of Europe is five times higher than in some of the poorest rural areas. The rate of unemployment in some of the worst affected regions (in Spain, for example) is ten times higher than in those least affected (e.g. in Austria and the Netherlands).

The evidence is mixed on whether these huge disparities have been narrowing or widening over time. The degree of dispersion tends to vary with the trade cycle, with differences narrowing on the upswing and widening on the downswing. Over the long period from 1950 to the present, there is evidence of per capita income convergence with poorer countries and regions slowly catching up with the richer (at a rate of roughly 2 per cent per annum), but the speed of convergence was more pronounced in the 1950s, 1960s and 1970s than in the 1980s and 1990s.

Productivity levels have converged slightly faster, but at the expense of unemployment. From 1986 to 1996, for example, GDP per head in the 25 poorest regions rose from 52 per cent of the EU average to 59 per cent, but unemployment rose from 20 per cent to 24 per cent. Unemployment (and low participation rates) reduces per capita income, of course, but not productivity. The consensus among economists would seem to be that the scope for convergence is not exhausted, but other factors continue to polarise regions including differences in industrial structure, research and development effort between regions and sectors of the economy, population density and migration, as well as unemployment. The predominance of agriculture is a serious obstacle to output growth in poor regions, because the

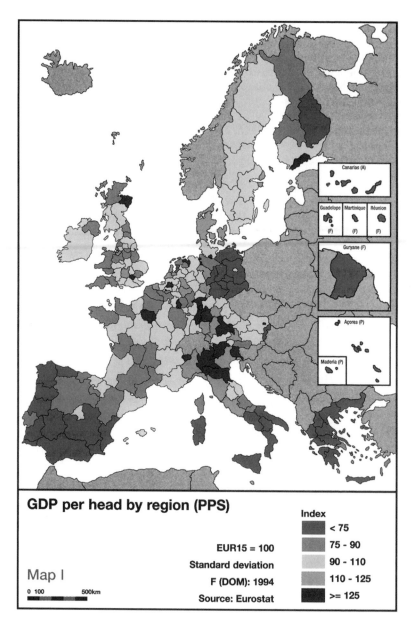

Map I   GDP per head by region (PPS)

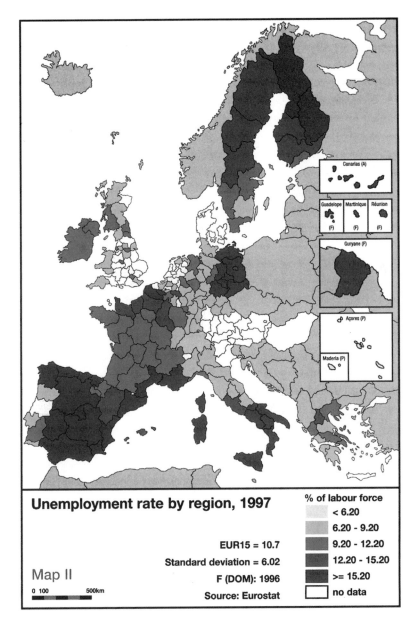

Unemployment rate by region, 1997

EUR15 = 10.7

Standard deviation = 6.02

Map II

F (DOM): 1996

Source: Eurostat

0 100   500km

% of labour force

< 6.20

6.20 - 9.20

9.20 - 12.20

12.20 - 15.20

>= 15.20

no data

Map II   Unemployment rate by region, 1997

scope for economies of scale and research and development is less than in industry and services.

With regard to unemployment, regional differences across the EU as a whole, and within individual countries, have remained remarkably stubborn over a long period. A pioneering study by Baddeley, Martin and Tyler[4] shows no evidence of 'global' convergence, and that the absolute dispersion of unemployment rates (measured by the standard deviation) tends to follow a pro-cyclical pattern, rising in the recession of the early 1980s, falling in the boom 1986–90, and rising again post-1990, as shown in Figure 2.1.

Notice also, however, that underlying these cyclical movements, the trend of dispersion has been upwards. Contrary to the conventional wisdom, it is difficult to interpret the persistence of these disparities as simply a prolonged disequilibrium in regional labour markets. Rather, they represent an *equilibrium* phenomenon associated with differences in industrial structure and the numbers of long-term unemployed. One half of the unemployed in the EU has been out of work for more than a year, and in the 25 regions with the highest unemployment, this percentage is 60 per cent.

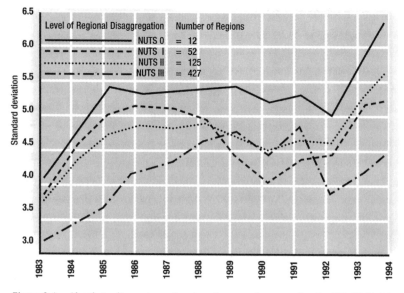

Figure 2.1   Absolute dispersion of regional unemployment in the EU, 1983–94

Regional policy

One of the explicit objectives of the EU is '(reducing) disparities between levels of development of the various regions and the backwardness of the least favoured regions, including rural areas'. Article 130A of the Treaty of European Union 1992 specifically instructs the Union to 'develop and pursue actions leading to the strengthening of its economic and social cohesion'. As a result of the Maastricht agreement, Article 2 of the Treaty also explicitly recognises economic and social cohesion as a fundamental principle of the Union. The case for regional policies should be self-evident. First, high unemployment represents a massive resource waste – a loss of potential output that can never be recouped. Regional differences in per capita income are systematically related to differences in unemployment rates, so that unemployment is a major cause of poverty and social deprivation.

Secondly, and related, there are substantial social costs associated with regional unemployment disparities. Unemployment itself imposes social costs through its link with poor health, crime and the need for income transfers, but disparities impose even greater costs. It is easier, for example, for communities to pool resources in a situation where overall unemployment is 10 per cent with no regional disparities than if unemployment is 5 per cent in some fairly large regions and 20 per cent in a series of smaller ones. Congestion in rapidly expanding areas imposes other types of well-known social costs.

Thirdly, regional imbalances in economic activity worsen the macroeconomic trade-offs in an economy, and particularly the relation between unemployment and the rate of inflation. A wide dispersion of regional unemployment around a given average rate is likely to lead to a much higher rate of increase of wages and prices because the inflationary pressures in regions with unemployment below the mean spill over to regions with unemployment above the mean. This is a powerful argument for active manpower policies regionally (and industrially). In modern parlance, large and persistent regional disparities in unemployment raise the non-accelerating inflation rate of unemployment (NAIRU) – in other words, the rate of national unemployment to keep the aggregate rate of inflation at a given level.

Finally, regional differences in living standards and employment opportunities can breed resentment that manifests itself in the form of regional political groupings, the growth of nationalism, and ultimately social and political unrest. If this scenario developed, it would jeopardise everything that the European Union stands for; and it is an ever-present danger in a Europe still rife with such deep economic and regional schisms, and the prospect of them worsening.

Up to 1975, there was no specific European regional policy. Regional policy was left to national governments, and the European Commission confined itself to supervising and coordinating national regional aid and preventing unfair competition. Then, in 1975, after the accession of the UK, Denmark and Ireland to the European Community, the European Regional Development Fund (ERDF) was established to provide assistance for infrastructure and industrial projects. But the Fund was limited and only acted at the request of national governments. At the same time, however, two other Structural Funds, the European Social Fund (ESF) and the European Agricultural Guidance and Guarantee Fund (EAGGF), were given an enhanced regional focus. In 1987, the Single European Market programme was then launched. Interestingly, it recognised that free trade and the free mobility of factors of production might hurt peripheral regions and called for a European-level regional policy. This led in 1989 to the reform and merger of the three Structural Funds (the ERDF, ESF and EAGGF). These now form the basis of regional policy in the EU, together with loans from the European Investment Bank and a Cohesion Fund created in 1992 to help the four less prosperous countries of Greece, Spain, Portugal and Ireland.

The reform of the Structural Funds in 1989 had three main purposes:

- to concentrate funding on a limited number of objectives and on the most vulnerable regions
- to increase the scale of funds available
- to improve the use of funds.

The first purpose was implemented by specifying seven policy objectives:

- help for regions with GDP per head less than 75 per cent of the EU average – so-called Objective 1 regions
- the conversion of declining industrial regions with high unemployment – Objective 2 regions
- combating long-term and youth unemployment
- the adaptation of workers to industrial change
- the adjustment of agriculture in the context of the Common Agricultural Policy

- development and structural adjustment of rural areas (Objective 5b)
- structural adjustment of regions with very low population density.

The second purpose of reform was implemented by doubling the Structural Funds available and increasing the Funds by another 50 per cent for the six-year period 1994–9. This expansion was financed by an increase in the size of the EU's budget from 1.05 per cent of EU GDP to 1.2 per cent. The third purpose of reform was introduced by switching from projects to programmes.

The allocation of Structural Funds across Objectives over the period 1994–9 is shown in Table 2.2.

It can be seen that 85 per cent of the Fund allocation was designated for Objectives 1, 2 and 5b, with the vast bulk concentrated on Objective 1 regions. The average GDP per capita in Objective 1 regions was 64 per cent of the EU average. Most of the regions are in Greece, Spain, Portugal and Ireland. It can also be seen that Objective 1 regions experienced higher than average unemployment. These regions have twice the share of employment in agriculture compared with the EU average, and their infrastructure is also poor.

The future allocation of the Structural (and Cohesion) Funds over the period 2000–6 was agreed at the Berlin Summit in March 1999. There is to be a greater concentration on the regions most in need of assistance. The seven objectives outlined above have been consolidated into three. Objective 1 regions stay and are based on the same criterion. The new Objective 2 will support economic and social adjustment in regions with structural difficulties up to a maximum of 18 per cent of the population of the Union covered – 10 per cent in industrial

Table 2.2   Expenditure on structural funds, 1994–9

	Objective 1	*Objective 2*	*Object 5b*	*All EU assisted regions*	*Rest of EU12*
Population share % 1994	26.6	16.8	8.2	51.6	48.4
Unemployment rate % 1993	16.7	12.1	7.3	n.a.	8.0
GDP per capita 1991 (EU Average = 100)	64	94	83	n.a.	116
Structural fund Allocation (%)	74	6	5	85	15

Source: Dignam (1995).

areas; 5 per cent in rural areas; 2 per cent in urban areas, and 1 per cent for areas depending on fishing. A new Objective 3 is designed to support education, training and employment outside of Objective 1 and 2 regions. Regions currently supported under Objectives 1, 2 and 5b, which are no longer eligible, will receive transitional support. The total allocation of funds is 213 billion euros, which, spread over seven years, is a smaller annual allocation in real terms than the amount allocated in 1999 of 28 billion euros.

At present, Structural Funds account for about 2 per cent of the GDP of all Objective 1 regions and 10 per cent of their investment. This is a sizeable contribution, and there is evidence reported by the Commission[5] that the Funds have contributed to the process of convergence by raising the growth rate by about 0.5 per cent a year. From 1989 to 1996, the GDP per head of regions with Objective 1 status rose from 63 per cent of the EU average to 69 per cent. It is notoriously difficult, however, to separate precisely the impact of Funds from other variables that might contribute to convergence, including structural change.

What is clear is that the Funds are a drop in the ocean in relation to the magnitude of the task to be tackled. If the EU is serious about regional convergence and cohesion, it needs substantially to increase the size of the budget, particularly to tackle unemployment.[6] The programmes financed by Structural Funds need to create sustainable comparative advantage in disadvantaged areas, by developing clusters of inter-linked activities which can generate self-sustaining growth and weather the vicissitudes of the trade cycle. There should also perhaps be more focus on the criterion of regional per capita income than on GDP per head, to highlight more the need for fiscal transfer mechanisms within the EU. In Objective 1 regions in countries such as Greece, Spain, Portugal and Ireland, the interregional transfers are weak which leads to wider regional differences in living standards relative to GDP per head, compared, say, to the UK, where interregional transfers are more well-developed. Fiscal transfers within the EU are miniscule compared to the United States, and this is one of the great worries if monetary union leads to greater regional disparities. There are not the fiscal mechanisms in place to act as partial automatic stabilisers.

What will the euro do to 'regional' differences?

Economists are divided (as they are on most things!) over whether the euro is likely to narrow or widen regional economic differences. In

LEEDS METROPOLITAN UNIVERSITY LEARNING CENTRE

orthodox economic theory, regional differences in levels of per capita income are supposed to be narrowed by the process of factor mobility and trade. Take two regions (A and B) both at the same level of development, and then assume that region A suffers an adverse shock that raises unemployment and reduces wages. Labour migrates from A to B in response to differences in opportunities which is supposed to lower unemployment and raise wages in A, and to raise unemployment and lower wages in B, leading to convergence. Capital, by contrast, is assumed to 'migrate' from B to A in response to a higher rate of return on capital where wages are lower, thus reinforcing the equilibrating tendency.

This is the orthodox story, or perhaps I should say fairy-tale, because it is immediately obvious that the story bears little relation to reality, and a number of qualifications need making. First, migration is usually a very selective process, which can have serious detrimental effects in the regions of origin and confer positive externalities on the regions of destination. Secondly, migration not only affects supply but also demand. When labour moves into a region, it demands goods and services which adds to labour demand and when labour leaves a region the demand for output falls. The supply and demand for labour is interdependent. Thirdly, and a related point, the (expected) rate of return on capital is determined by demand as well as by the cost of labour. Capital is just as likely to flow to high wage regions to which labour is migrating as to low wage regions where investment opportunities (at least for the provision of local goods and services) are diminishing. Expanding markets act as a powerful magnet for new investment, particularly if there are extensive agglomeration economies and transport costs are low.

In short, factor movements may not be equalising. On the contrary, they may be disequilibrating through a process which the great Swedish economist, Gunnar Myrdal, first coined 'circular and cumulative causation'. This is nothing more than the idea of virtuous and vicious circles based on positive and negative feedback mechanisms. The cumulative causation school seems to me to have the evidence on its side. How else is it possible to explain the persistent differences in unemployment rates and living standards across regions of countries despite years of migration from poor to rich regions, and years of regional policy implementation? Labour migration cannot be regarded as an automatic safety valve for regions and countries of high unemployment which suffer adverse shocks and which have relinquished all instruments of economic policy for the sake of a single currency.

Orthodox economic theory also teaches that trade is equilibrating. In the absence of factor mobility, trade is supposed to act as a substitute, with poor, low-wage regions specialising in labour intensive goods, and rich, high-wage regions specialising in relatively capital intensive goods. The returns to factors of production should then equalise across regions. What the story forgets to tell is that labour productivity is assumed to be the same across regions, and that free trade does not cause unemployment. Two major factors can cause unemployment with the freeing of trade. The first is a limit to employment in activities, such as agriculture and other land-based activities, which some regions are forced to specialise in. The second is balance of payments problems if the balance of payments consequences of trade are not self-rectifying.

The other point to make about the consequences of freer trade is that if there is factor mobility, regions will compete on the basis of absolute advantage not comparative advantage. In this scenario, it is possible that many regions will have no production role at all. Their fate is 'desertification'.

Research on regional disparities across Europe shows that what happens to regional differences in living standards and unemployment depends largely on what happens to the relative performance of individual countries. In other words, movements in regional convergence/divergence have much more to do with what is happening to growth performance *between* countries than what is happening to regional performance *within* countries. If the interest rate and the exchange rate are no longer available to address country-specific shocks, regional disparities across Europe as a whole will automatically widen. Shocks to countries also have asymmetric effects on regions. The poorer the country, the greater the asymmetric shock to regions is likely to be because regions in poor countries are less diversified and less integrated with the rest of the economy.

In considering, therefore, what is likely to happen to regional disparities with the introduction of the euro, there are two basic questions. Firstly, is there likely to be real convergence between the countries of Europe that make up Euroland? Secondly, will regional policies be strong enough to offset divergent tendencies if countries adversely affected by shocks find difficulty in adjusting because they have lost sovereignty over monetary and exchange rate policy?

This raises the whole question, in turn, of whether the countries that have decided to adopt a single currency, and other countries contemplating joining (including the UK), constitute an optimum currency area. In other words, do they comprise a sufficiently homogeneous economic entity in which it is sensible to have just one currency instead of multiple currencies, and to operate a single economic policy as opposed to each country operating its own independent economic policy. This clearly depends on the benefits and costs of a single currency, and whether the benefits outweigh the costs, where the benefits and costs are measured in terms of output gains and losses within the area as a whole.

The costs of a single currency relate to: the loss of the exchange rate as an instrument of policy to maintain a country's competitiveness; the loss of the interest rate as an instrument of economic policy; and the loss of fiscal discretion. These are all powerful weapons of economic policy that countries entering a single currency surrender. The potential benefits of a single currency relate largely to the promotion of trade and a more efficient allocation of resources. The question then is: under what circumstances are the costs likely to be minimised and the benefits maximised, so that one can be sure that the currency area is an optimum? Four conditions are normally specified.

The first condition to minimise costs is that economies should be roughly similar and synchronised so that shocks are symmetrical in the sense that if a shock to the system takes place (e.g. a world recession or an oil price increase, etc.) all the countries are affected in roughly the same way so that countries do not require specific individual policies applied to them. This, of course, is the reason why so much attention in the run-up to monetary union on 1 January 1999 focused on countries reaching certain convergence criteria. Note, however, that all the convergence criteria were *monetary* in nature, relating to inflation, interest rates, budget deficits and the size of the national debt. But monetary convergence is no guarantee of real convergence, nor any guarantee that future shocks will be symmetrical. The more that countries and regions are specialised, the less symmetrical shocks are likely to be. Indeed, given the diverse nature of the economies of the EU, and differences in institutional arrangements, it is probable that any future shocks will be asymmetrical. Real convergence will require monetary *divergence* that is precluded by a single currency.

If costs are incurred in particular countries or regions, in terms of lost output and unemployment, a second condition to minimise costs in an optimum currency area is that there should be sufficient labour market flexibility and capital mobility to mitigate the costs. The orthodox presumption is that if wages are sufficiently flexible, and labour and capital are freely mobile, the under-utilisation of resources in depressed areas can be eliminated. There are two responses to this argument. The first is that wages may not be flexible downwards, and, even if they were, Keynesian theory teaches that wage flexibility may not be an efficient adjustment mechanism in the case of demand shocks. The euro may actually reduce wage flexibility. Firstly, by increasing transparency, there may be pressure from workers and trade unions for greater equality of nominal wages across Europe, which on an orthodox view of the world would worsen regional disparities in unemployment. Secondly, the lower and more uniform the rate of inflation in Europe as a whole, the less the flexibility of *real* wages across countries. The second response is that labour and capital mobility may not be equilibrating, as argued earlier. Even if the orthodox adjustment mechanisms are allowed to work, they may turn out to work perversely.

A third condition to minimise costs is that fiscal transfer mechanisms exist which automatically come into operation if countries within the single currency area become depressed and unemployment rises – as, for example, in an individual country where government expenditure on unemployment and social security automatically rises as unemployment rises which cushions consumption in depressed regions. At present, these mechanisms between the countries of Europe simply do not exist.

Finally, a fourth condition for an optimum currency area is that multiple currencies are seriously impeding trade and the efficient allocation of resources. Under these circumstances, moving to a single currency would maximise benefits. No one disputes that trade is an important engine of growth, and can be of mutual benefit to countries but, as pointed out at the beginning, trade has grown and flourished in Europe for the last 50 years with multiple currencies, and there is no firm evidence that fluctuating exchange rates discourage trade. All that can really be said on the benefit side is that there will be a saving of transaction costs, estimated at about $30 billion a year. This is a big saving absolutely, but very small in relation to the combined GDP of the EU countries, and set against the potential costs of monetary union. I know no one who believes that the current 11 countries of Euroland constitute an optimum currency area. This being so, monetary union is unlikely to lead to the real convergence of member countries. If anything, increased divergence is more likely. Therefore, greater regional divergence is also more likely given that regional disparities are more closely related to differences in performance between countries than to regional disparities within countries. All this, of course, is quite independent of the accession of new states to the EU that raises a whole set of different issues and is another story.

The picture I have painted for the future of Euroland may look bleak, but I see no redeeming features except small savings for businesses and tourists in exchanging currencies. The economic and political risks are enormous for such trivial gains. The great challenge in Europe at this present time is to boost growth and to create jobs. I see nothing in the single currency itself that is going to produce a more dynamic European economy (although I hope I am wrong). In my view, what regions and countries require as far as possible are individually tailored economic and social policies to suit their own particular needs. This is the direction in which economic policy-making ought to be moving for economic success and a more harmonious Europe, not the opposite of imposing an economic straitjacket on all countries, however dissimilar. The result may be irreparable damage to the cause of European integration.

The UK and the euro

As far as the UK is concerned, the promised benefits of ever-closer union with the rest of Europe have always been exaggerated, although I support continued membership of the EU. When there was a referendum on the Common Market in 1975 on whether the UK should accept the revised terms of membership, I (along with 7 million others) voted against, not out of anti-European sentiment in a petty nationalistic sense but because I thought the new terms would still damage the country's long-term economic interests. I believe the scepticism was justified. It is very difficult to demonstrate that the welfare of ordinary UK citizens has benefited significantly from full membership of the EU. The trading benefits could have been obtained from associate status without signing up to the Common Agricultural Policy and other arrangements that have made the UK one of the largest contributors to the European Commission budget. It was much to the credit of Mrs Thatcher that she renegotiated our budgetary contribution, but it is still not widely appreciated that each individual in the UK pays, on average, roughly £250 a year more for food than if the same goods were bought on the world market.

Even on the trade front, our European partners have penetrated the UK market much more successfully than UK producers have penetrated European markets with the consequence that massive trade deficits have arisen which have contributed significantly to the deindustrialisation of

Britain. This is a far cry from the promises held out in the two White Papers preceding entry into the European Community in 1973 which talked of the 'dynamic effects of a much larger and faster growing market' and 'the growth of industrial exports outpacing the growth of imports with corresponding benefit to the balance of payments'. The growth rate of output since joining the Community has not been the miracle promised. The growth of manufacturing output has been abysmal and the average growth of GDP since 1973 has been no more than 2 per cent per annum, lower than in the period 1950–73, and reduced by the deep recession between 1990 and 1992 as a result of the pound sterling being locked into the European Exchange Rate Mechanism (ERM) at an uncompetitive rate. That in itself should surely be a salutary warning to those pressing Britain to abandon the pound sterling and to adopt the euro as soon as possible.

Outside the confines of a single currency area, Britain has a wonderful opportunity to become the economic success story of Europe. There is no reason to suppose that trade, inward investment or the City of London would be adversely affected by staying out,[7] provided the country remained competitive. It is the last refuge of the scoundrel to argue that one of the largest economies in the world, after the US, Germany and Japan, cannot survive and prosper unless it surrenders its economic independence. What matters above all for the economic performance of nations are sensible macroeconomic policies underpinned by solid micro foundations. Macroeconomic policy mismanagement can easily negate the benefits of microeconomic reforms. This was no more evident than in the UK in the 1980s when, despite some very sensible supply-side reforms, misguided macroeconomic policies completely nullified their effects, leading to over 3.5 million unemployed in 1985. This should be a warning to the European Union, where unemployment averages 10 per cent, that no amount of reforming labour markets and reducing market imperfections will create jobs if there is inadequate demand for labour in the economy as a whole.

In contrast to most of the rest of Europe, the UK economy is currently in a relatively healthy state with inflation low, unemployment falling, and the growth of output improving. If Britain retains control of its own currency and exchange rate, and is able to decide its own interest rate and fiscal policy, it has the prospect of continuing the economic performance of the last four years. To sign up to the euro, and to lose control over the weapons of economic policy, would serve no useful purpose. We would be at the mercy of a European Central Bank whose sole purpose is to keep the lid on the price level despite the fact that there is no scientific empirical evidence that price stability is a precondition for faster growth or the creation of jobs. On the contrary, inflation and growth appear to be positively correlated within the range of 0–8 per cent inflation.

It would be churlish to wish the euro ill, but I fear that it is going to do great damage to the economies of Europe and to the noble objective of greater European harmony and cooperation. Economic and social disparities between the countries and regions of Europe are still vast, and there is nothing in the euro itself which is going to eliminate these disparities. If anything, without an effective regional policy and fiscal transfer mechanisms, they are likely to widen, making the task of political integration – if that is the ultimate aim of the euro – that much more difficult. The United Kingdom government would do well to steer clear of this risky venture for more than the lifetime of even the next Parliament.

Notes

1. Germany, France, Italy, Netherlands, Belgium, Luxembourg, Ireland, Spain, Portugal, Austria and Finland.
2. *The European Single Currency: A bad idea*, New Europe, 1999.
3. NUTS is the French acronym for Nomenclature of Statistical Territorial Units.
4. 'European Regional Unemployment Disparities: Convergence or Persistence?', *European Urban and Regional Studies*, July 1998.
5. *Sixth Periodic Report on the Regions: Summary of main findings*, February 1999.
6. See the MacDougall Report, *Report of the Study Group on the Role of Public Finance in European Integration* (Commission of the European Communities, Brussels, 1977).
7. See D. Lascelles, *Confidence in the City outside the Euro*, New Europe, 1999.

Selected Bibliography

Baddeley, M., Martin, R. and Tyler, P. (1998) 'European Regional Unemployment Disparities: Convergence or Persistence?', *European Urban and Regional Studies*, July.

Ball, J. (1999) *The European Single Currency: A bad idea*, New Europe.

Dignam, T. (1995) 'Regional Disparities and Regional Policy in the European Union', *Oxford Review of Economic Policy*, Vol. 11, No. 2.

European Commission (1999) *Sixth Periodic Report on the Regions: Summary of main findings*, Brussels, February.

Lascelles, D. (1999) *Confidence in the City outside the Euro*, New Europe.

Thirlwall, A. P. (1980) 'Regional Problems are Balance of Payments Problems', *Regional Studies*, No. 5.

Thirlwall, A. P. (1998) 'The Folly of the Euro', *European Journal*, March.

3

British Trade and Europe since the 1960s*

Martin Holmes

Introduction

I would like to take the opportunity to look at Britain's relationship with the European Union in economic terms over the last 50 years or so. I often find, when taking part in debates with supporters of European integration on economic topics, that they are eager to avoid discussing the Common Agricultural Policy, the Common Fisheries Policy, and Britain's gross budgetary contribution to the European Union, which has been averaging £7 billion a year. When these matters are raised there are two alternative topics that they do want to discuss; firstly trade and secondly monetary policy or the European single currency. So for the sake of argument I will leave aside the CAP, the CFP and the budgetary contribution because I know that many Eurosceptics will agree with me that they are iniquitous and in themselves are reasons for us not to be members of the European Union. Instead I am going to attack head-on the arguments that are always trotted out in every TV studio and newspaper article by the supporters of economic integration who prefer to concentrate exclusively on trade and on the single currency.

Trade policy – 1960s expectations

As far as trade is concerned the argument goes back to the 1960s, to the days of Conservative Prime Minister Harold Macmillan[1] and George Brown, the sometime Foreign Secretary in the Wilson administration. These two politicians did more than anyone else to inject into the

*First published in *The European Journal*, May/June 2000.

political bloodstream the idea that joining the EEC was all about trade, and in particular about an expanded home market for our manufactured goods. If only Britain could join the EEC's enlarged home market they argued, then the balance of payments problems which had bedevilled us since World War II would evaporate. Backed by much of big business and the civil service this view became the new orthodoxy. Some of you might remember the then Chairman of the British Motor Corporation, soon to be British Leyland, Lord Stokes, saying if only we could become a member of the European Economic Community we could then sell our Morris Marinas and Austin Allegros to the continent without facing the EEC tariff. The objective was to penetrate a bigger home market, rising from 55 million to 320 million people.

But I believe that from the start this argument was flawed. For one thing, our problems with the balance of payments in the 1950s and 1960s did not stem from lack of markets. After all, in contrast to 1930s protectionism, GATT had successfully opened markets on a global basis. They stemmed from the fact that the pound was hideously overvalued against the dollar in the old Bretton Woods system of fixed exchange rates. Each time there was a devaluation it was too little too late. If Rab Butler in 1952 had won the ROBOT battle with his Cabinet colleagues, and if the pound had been allowed to float, I suspect we would never have joined the European Economic Community as an escape from the balance of payment constraint.[2] Nor would we have joined if North Sea oil had been discovered a decade earlier.

The other reason why the argument for EEC membership was flawed was the poor quality of some products in the manufactured sector. I am not surprised that Austin Allegros and the Morris Marinas didn't sell in Europe, or around the world, because the quality was deficient, car industry industrial relations were appalling, the unions would go on strike as a first resort before negotiations had begun rather than when negotiations had broken down, and Lord Stokes and his colleagues in management were weak and ineffective leaders. In that era of nationalised industries, the industrial relations jungle, penal taxation and regulatory overload, not surprisingly the performance of British industry was often uncompetitive. Joining the Common Market, as it was then called, would have solved none of those problems, because it would not have addressed the over-valued pound and the Bretton Woods system, nor did it address the structural underperformance of British industry.

The first problem was finally addressed when the Bretton Woods system broke apart in the early 1970s and the second problem was finally addressed after 1979 when Margaret Thatcher came to power. But from the beginning the argument that it was necessary to join the European Economic Community in order for the balance of payments problems to be solved was always flawed because predicting trade patterns is so difficult. In the current decade the British economy is very different in terms of its export profile from the 1960s. No longer is Britain primarily exporting volume manufactured goods. If we look at the current composition of our exports, they are divided into four categories.

A global surplus

Firstly there is oil which is priced in dollars, and which trades in a global market as the increase in oil prices since early 1999 has indicated. Secondly there is financial services, which again is a global market. Britain has benefited from the massive expansion of financial services, 24-hour-a-day equity and foreign exchange markets, Big Bang in the City in 1986, the telecommunications revolution, and the increase in foreign direct investment, none of which were foreseen in the 1960s and 1970s when Britain joined the European Economic Community. This engine of foreign exchange earning for Britain is global and is irrespective of our membership of the European Union.

Thirdly, there is tourism. Again if we are looking at the debates in the 1960s and 1970s it hardly appeared on the economic radar screen. But tourism has changed in its nature since then. We now have the rise of the intelligent tourist who comes to Britain not for the sea and the beaches, but for the culture, the arts, the country houses, the pageantry and royalty, visiting particularly Oxford, Cambridge, Bath, Edinburgh, York and London. And where do these tourists come from? Primarily from the English-speaking world, plus our Japanese friends with their thousands of tiny cameras. In other words this is another engine of foreign exchange earnings for Britain which is global and has very little to do with the European Union.

Fourthly, there is specialised manufacturing. As we are aware, volume manufacturing has largely shifted towards the Pacific Rim countries and the NICs over the past 20 years or so. The British manufacturing sector is leaner, meaner, and fitter, and its range is global. Not surprisingly if we look at the balance of payments figures over the past 27 years while we have been a member of the European Union, we have regularly had a deficit with Europe while we have a surplus with every other continent on the planet. As Brian Burkitt has argued, the Single Market has not affected this outcome.[3] In other words, it is in

Europe where we spend our money, because we have a propensity to import European products, but we make it primarily by exporting to the rest of the world. Our exports to EFTA and NAFTA have grown faster than to the EU–14. Consequently I would argue that the process of globalisation is far more important for the prosperity of British economy than membership of the European Union.

Demise of regionalism

As such, European Union membership was based on the mid-twentieth-century notion that trade was primarily determined by geographic proximity. Not surprisingly this notion prospered when the world was divided into geographic blocks. The great ideological contest between East and West, between democracy and Communism, was a geographic strategic confrontation. NATO and the Warsaw Pact reflected the importance of geography. COMECON in Eastern Europe, and the European Economic Community in Western Europe reinforced that notion. In the 1980s there was a last hurrah for this form of geographical economics, with the moves towards ASEAN and APEC in Asia Pacific and towards NAFTA in the United States.

But the great economic changes that have taken place over the past decade, particularly technological changes, have shifted economics from favouring the risk-averse to favouring the risk-takers. It is this change that enables Britain to be in such a strong position to take advantage of globalisation. Indeed I would argue that the whole notion of a geographically based customs union model is obsolete. That is the model of the European Union which has now been superseded by globalisation. The EU has prized the stability of its economies of scale regionalism; but that stability is now a rigidity in the age of entrepreneurial dynamism which, more often than not, originates in small and medium-size firms, whose commercial reach transcends regional blocs.[4]

It has become a cliché to state that '60 per cent of our trade is with Europe'. This is meant to silence Eurosceptics, to excuse the CAP, the CFP, the budgetary contribution and the loss of parliamentary sovereignty. The approach of the euroenthusiasts is that other matters are unworthy of consideration because, as Tony Blair told the 1999 CBI conference, the EU 'takes nearly 60 per cent of our trade'. It is about time that this claim is subjected to some intellectual scrutiny. The 60 per cent figure is accurate as far as the volume of trade is concerned. But that is a figure which includes both exports and imports and primarily measures our propensity to import from Europe. What the 60 per cent measures is the fact that we wear Italian suits, drive German motor cars, and drink French wine and Danish beer. It is a measure of how we spend our money, not how we earn it. Thus it is possible to obtain a figure as large as 60 per cent.

But much more significant is the figure for British exports. If we look at 1998 total exports, visibles and invisibles, 48 per cent went to the European Union and 52 per cent to the rest of the world. But those figures themselves contain a massive distortion known as the Rotterdam/Antwerp effect.[5] Products which we export around the world are routed via Rotterdam and Antwerp on containers, and are then repackaged for final destination. But in the balance of payment figures they count as exports to the Netherlands or Belgium. Consequently the statistics are hopelessly skewed to the extent that every Belgian or Dutch person is consuming three times as much British produce as the average German or Frenchman. If the Rotterdam/Antwerp effect is taken into account we can adjust the export percentages accordingly down to 41 per cent exports to the EU and consequently 59 per cent to the rest of the world. Yet in the context of total GDP, as one authoritative study has shown, 90 per cent of the UK economy is not EU-related at all.[6]

In other words the trend of British exports would bear out that, although we are members of the European Union, our economic future does not lie there. It lies in globalisation not only because the fourfold division of our exports provides an excellent position to take advantage of world markets, but also because of the declining importance of geographical proximity in trade, investment and commerce.

Economic divergence

There is another important factor I want to raise in connection with Britain's economic relationship with Europe. If you consider the British economy up to 1979 an argument can be made that our political economy was converging with the European 'Social Model'. Convergence was towards more nationalisation, higher taxes, uncontrolled welfare spending, bigger budget deficits, and more socialism. Whether described as the European Social model, or the Rhineland capitalist model, the policies pursued by British governments were moving in that direction, in particular in the 1970s, not only under Labour governments but under Ted Heath.[7] The same argument cannot be made today. Since 1979 we have diverged in terms of our economic model from the continent. We have privatised and deregulated, we have opted for the free market and free trade. As Lionel Jospin bemoans, the Thatcher revolution was deeply hostile to values which are still held dear in France.[8] Continental Europe has retained its social model which in trade terms is less globalised and much more autarchic, as the never-ending addiction to the Common Agricultural Policy indicates. Our model of political economy now is fundamentally different from that on the continent, which is one of the reasons why our economy is now so much better oriented to globalisation than the continental economies.

Moreover the continentals tend to trade, with the exception of Germany, largely with themselves and they invest predominantly in Europe. We invest far more in the rest of the world which in turn invests more here in Britain. In 1998 nearly 60 per cent of inward FDI came from the Americas; in turn 70 per cent of UK outward FDI went to the Americas.[9] Many American and South East Asian companies invest in Britain despite the EU not because of it. They are attracted by our lower taxes, our flexible labour market, our regulatory environment that is more understanding of the needs of business, and the growing importance of English as the global business language. The arguments that have been advanced in favour of greater integration because our economic destiny lies in Europe, that our prosperity is tied up with Europe, are now obsolete. The scare that 8 million jobs would be lost, according to Simon Buckby of BIE, if Britain wasn't in the European Union was refuted even by the NIESR which had been asked to carry out the research. Over the years, Eurosceptics were always asked what was their alternative to Europe. There is now a very clear, powerful and intellectually coherent answer – the rest of the world, or globalisation.

Monetary policy – 1970s expectations

A second argument that has been advanced over the years in favour of greater integration with the EU relates, of course, to Monetary Policy. But significantly the EU integrationists have only in the last decade become fanatical about this particular project. Indeed if we look at the 1970s even supporters of membership of the EEC were cautious about the original proposal for a single currency contained in the 1970 Werner Report. Pierre Werner, the Prime Minister of Luxembourg, predicted that monetary union leading to the single currency could be created by 1980. Those of you that remember the 1975 referendum will know that the supporters of the 'Yes' campaign never discussed that plan. In as far as they did refer to it, it was contained in the HM Government document which stated that 'there was a threat to British jobs and growth posed by membership of a fixed currency area' – i.e. the Werner Report – 'that threat has now been removed'. So in 1975 we were not being promised monetary union even by those who urged a 'Yes' vote.

When the European Monetary System was concocted by Roy Jenkins, Giscard D'Estaing and Helmut Schmidt in 1978/9 Jim Callaghan made it clear that the pound would not be joining, and in his memoirs stated that he made that decision because joining would have damaging effects on British employment and growth. For these obvious reasons he did not allow the pound to join the ERM. Similarly in the early Thatcher period, the then Chancellor of the Exchequer, Sir Geoffrey Howe, declined to favour membership of the ERM. Initially the supporters of European integration, in the UK at least, did not appear to be enthusiastic about monetary union. So why did they change their minds and why is this now regarded by so many of them as the great economic panacea?

Consequences of Mr Lawson

The answer lies in the chancellorship of Nigel Lawson. It was Lawson who believed that joining the ERM was crucial to an anti-inflationary strategy. In the technical jargon he switched from domestic monetarism to exchange rate monetarism, believing that if the pound was targeted against the Deutschmark it would exert on the British economy the disciplines of the German monetary regime, supervised by the Bundesbank, so that Britain would conquer inflation. Lawson, to be fair to him, has never been a partisan of the single currency, but what effectively he did was to open the door ajar for the supporters of European integration to pour through who knew little of the arguments about inflation and the different types of monetarism. Some were intent on increasing the scope of European integration for political reasons, because they were aware that ultimately the plans for a single currency were pregnant with plans for political union as well. Others were bedazzled by the continental economic model which they wished the UK to emulate. Towards the end of the 1980s Margaret Thatcher's arm was twisted, not just by Nigel Lawson, and his successor at the Treasury John Major, but by the Foreign Office, the CBI, the *Financial Times*, the BBC, *The Economist* and many in the City and academia who advocated ERM membership.

The thing I find remarkable about the experience of the ERM is that we were aware all the time why it would go wrong. From the start we Eurosceptics said it was fatally flawed. We agreed with Mrs Thatcher that you cannot buck the markets. We predicted that it would fail. What I find amazing is that even when it ended in tears, even when it was such a disaster, even when it induced the longest and deepest recession since the 1930s, the supporters of the ERM seemed to learn so little. When economic meltdown finally led to the ejection of the pound from the ERM, as the markets would no longer accept its parity at 2.95 Deutschmarks, the same people who were the architects of that failed policy have ever since told us we have to accept the European single currency. The same *dramatis personnae*, the *Financial Times*, the BBC, *The Economist*, the *Guardian*, the TUC, the CBI, and many in the City and academia, urge the euro in the same language of 'stability' and 'reducing exchange rate risk' which underpinned the ERM. This brings me on to the three main arguments I have against the single currency. The first relates to the principle of exchange rates targeting.

Supporters of the euro told us, in the period September 1992 when the pound was ejected from the ERM, up to 4 January 1999 when the euro was launched on the Foreign Exchange Market, that the pound was weak, feeble, pitiful, on the floor, out of it, finished, inflation prone, and declining. Whereas the euro would be strong, powerful, and virile, sweeping aside the pound, Swiss franc and the yen before overtaking the dollar. That was the way that the euro was described to us, by its partisans such as Christopher Johnson, whose 1996 book *In with the Euro, Out with the Pound* relished the exchange of the weak pound for the strong powerful euro. But now that same combination of people over the past 16 months has been spinning us a different tale. They shamelessly argue, especially the CBI and TUC, that the pound is now overvalued, and if only we could ditch it in favour of that export-friendly euro.

This familiar style of reasoning proves that the supporters of European integration have made a fundamental flaw with regard to exchange rates. They are instinctive exchange rate targeters. They believe that you target the exchange rate first and then adjust the economy afterwards. They want to micro-manage the exchange rate; sometimes they may want to micro-manage it up, on other occasions, as we've seen in the last 16 months, they might want to micro-manage it down. Micro-managers of the exchange rate, like Nigel Lawson in the late 1980s, think they can buck the market. I do not believe that this approach is desirable or actually possible in the modern age. It was barely possible in the days of Bretton Woods in the 1950s and 1960s. Then the politicians thought they had near monopoly powers to control the circumstances of international finance, even though the speculative pressures were intense as the UK discovered in 1949, in 1956 during the Suez crisis, and in 1967.

But it is not possible for politicians any longer to fool and second guess the foreign exchange markets. The global capital flows are too great, the process of globalisation too far advanced, and those clever chaps in the market know what the politicians and the central bankers are up to. The politicians and central bankers, the exchange rate micro-managers, have been rumbled. And for this reason I think that it is a fatally flawed argument from the supporters of the euro either way, to try to micro-manage and ultimately to abolish exchange rates. In fact I take the opposite view, long live Exchange Rates, and long live exchange rate variations, because the Exchange Rate is an excellent economic shock absorber. Especially in bad times when there is a recession, the exchange rate takes the pressure off growth and employment.[10] If the exchange rate can't take the strain there will be higher unemployment and lower growth, which means more spent on social security, and greater pressure on budget deficits. Exchange rate stability can too often become a rigidity which diminishes economic performance and reduces living standards.

For these reasons the best policy towards the exchange rate is leave it alone. You can't create a strong economy by artificially creating a strong currency. The truth is the other way round. Let the market decide the exchange rate, because intervention on the currency market does more harm than good. There is no substitute for benign neglect. Of course, this is an argument that means we reject on principle any attempt to abolish the pound and to join the fixed exchange rate system which is the euro.

Cyclical objections

The second argument concerning the single currency concerns the cyclical movements of the UK economy in relation to Europe. This is an argument that I think is very important for Eurosceptics because it is pregnant with a number of dangers and pitfalls. It is true that our business cycle is out of line with the continent, and has been since 1976, and it is true that our business cycle is much more in line with the United States. UK interest rates are far closer at 6 per cent to those in the United States than interest rates on the continent which are 3.75 per cent. The argument can be made that in cyclical terms we tend to track the American economy rather than the continental economies, and that, for example, we certainly don't track the German economy. But this is an argument that cannot be relied upon. It is a secondary argument for the following reasons. We are now in an era of very low global inflation. It is possible that over the next decade or so, interest rates around the world may converge at a lower level. The circumstances of low inflation may enable the Federal Reserve, the Japanese Central Bank and the ECB to set interest rates that are very close to each other. Cyclical divergence has often been a function of high inflation which in today's low inflation economic environment may be much less significant.

Consequently it is vital for Eurosceptics not to be complacent about the current situation despite the latest opinion poll indicating 69 per cent of the British people favour retaining the pound. The greatest threat to the pound's popularity comes from the recent decisions of the Monetary Policy Committee of the Bank of England to increase interest rates. What I fear more than anything else could jeopardise the retention of the pound is an unnecessary recession in Britain while on the continent, because interest rates are lower, unemployment falls and the rate of economic growth increases. I do not think the Bank of England has necessarily got it right. There has been too much self-congratulation, including from within the Blair administration. The reasons given by the Monetary Policy Committee for interest rate rises have been highly dubious.[11] The claim that an increase in economic growth is by itself inflationary is not true. There are many examples of non-inflationary growth, not least contemporary UK and US experience. Theories of 'trend' growth are unduly pessimistic, reflecting the inflationary 1970s in which the models were devised. The assertion that a rise in house prices is in itself inflationary is hard to sustain over the late 1990s. The claim that an increase in wages is automatically inflationary, is unproven. Such a theory depends on how flexible the labour market is and whether there is a corresponding increase in the money supply. The claim that an external depreciation is inflationary is easily disprovable.[12] Alan Greenspan sees the rising US stock market as inflationary, as apparently does the MPC's Professor Vickers. On that basis America would have hyperinflation given the 1990s Wall Street bull run.

I am not of the view that the current generation of British and American central bankers, schooled in the 1970s inflation, are accurate in their recent projections that we are on the verge of a great inflationary surge. On the contrary it is much more likely that there will be a period of very low inflation in this country and worldwide. Indeed at 2.0 per cent in March 2000, UK inflation was at its lowest for 25 years. Roger Bootle, who spoke to the Bruges Group meeting last year, was right to pronounce the death of inflation in current circumstances. I cannot see the great monetary expansion leading to the inflation which the Bank of England anticipates. My fear is that eurosceptics may get too addicted to the cyclical argument, leaving us vulnerable to a recession in which our opponents portray continental Europe as more prosperous, with unemployment falling and with a high rate of economic growth. Thus we need to treat the cyclical convergence/divergence argument with caution.

Structural objections

That brings me to what I regard as the most powerful argument of all against the single currency, which is based on the divergent structure of the British economy. Our economy is structurally different from the continental economies. For example, we have a global trade investment pattern unlike the continentals. The pound has petro-currency status unlike the euro which is a crucial difference when energy prices are volatile or during an oil crisis. Our housing market is completely different from that on the continent and especially sensitive to changes in interest rates. We have 67 per cent rate of owner occupation, most of whom pay variable rate mortgages. We have a lower proportion of taxes as a percentage of GDP than on the continent, 37 per cent in the UK (it was 35 per cent at 1 May 1997), but 44 per cent on the continent. Our pensions funding is totally different. Because of our well funded contributory system we avoid the continental pension debt overhang. We have a flexible labour market as a result of the Thatcherite reforms of the 1980s while on the continent rigid and sclerotic labour markets persist. We have far more privatisation and deregulation and a far larger small business sector than on the continent. The continental economies emphasise economies of scale, the disadvantage of which can lead to 'dinosaur theory', huge corporations with a pea-size brain. The UK has a better balance between small, medium and larger companies to take advantage of high-tech innovation. For all these structural reasons which are features of the Anglo-Saxon model, our economy is fundamentally and structurally different from the continental economy and for that reason we need to set our own interest rates, impose our own taxes only through Parliament, and maintain our own currency.

Conclusion

That leaves the final point that I wish to make. So often the supporters of European Integration say that unless we sign up to greater integration, including the euro, we will be left out and left behind, in the great adventure of European integration.[13] In the familiar overused phrase, 'we will be isolated'. To this I would retort that not so long ago I was in a European country with 2 per cent unemployment, 2 per cent inflation, 5 per cent economic growth, control over its own fishing limits, and with a democratic parliament accountable only to its own people. If the 278,000 people of Iceland can do it, then we can do it, as the fourth largest economy in the world, superbly equipped to take advantage of globalisation, and with a democracy worthy of the name.

Notes

1. For further consideration of Macmillan's role see M. Holmes, *The Conservative Party and Europe*, Bruges Group publications, 1994.
2. Butler's own account of ROBOT is powerfully argued in *The Art of the Possible*, Hamish Hamilton, 1971.
3. Article in the *European Journal*, May/June 1999. Dr Burkitt assessed the cumulative deficit with the EU between 1992 and 1997 at £64 billion while over the same time period there was an aggregate surplus with the rest of the world of £48 billion.
4. For an intriguing analysis of the Baden-Württemberg economy's stability/rigidity see Charles Leadbeater, *Living on Thin Air*, pp. 147–8, Penguin Books, 2000.
5. For further analysis see *UK Trade in 1998*, pp. 30–1, Global Britain, 1999.
6. 'How "Dependent" is the UK on exports to Europe?', *Eurofacts*, 19 November 1999.
7. For further consideration of 1970–4 see M. Holmes, *The Failure of the Heath Government*, Macmillan, 1997.
8. See the *Guardian*, 16 November 1999. M. Jospin wrote that: 'Great Britain has always been more "globalised" than France. It is the country that invented free trade and gave it life – while at the same time knowing how to manipulate imperial preferences when this was in its interests. The

Thatcher revolution was deeply hostile to values that are still held dear in France ... We fully recognise globalisation. But we do not see its form as inevitable. We seek to create a regulatory system for the world capitalist economy. We believe that through common European action – in a Europe fired by social democratic ideals – we can succeed in the regulation of key areas, whether finance, trade or information.'

9. Surprisingly Christopher Huhne, The Liberal Democrat MEP and strong partisan of the euro, has sought to diminish the importance of investment income and capital flows to the UK economy. See his letter to *The Times*, 28 March 2000.

10. In contrast to his predecessor as Conservative leader William Hague has fully understood this point. For further analysis see M. Holmes, *William Hague's European Policy*, Bruges Group publications, 2000.

11. I exclude the contribution of Dr DeAnne Julius. See 'Low Global Inflation', Birmingham University lecture 20 October 1999, in which she argues that, '... intensified international competition – what some call globalisation – and the spread of the new technologies may be thought of, not as elements of a new paradigm, but rather as the current drivers towards low global inflation'.

12. Following the pound's exit from the ERM there was no inflationary increase as the exchange rate depreciated against the Deutschmark and the dollar. Similarly, the USA experienced a 28 per cent devaluation 1985–7 though inflation moved from only 4.3 per cent to 5.0 per cent. The Italian depreciation 1990–3, 20 per cent, witnessed a fall in inflation from 6.4 per cent to 5.4 per cent. Finland's inflation fell from 6.1 per cent to 1.0 per cent during its 24 per cent devaluation 1991–3 and Spain's 18 per cent devaluation 1992–4 was accompanied by a reduction in inflation from 5.9 per cent to 3.6 per cent.

13. For contrasting views see *Continent Cut Off?*, NIESR, 2000; and *EU Membership: What's the bottom line?*, IOD, 2000.

4
The UK and Euroland: Ships Passing in the Night

Graeme Leach

Introduction

The Economist has described the controversy over UK convergence with Euroland as 'the debate that will not die'. The government has stated that it will not consider joining the euro until the five economic tests (FET) have been satisfied. Any assessment of the FET is likely to follow the next General Election and to take place against the backdrop of a convergence in output gaps between the UK and Euroland. Recent projections from the OECD[1] show the output gap differential falling to zero in 2001.

The received wisdom regarding the FET has been well summarised by David Walton of Goldman Sachs. Walton has stated that,

> the Treasury can do some analysis but this is still a very political question ... these economic tests will provide a bit of cover: if the politics are not right then the Government can hide behind the economics. But if the politics are right, then the economics won't stand in the way. (*Financial Times*, 21 June 2000)

This chapter explains why economic forces may yet stand in the way of UK participation in the euro. It shows that sustainable, as opposed to transient convergence, is a long way off.

The IMF has supported the wait-and-see approach of the government, arguing that it will take time to see whether concerns over economic convergence and wage flexibility can be met. The IMF state that 'an over-riding case for or against entry could not be made at the present time'.[2] The Institute of Directors (IoD) takes issue with this

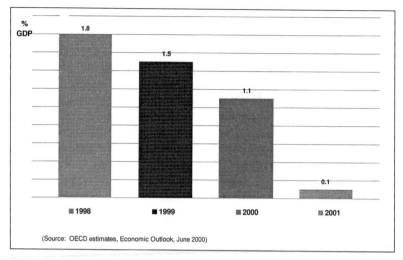

(Source: OECD estimates, Economic Outlook, June 2000)

Source: OECD estimates, *Economic Outlook*, June 2000.

Figure 4.1   UK–Euroland output gap differential

claim, arguing that an overriding case against entry can be made at the present time.

The five economic tests

To recap, the FET as set out by HM Treasury are:

- Are business cycles and economic structures compatible, so that we and others could live comfortably with euro interest rates on a permanent basis?
- If problems emerge, is there sufficient flexibility to deal with them?
- Would joining EMU create better conditions for firms making long-term decisions to invest in Britain?
- What impact would entry into EMU have on the competitive position of the UK's financial services industry, particularly the City's wholesale markets?
- In summary, will joining EMU promote higher growth, stability and a lasting increase in jobs?[3]

If one reads the HM Treasury report on the FET the scepticism of the most powerful department in Whitehall is all too clear. HM Treasury states very clearly that temporary convergence is insufficient and that there should be a 'period of stability'. Without convergence, HM Treasury states that the 'resulting turbulence could cause considerable damage' and the UK economy needs to have displayed 'sustainable convergence'.

The language and tone of the October 1997 report on the FET strongly suggests that HMT caution regarding UK participation in the near term remains firm. Moreover, strong opposition can be found in Threadneedle Street as well.

The Governor of the Bank of England, Sir Eddie George, commented on his relief that Britain had not joined EMU in January 1999, because 'we could have been the elephant in the rowing boat'. Sir Eddie George went on to state that, 'if we had joined EMU from the start ... it is very difficult to envisage how we would have avoided another inflationary boom in this country'. More recently (*Financial Times*, 24 July 2000) the Governor has challenged the view of the ECB President that there is a 'window of opportunity' to join the euro. George stated that 'we must put the emphasis on sustainability rather than transient opportunity'.

The emphasis on sustainable convergence reflects the fact that economies can appear to be converged in much the same way as 'ships pass in the night'. In other words, economies can at any point in time display similar rates of output growth, inflation or interest rates, but this tells us nothing about the future direction and speed they are heading.

The House of Commons Treasury Select Committee, to which Ruth Lea, Head of the IoD Policy Unit, gave evidence, states that 'our witnesses agreed that sustainable convergence is the most critical of the five tests and that it should be more than a short term cyclical coincidence'.[4]

What is convergence?

The standard dictionary definition of convergence is 'moving towards', but how a country moves towards in an economic sense is far less transparent. This lack of clarity and precise definition is apparent in the way in which ECB President Wim Duisenberg has been able to engineer a flip-flop in his views regarding UK convergence.

In a BBC *Money Programme* interview in early 2000 he stated: 'if ever the UK were to decide to join, you are talking about a moment in time which is years from today, well it has to be, one of the prerequisites for joining monetary union is to have demonstrated that your economic performance has converged [with the euro area]'.

However, by June 2000 the ECB President had shifted his view (*Financial Times*, 21 June 2000), stating that there was a window of opportunity and that 'UK economic conditions in terms of inflation, in terms of budgetary policy, in terms of interest rates, more and more point in the direction of the UK joining forces with the euro area'.

Which convergence test is best?

The House of Commons Treasury Select Committee has reported that, 'there is broad agreement that the UK meets all the Maastricht criteria, bar that of exchange rate stability'.[5] Nevertheless, what matters in the UK context is what the government has decided will be the criteria for entry, namely the FET. As we show below, the concern of the IoD is that until there is far greater convergence in monetary policy transmission mechanisms, together with structural or natural rates of unemployment (the NAIRU), any convergence can only be seen as ephemeral.

Why sustainable convergence is crucial

The costs and benefits of a monetary union are illustrated in Figure 4.2. Real divergence is shown on one axis (the extent to which countries face asymmetric shocks) whilst the adjustment mechanism is shown on the horizontal axis. In simple terms, the more flexible the economy is, the less costly is the loss of national monetary policy. Here the aim

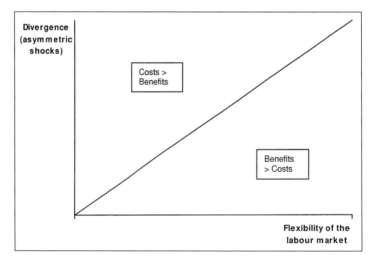

Figure 4.2   Costs and benefits of a monetary union

is to show that the UK economy is positioned above the line, i.e. there are likely to be frequent asymmetric shocks. Moreover, deeper economic integration is likely to weaken the adjustment mechanisms by increasing labour market inflexibility.

The first two economic tests which are concerned with economic cycles, structures and flexibility can be examined within the context of:

- The NAIRU (non-accelerating inflation rate of unemployment)
- The monetary policy transmission mechanism.

Both considerations are important in order to have an effective economic policy. For example, even if two countries were to have the same NAIRU, economic problems would still emerge if they had profoundly different transmission mechanisms in monetary policy – the obvious example being where one country had a large exposure to fixed rate debt whereas the other country was far more exposed to variable rate debt.

Alternatively, even if the two countries had the same transmission mechanism, it could engage at different times or speeds if their NAIRU differed. Inflationary pressures would emerge earlier in the economic cycle – and interest rates would need to rise – for the country with the higher NAIRU.

The NAIRU

If different economies have a different NAIRU then inflationary pressures will emerge at different stages in the economic cycle – sooner or later depending on whether the NAIRU is higher or lower in the countries concerned.

Whilst the NAIRU has fallen during the 1990s in the UK, in the EU it has increased over the same period. Figure 4.3 shows IMF estimates that structural (NAIRU) unemployment fell by 1.3 percentage points in the UK in the 1990s whereas it rose by 2.7 percentage points in Germany over the same period.

A significant part of the explanation of different NAIRU estimates is the different labour and product market regulatory structures across the EU.

Research by Koedijk and Kremers[6] shows a powerful link between the degree of regulation in the economy and growth in output. Over recent decades deregulation in the Anglo-Saxon economies has not been matched in the EU economies. The work of Koedijk and Kremers shows the UK has a high ranking – light regulation – in both product and labour markets. Koedijk and Kremers show there is a strong link

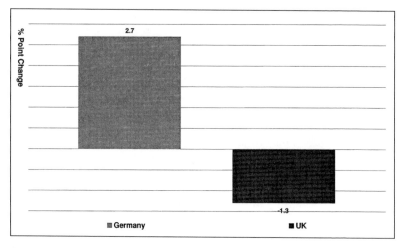

Source: IMF *World Economic Outlook*, October 1999.

Figure 4.3   Changes in structural unemployment (NAIRU) in the 1990s (% point increase/decrease)

between the degree of regulation and economic performance. Cluster analysis shows the alternative economic models in terms of their regulatory burden – Anglo-Saxon, Iberian, Rhineland and Mediterranean (see Figures 4.5 and 4.6).

These alternative models can also be grouped by GDP growth, with the least regulated economies displaying the fastest economic growth – and the smallest output gaps. Euro participation and deeper economic integration risks a higher NAIRU and lower GDP growth rate for the UK economy in the future.

Transmission mechanism

The importance of the monetary policy transmission mechanism can be seen in the various ways in which it can impact on an economy:

- An increase/decrease in interest rates leads directly to a decrease/increase in consumption and investment.
- An interest rate adjustment leads indirectly to a change in consumption via wealth effects emanating from equity and property markets – in accordance with the life cycle hypothesis of consumption.
- An interest rate adjustment leads indirectly to a change in investment via Tobin's Q – higher equity prices increase the value of Q

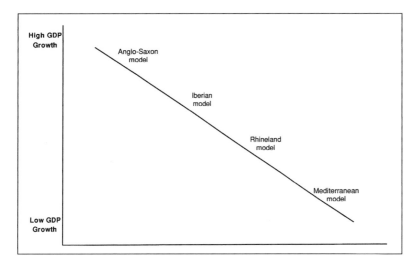

Figure 4.4 Economic models and GDP growth

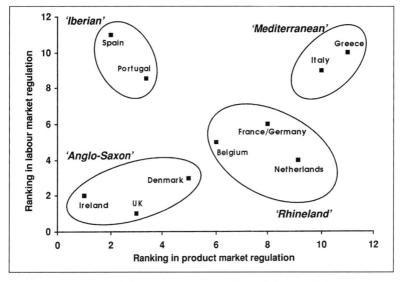

Note: Countries are ranked in increasing order of regulation: 1 = light regulation.
Source: K. Koedijk and J. Kremers, *Economic Policy*, 23, October 1996.

Figure 4.5 Alternative economic models (Degree of product and labour market regulation in Europe)

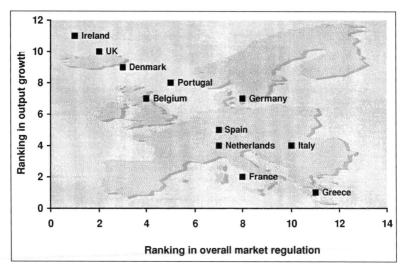

Source: K. Koedijk and J. Kremers, *Economic Policy*, 23, October 1996.

Figure 4.6   Economic growth and regulation

(the ratio of a firm's market value to the replacement cost of capital) and make it easier to issue equity to finance investment.

- An interest rate adjustment leads to a movement in the exchange rate which changes the balance between domestic demand and imports.
- Interest rate movements alter the disposable (wages and income from saving) and discretionary (available income for spending after paying for mortgages and borrowing) income of consumers.
- Interest rate movements impact differentially depending on the proportion of liabilities and assets at fixed or variable rates of interest.
- Interest rate movements impact differentially depending on holdings of equities and bonds by consumers.
- Interest rate movements impact differentially depending on the population profile and generational holdings of saving and borrowing.

There is a considerable economic literature showing that interest rate movements have a different impact on the UK economy from Euroland. For example, Oxford Economic Forecasting model simulations 'show that the impact on UK GDP [from a rise in interest rates] is considerably higher than for other EU countries'.[7]

The CEPR, in reporting a number of studies, have reported that:

a country where changes in interest rates have effects similar to those in other EMU members will be a country that has less difficulty in living with a common monetary policy. The transmission mechanism of monetary policy in the UK is however far from average ... unless UK balance sheets become more European, inside EMU, the UK would be more sensitive to changes in short term interest rates.[8]

Recent research by Maclennan, Muellbauer and Stephens analysed the contrasting nature of the UK housing market and how institutional characteristics influence asset prices and thereby produce 'substantially different responses to both interest rate changes and to worldwide equity price changes'.[9]

Despite these findings, the empirical evidence is also characterised by other results which seem to make the picture less clear. Table 4.1 summarises the empirical evidence of the impact on output of changes in monetary policy. The findings for single and multi-country models do suggest significant differences for the UK economy. However, the findings from small structural, reduced form and VAR models tend to

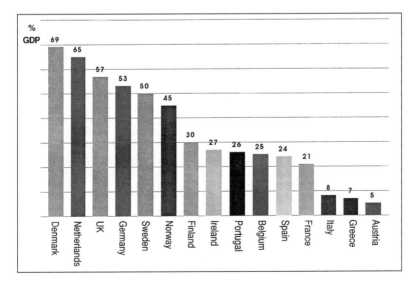

Figure 4.7   Outstanding residential mortgage debts as % of GDP (1998 figures)

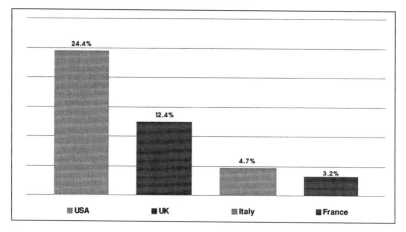

Source: 1997 figures, published in 'Stock Market Fluctuations and Consumption Behaviour', OECD Working Paper 98, 1998.

Figure 4.8   Household equity holdings as % of net wealth

Table 4.1   The impact of monetary policy on output

Study	France	Germany	Italy	UK
Single Country Models (BIS, 1995)	−0.4	−0.4	−0.4	−0.9
Fed's Multi-country macro model (BIS, 1995)	−0.7	−0.7	−0.3	−1.2
Small Structural Model (Britton and Whitley, 1997)	−0.5	−0.5	–	−0.3
Reduced form models	−1.5	−1.4	−2.1	−0.9
(Dornbusch et al. 1998;	−1.3	−1.2	−0.6	−0.5
Cecchetti, 1999)				
Structural VAR model (Gerlach and Smeth, 1995)	−0.5	−1	−0.5	−0.7

Source: C. W. Eijffinger and J. De Haan, *European Monetary and Fiscal Policy*, Oxford University Press, 2000, Table 6.2.

suggest that interest rate effects are weakest in the UK. This surprise finding suggests we should treat these results with caution. Maclennan et al. state that,

> simulations with large macromodels show large interest rate effects on output in the UK, consistent with economic reasoning. The fact

that research using VAR methodology has arrived at less conclusive results has persuaded some economists that these are minor issues ... however, research using VARs is seriously flawed.[10]

The limitations of VAR modelling have also been highlighted by the European Commission.[11]

The thesis that the UK has a significantly different monetary policy transmission mechanism is therefore based on single and multi-country econometric modelling together with available evidence regarding the proportion of debt at variable versus fixed interest rates. The case against is based on a very small number of studies with serious empirical deficiencies, with results highly sensitive to initial conditions.

Table 4.2 shows that there are significant variations across the EU in the proportion of credit at adjustable interest rates, ranging from 25 per cent in the Netherlands to 74 per cent in Austria. With reference to households alone, the UK is far and away at the top of the league with 90 per cent of borrowing at variable rates. UK consumers also have the highest proportion of household sector liabilities – as a percentage of disposable income – in the EU. Liabilities account for 111 per cent of disposable income in the UK, compared with 79 per cent in Germany, 75 per cent in France and only 28 per cent in Italy.[12]

Because the proportion of credit at variable rates is broadly comparable for the corporate sector between the UK, Germany and France, the result is that any one-size-fits-all ECB monetary policy would have a disproportionate impact on the household sector in the UK – this is an important political lesson the Government should be aware of.

Table 4.2 Credit at adjustable interest rates in the EU (% of total credit)

Country	All Sectors	Households	Firms
Austria	74	–	–
Belgium	44	18	67
Germany	39	36	40
France	44	13	56
Italy	73	56/59	77
Netherlands	25	8	37
Spain	43/64	–	–
Sweden	35	–	–
UK	73	90	48

Source: BIS, 1995.

Ex post and *ex ante* convergence

The foregoing has explained in conceptual terms why convergence in NAIRU rates and monetary policy transmission mechanisms is fundamental to sustainable convergence – without both any convergence will only be transient. However, it must also be considered that a country might be more likely to satisfy the optimal currency area criteria for creating a monetary union ex *post* rather than ex *ante*. In other words, euro participation of itself might accelerate the convergence process via:

- Financial markets
- Price convergence.

Financial markets

We will first consider whether the introduction of the euro is of itself likely to have an endogenous effect on the future financial system. An obvious possibility arises from so-called matching rules – when EU life insurance companies have had to match 80 per cent of their assets to the currency of their liabilities. This has led to virtually all assets being held in national currencies. The euro clearly enables companies to diversify their portfolios across Euroland. However, there are also deep-seated structural impediments to convergence in financial systems.

One school of thought[13] suggests that the financial structure of a country reflects the legal system and so variation in financial intermediation is a consequence of dissimilar legal structures. If this is true, then for as long as the legal systems of EU countries differ, then so too will the impact of ECB interest rate changes. Table 4.3 shows an index where a higher number indicates: (1) it is less costly for shareholders to exert influence on managers; (2) creditors can more easily reorganise or liquidate a company. The central message of the table is that countries with a common law system generally support the greatest investor protection and the most developed equity markets.

Price convergence

Professor S. Hall argues that the loss of an independent monetary policy is not the concern suggested by opponents of UK participation, because of the 'fundamentally different way that prices work inside a single currency zone. Within a single currency area it is simply impossible for two regions to experience different inflation rates for a prolonged period of time' (*Financial Times*, 5 July 2000). Hall makes the point that over the long term, inflation rates will need to converge

Table 4.3 Differences in EU legal systems

Country	Shareholder rights	Creditor rights	Enforcement
Austria	2	3	10.00
Belgium	0	2	10.00
Denmark	3	3	10.00
Finland	2	1	10.00
France	2	0	8.98
Germany	1	3	9.23
Greece	1	1	6.18
Ireland	3	1	7.80
Italy	0	2	8.33
Netherlands	2	2	10.00
Portugal	2	1	8.68
Spain	2	2	7.80
Sweden	2	2	10.00
UK	4	4	8.57

Source: La Porta et al. (1997), in C. W. Eijffinger and J. De Haan, *European Monetary and Fiscal Policy*, Oxford University Press, 2000.

within the euro zone. Consequently, he asserts that 'this simple point is profoundly important for Mr Brown's business cycle criteria. If inflation cannot be different across the euro zone, to any important degree, there is no need for an independent interest rate policy to control differential inflation pressures in the UK.'

The essential argument is that wage and price convergence will involve labour market restructuring and a convergence in NAIRU rates. The difficulty with this approach is the time scale involved. At present there are very substantial differences in NAIRU rates and little evidence of convergence or deregulation – witness the recent introduction of the 35-hour week in France. The theory also fails in the context of the monetary policy transmission mechanism – since the introduction of the euro there has been an increase in inflationary divergence across Euroland. Inappropriate monetary policy in Ireland, for example, has fuelled inflationary pressures. The European Commission (April 2000) has recently warned of the inflation threat and that five of the Euroland economies are in danger of overheating.

There are divergent views (see Figure 4.9) over the impact of the euro itself on economic convergence across Euroland. On one side lies the European Commission which argues that greater economic integration will lead to less divergence due to the promotion of intra-industry

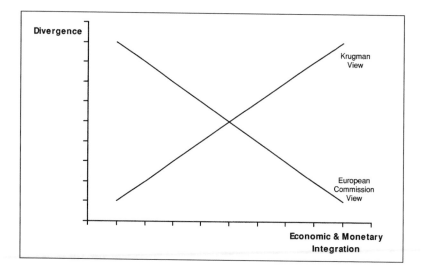

Figure 4.9   Economic divergence or convergence?

trade and income convergence – which is likely to reduce national specialisation.

In contrast, economists such as Professor Paul Krugman[14] argue that the euro will lead to greater divergence as a result of regional specialisation. Krugman argues that the combination of a single market and a single currency will lead to greater vulnerability to region-specific disturbances – although the 'region' in this sense may not necessarily coincide with the 'country'. However, at the very least the existence of such a debate suggests the UK should proceed with great caution when considering participation in the euro.

Finally, it should also be pointed out that supporters of UK participation often argue that even though one size does not fit all at the Euroland level, neither does it within the UK – for example because of a north–south divide. In other words, Euroland is not an optimal currency area, but neither is the UK.

The obvious response to this has come from David Smith, Economics Editor of the *Sunday Times*, who has written that, 'Some will say one size does not fit all in the UK and the MPC doesn't set interest rates appropriate for the North East. That may be true but two wrongs don't make a right' (*Sunday Times*, July 2000).

The UK is closer to being an optimum currency area than is Euroland – within countries there is greater scope for migration and regional fiscal transfers. If an area such as Euroland is too big to be an optimum currency area, then making it bigger must make things worse.

The five economic tests

Here I examine HM Government's five economic tests (FET) and whether or not they can expect to be satisfied over the coming years.

HM Government states that 'at present the UK's business cycle is not convergent with the rest of our European partners'.[15] However, as we have seen, OECD output gap projections do at face value suggest the UK economy is converging with Euroland. In Figure 4.1 OECD output gap projections showed the UK/Euroland differential falling from 1.8 per cent of GDP in 1998 to zero in 2001. The 2001 figure is significant because this is the order of magnitude that HM Treasury are likely to use in any post-general election assessment of the FET.

Generally the OECD is very bullish about the UK's prospects for participation in the euro. The OECD has stated that, 'on several scores, even as an "out", the UK is projected to be as close or even closer to the economic centre of gravity of the euro than some of the ins'.[16] Acknowledging that UK short-term interest rates are higher than euro rates the OECD states that, 'this would change should the prospect of joining become a reality'.

In this chapter the IoD challenges the OECD view that the UK economy has converged with Euroland. Indeed, the reason that we have an element of convergence in GDP growth rates at present is primarily attributable to *divergent* monetary policy.

It is very obvious that countries which have previously followed divergent economic cycles, could converge with each other with very close rates of growth. However, this merely reflects 'ships passing in the night'; it tells us nothing about:

- Whether the economies are sailing in the same direction – one might be slowing whilst the other accelerates.
- Whether the convergence is sustainable.

We consider four key economic indicators which suggest that:

1. Any short-term GDP convergence is transient and unlikely to reflect a sustainable trend.
2. Since the introduction of the euro inflation has diverged between the UK and Euroland.

The four indicators are:

- GDP correlation coefficients
- Inflation rates
- Interest rates
- Output gaps.

GDP correlation coefficients

HMT highlighted the fact that over the 1982–93 period UK and German GDP growth had a negative correlation coefficient.[17] Moreover, HMT's correlation coefficient estimates show the desynchronisation of UK and German GDP increasing over time.

More recent estimates by the IoD – over the 1990–8 period immediately prior to the introduction of the euro – show the UK's GDP correlation coefficient with Germany was –0.52, with France 0.3 and Italy 0.2. With Euroland as a whole over the 1990–8 period the GDP correlation coefficient was –0.03. In contrast, the GDP correlation coefficient between the UK and the US over the same period was 0.8.

UK GDP performance remains weakly associated with that on the continent. This has even prompted some to argue that divergent economic cycles are beneficial to the EU, since the UK can then perform a function as 'importer of the last resort' when GDP growth on the continent is poor.

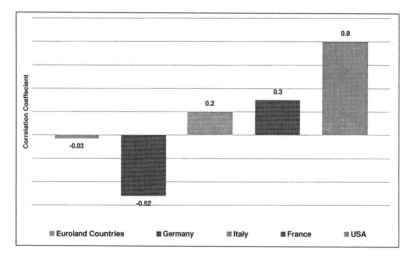

Figure 4.10   UK GDP correlation coeffecients pre-Euroland, 1990–8

Table 4.4 Inflation divergence (HICP measure) (% change year-on-year)

Date	UK	EU-15	Euroland	UK/EU gap	UK/Euro gap
January 1999	1.6	1.0	0.8	0.6	0.8
2001 Latest	1.1	2.3	2.6	-1.2	-1.5

Source: ONS CPI June 2000 release.

Inflation rates

Table 4.4 shows the relative inflation rate – harmonised index of consumer prices (HICP) measure – in January 1999 at the introduction of the euro, and latest data for March 2001. Table 4.4 shows that over the past 18 months the UK has transformed from having an inflation rate double that in Euroland to one that is less than half the average Euroland rate and the lowest in the EU – hardly synchronisation.

The Irish economy was the fastest growing economy in the world at the end of the 1990s. Despite this, interest rates were reduced in order to squeeze inside the euro. The end result has been a housing boom, 20 per cent plus growth in the money supply and an HICP inflation rate four times that in the UK – UK 1 per cent, Ireland 4.1 per cent inflation. Moreover, the inflationary pressures in Ireland have probably been muted by an exceptional boost to the labour supply from inward migration.

Interest rates

In 1997 the gap between UK and German/French short-term interest rates was around 4 per cent. The gap between UK and euro short-term rates was around 3 per cent. This fell to 2.4 per cent in 1999. Latest figures for May 2001 show the differential at 1.5 per cent.

However, the clear lesson of contemporary policy is that we have convergent economic cycles because of divergent monetary policy i.e.

Table 4.5 Interest rate differentials, UK versus Euroland (UK less Euroland rate)

	1993	1994	1995	1996	1997	1998	1999	2000	2001
Short-term rates	-2.7	-0.8	0.2	1.2	2.6	3.4	2.4	2.3	1.0
Long-term rates	-0.5	0.2	-0.2	0.8	1.1	0.8	0.5	-0.2	-0.1

Source: OECD Economic Outlook, June 2000.

higher interest rates and a high pound. Without this divergent monetary policy UK growth would be very much higher in 2001.
    The narrowing in the interest rate differential needs to be placed
in context:

• The interest rate gap at the short end is still significant. If UK rates
  were to fall by 1.0 per cent tomorrow, a boom–bust scenario for the
  housing market would become very possible.

• Falling interest rates could also herald a depreciation in the pound – in
  advance of euro membership – which accentuates inflationary pressures. Based on current indications, the MPC would wish to respond
  to any depreciation in the pound with higher interest rates. Instead,
  euro participation could facilitate lower interest rates and a lower
  pound against the background of an already tight labour market with
  claimant unemployment falling below the 1 million level.

• NIESR estimates of the FEER (fundamental equilibrium exchange
  rate) suggest the pound is more than 20 per cent overvalued. There
  is no guarantee that an overvaluation of this magnitude can be
  reversed. Consequently we may be forced to join the euro at an
  overvalued exchange rate – which does not suggest sustainable convergence.

Output gaps

According to OECD estimates, output gaps in 2000, across the EU,
ranged from plus 4 per cent (4 per cent of GDP above potential output)
in Ireland to minus 1.7 per cent in Italy (1.7 per cent of GDP below
potential output). [18] The UK was estimated to have an output gap of
plus 1 per cent. Cross-sectional comparisons such as this only partly
describe the degree of sustainable convergence – or lack of it.
    In order to assess sustainability, we need to examine the time series
of output gaps. Figure 4.11 shows the cumulative output gap of the UK
with Euroland. The cumulative output gap differential over the 1992–9
period (when the UK was outside the ERM) amounts to over 6 per cent
of GDP. In other words, if the UK had pursued a monetary policy
appropriate to Euroland there would have been a reduction in potential output of the order of £50 billion.
    It is possible to argue that the Maastricht criteria unduly constrained
EU output growth over this period. However, there is also a counter
argument that looking at cumulative output gaps fails to capture the
full impact of economic divergence – because of a lack of cyclical synchronisation.

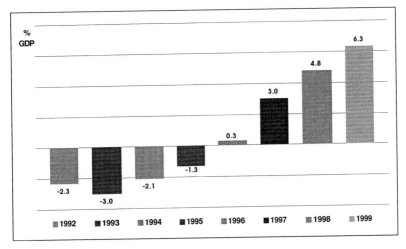

Source: IoD calculations based on OECD estimates.

Figure 4.11 UK–Euroland cumulative output gap differential (sign)

For example, the cumulative output gap over a ten-year period might be zero, because for half the period UK growth rate exceeded the EU rate by 5 per cent and for the other years was less than the EU by the same amount. Obviously, in this example, the economies were always divergent and so it is more realistic to examine absolute measures of cumulative output gaps – ignoring positive and negative signs.

This analysis shows (see Figure 4.12) that the absolute cumulative output gap was over 13 per cent of GDP. Note that the loss of potential output would not equate to the output gap in this example, because of both higher and lower relative growth. What the absolute measure shows is the potential for greater volatility in the UK economic cycle within Euroland.

Inward investment

Previous IoD reports have argued that only a small proportion of FDI into the UK is dependent on the single market, and even less on the single currency.[19] However, the debate over the impact on FDI of staying outside the euro shows no sign of abating. Drawing conclusions from individual corporate announcements is very difficult. At the same time that Toyota was instructing its suppliers to invoice in euros, Honda was announcing it is to double production in the UK. Just as the

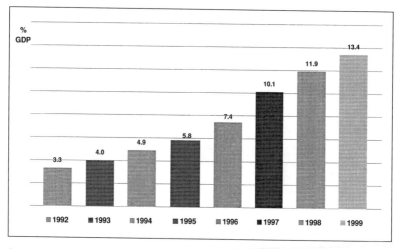

Source: IoD calculations based on OECD estimates.

Figure 4.12 UK–Euroland cumulative output gap differential (no sign)

President of Matsuchita suggested that his company's problems in the UK would be solved by joining the euro, the President of NEC stated that the UK and the euro 'is not so big an issue for us' (*Sunday Business*, 6 August 2000). The President of Matsuchita failed to mention that much of their TV production has already been moved to the Czech Republic – a low-cost base outside not just Euroland but the EU as well!

Latest statistics from Invest UK (formerly IBB) show that the total stock of foreign assets in the UK continues to rise, reaching £252 billion in 2000 – an increase of £100 billion over the past five years. The number of inward investment projects has increased strongly, reaching 757 according to latest figures. Invest UK also reports that interest from potential investors remains strong (*Financial Times*, 30 May 2000).

Figures from Dun & Bradstreet show the number of companies owned by foreign firms has increased by almost 24 per cent over the past two years. The number of foreign-owned companies doing business in the UK increased to 28,777 in 2000, from 25,802 in 1999 and 23,300 in 1998. Given the strength of sterling over this period, against the euro, this is a considerable vote of confidence in the UK.

Business surveys of FDI confidence by AT Kearney show the UK is only eclipsed by the US. The *Financial Times*, 25 January 2000 has

Table 4.6   Direct investment in the UK

		Total stock of foreign assets
1995	Q4	£137.9 billion
1996	Q4	£147.6 billion
1997	Q4	£ 167.1 billion
1998	Q4	£ 192.8 billion
1999	Q4	£ 243.1 billion
2000	Q1	£ 252.4 billion

Source: Invest UK.

reported that 'Investors prefer UK despite euro uncertainty.' The AT Kearney survey of chief executives shows that the UK is the second most attractive location in the world for inward investment, after the US.

One study, by Ernst & Young, does suggest that the UK's market share of inward investment into Europe has fallen over recent years. Ernst & Young report that the UK's share of inward investment fell from 28 per cent in 1998 to 24 per cent in 1999 – these figures exclude mergers and acquisition activity. This report is out of line with surveys by Invest UK and the United Nations Conference on Trade and Development (UNCTAD). Moreover, even if the figures are correct, they say little about the cause of the fall in market share. It is quite plausible to argue that any loss of attraction for the UK could be attributable to the greater regulatory burden on business introduced in recent years.

Britain in Europe argues that because of long lead times, it will only be in the years to come that we will begin to see the impact on FDI of the UK staying outside the euro. Against this argument is evidence from Invest UK that international interest remains high despite the fact that UK politics are likely to prevent participation for the foreseeable future. Moreover, the NIESR report that, 'When FDI plans were struck there were certainly many people who believed that Britain would be a late entrant rather than a permanent non participant.'[20]

However, the NIESR assert this view without presenting any evidence. At present, much of the debate about the costs of being outside the euro is based on the weakness of the euro against sterling. Many of those who presently support UK participation are in reality arguing for a weaker exchange rate. Unfortunately, joining the euro does not necessarily mean that the pound will weaken substantially. Lower interest rates might bring about a limited depreciation against the euro, but the

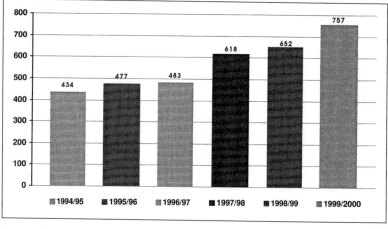

Source: Invest UK.

Figure 4.13   Inward investment: number of projects

currency could still be irrevocably locked at an exchange rate ill-suited to UK exporters.

The City

The IoD has reported elsewhere[21] that the City is just as likely to gain as it is to lose from being outside the euro. Since this report over a year ago no evidence has emerged to undermine that conclusion. Latest evidence reaffirms this view. The House of Commons Treasury Select Committee concluded that

> witnesses from the financial services sector were united in the opinion that they and in particular the City of London as a global financial centre, have not yet been adversely affected by the UK decision not to participate ... we are of the view that the success of the City will not be much affected if the UK chooses to join the euro or stay outside.[22]

In their evidence the British Bankers Association stated that: 'There are no areas of business which have manifestly suffered and there are some which have manifestly grown since the euro was launched.'

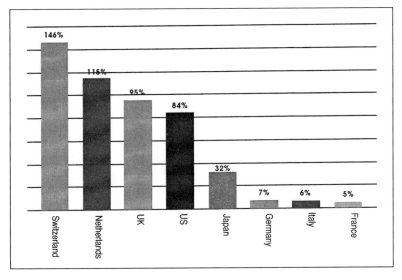

Source: InterSec Research Co., CCF Charterhouse.

Figure 4.14 Pension assets as % of GDP, 1999

Across many products, from asset management to forex, from OTC derivatives to bond issuance, the City's position is strong and improving.[23]

Despite the depth of financial markets in the UK (see Figures 4.14, 4.15 and 4.16), prior to the launch of the euro-concern regarding the City's future prospects centred on:

- The general development of EU capital markets, which have considerable potential for growth, thereby losing market share for the City
- The Target real time gross settlement system and the lack of full access to non-EMU countries
- The location of the ECB in Frankfurt.

Thus far, however, neither Target (which the City has access to via Chaps Euro), the ECB or the deepening in Euroland capital markets appears to have had a sizeable impact (see Seifert et al., 2000).[24] Some of the fears were always misplaced. For example, US banks have not moved to Washington to locate alongside the Federal Reserve. Confidence in the City's future prospects is best summed up by

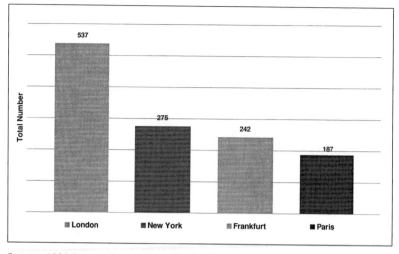

Source: 1999 Figures from Bank of England.

Figure 4.15   Bank representation (bank branches, subsidiaries and representative offices)

Deutsche Bank's decision to invest around $500 million in a new international investment banking HQ in London.

The Bank of England has reported that 'all the available evidence confirms that London has to date fully maintained its position as the main international financial market in the European time zone'.[25] The BoE acknowledges that the location of activity in many wholesale financial markets can be hard to pin down, but says that capital market activities, treasury and risk management operations, trading, fund management and research are all concentrating in London.

AT Kearney report that banks continue to rate the UK as the most attractive place in the world to invest (*Financial Times*, 25 January 2000). As a result, there are almost twice as many banks in London as New York, and more banks than in Frankfurt and Paris combined. One voice of concern over the City's future prospects was that of Lord Levine, the former Lord Mayor of London. In February 1999 Lord Levine stated that 'London's business would, in time, be eroded if the UK's entry into EMU is long delayed.' However, by the end of 1999 he had revised his views, saying that '[the launch of the euro] has been positive for the UK financial services sector ... the Government would have to look to other parts of the economy to support the case for joining'.

Two recent reports provide additional confidence. Research produced by the NIESR, for the London Chamber of Commerce, concluded that 'the City of London will prosper whether or not the UK joins the single currency'. Another report concluded that, 'provided the race is run fairly, being out should be no handicap'.[26]

The City retains huge strengths as the only true world financial centre. The depth of expertise and agglomeration economies located in the City are enormous – in most areas of the City's business it has five times the number of employees of Frankfurt or Paris.[27] Moreover, information technology suggests that existing financial centres should be able to serve wider hinterlands in the future. The share of pension assets in GDP is massive in the UK, compared with Germany (Frankfurt) and France (Paris).

There are very real concerns that participation in the euro might lead to a greater regulatory intensity being imposed on UK financial services. Clearly, the experience of the Withholding Tax illustrates that greater regulatory interference, including taxation in the City, is not prevented by staying outside the euro.

The IoD argues that UK participation in the euro will hasten EU integration and that there must be concern for a future scenario that entails UK participation in a single currency, followed by deepening moves towards a single financial market involving some form of super Euro FSA – such a body could well be established anyway regardless of the UK's participation in the euro.

The risk in euro participation is that it might encourage bolder moves towards a less market orientated regulatory environment. Seifert et al. have pointed out that one of the objectives of the FSA is to protect 'innovation and international competitiveness' in the City,[28] a requirement that has no match in any of the statutes for regulators on the continent.

Political convergence and future fiscal policy

Ultimately EMU is a political project and as yet, as Figure 4.17 shows, there is very little political convergence in the UK electorate's support for euro participation, as compared with our EU partners.

Figure 4.18 shows the future income tax rises required to maintain generational balance in the fiscal positions of six EU countries. The tax rises are based on inter-generational accounting estimates produced by L. Kotlikoff and N. Ferguson, published in *Foreign Affairs* (March/April 2000). The estimates suggest that the already large gap – in the share of

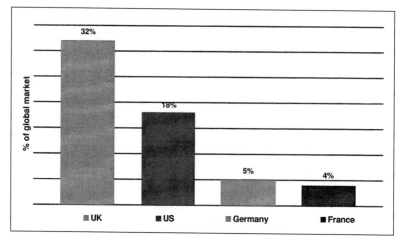

Source: Bank of England, *Practical Issues Arising from the Euro*, December 1999.

Figure 4.16   Foreign exchange turnover: global market share

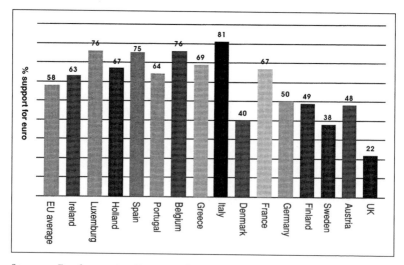

Source: Eurobarometer, European Commission, July 2000.

Figure 4.17   No political convergence (% population who support the euro)

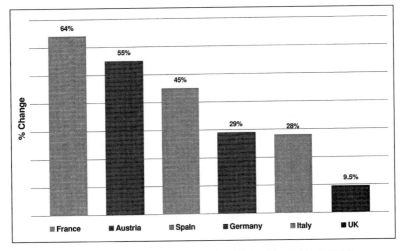

Source: L. Kotlikoff and N. Ferguson, *Foreign Affairs*, March/April 2000.

Figure 4.18 Generational balances (future income tax rises required to maintain generational balances)

public expenditure in GDP – between the UK and the rest of the EU will widen further in the future. OECD figures show that taxes accounted for 40 per cent of GDP in the UK and 45 per cent in the EU in 1999.[29]

Consequently, in the future we are likely to see expanding political divergence between the UK and the EU as a result of the fiscal implications of deeper EU integration. In other words, the electorate is likely to connect future monetary and fiscal policy harmonisation – with the former hastening the latter – as the price of euro participation.

Appendix: the IoD Convergence Contract

In August 1999 the IoD attracted considerable media attention when it published its 'Convergence Contract' (the contract was 'adopted' by the *Sun* newspaper!).

The IoD published the contract in order to highlight the structural changes required to provide sustainable convergence with Euroland. Moreover, key elements of the contract stress the need for reform across Euroland and why the UK alone cannot generate sustainable convergence.

The convergence contract shows that the only sensible way the UK economy can converge with Euroland is if Euroland itself changes towards an Anglo-American style system. This is highly unlikely to happen and explains why the IoD says the UK should stay outside the euro for the foreseeable future.

The contract criteria were:

- The GDP correlation coefficient between the UK and Euroland should exceed that with the US for a decade
- Euroland should account for more than half of total current account earnings for a sustained period
- The proportion of the UK mortgage stock at fixed rates should converge with Euroland
- The gap between UK and Euroland unemployment rates, activity rates and employed populations should halve, but without a deterioration in the UK's position
- The gap between UK and Euroland tax shares should halve, but without a deterioration in the UK's position.

Notes

1. OECD, *Economic Outlook*, No. 67, June 2000.
2. IMF, *World Economic Outlook*, March 2000.
3. HM Treasury, *UK Membership of the Single Currency – An assessment of the Five Economic Tests*, October 1997.
4. House of Commons Treasury Select Committee, *8th Report*, July 2000.
5. Ibid.
6. K. Koedijk and J. Kremers, *Economic Policy* 23, October 1996.
7. Reported in *Strainspotting*, HSBC James Capel Economics, November 1997.
8. CEPR, *The Ostrich and the EMU – Policy choices facing the UK*, 1997.
9. Maclennan, Muellbauer and Stephens, 'Asymmetries in housing and financial institutions and EMU', *Oxford Review of Economic Policy*, Autumn 1998.
10. Ibid.
11. European Commission, *Economic Policy in the EU – A study by the European Commission Services*, Oxford University Press, 1998.
12. OECD, *Economic Outlook*, annex table 58.
13. La Porta et al. 1997, in C. W. Eijffinger and J. De Haan, *European Monetary and Fiscal Policy*, Oxford University Press, 2000.
14. P. Krugman, *Geography and Trade*, MIT Press, 1991.
15. HM Treasury, *UK Membership of the Single Currency*.
16. OECD, *EMU One Year On*, February 2000.
17. HM Treasury, *UK Membership of the Single Currency*.
18. OECD, *Economic Outlook*.

19. IoD, *The UK and the Euro – Better out than in?*, April 1999.
20. NIESR, *Economic Review*, No. 173, July 2000.
21. IoD, 'Protecting the City', in *The UK and the Euro*, April 1999.
22. House of Commons Treasury Select Committee, *8th Report.*
23. W. C. Seifert et al., *European Capital Markets*, Macmillan, 2000.
24. See ibid.
25. Bank of England, *Practical Issues Arising from the Euro*, December 1999.
26. CFSI, *La Prix de l'Euro*, February 1999.
27. See Seifert et al., *European Capital Markets.*
28. Ibid.
29. OECD, *Economic Outlook*, annex table 29.

5
Towards 'A Treaty of Commerce': Euroland and NAFTA Compared

Keith Marsden

Introduction

> What has made the European family of nations an improving instead of a stationary portion of mankind? Not any superior excellence in them, which, when it exists, exists as the effect, not as the cause; but their remarkable diversity of character and culture. Individuals, classes, nations, have been extremely unlike one another; they have struck out a great variety of paths, each leading to something valuable ... Europe is, in my judgement, wholly indebted to this plurality of paths for its progressive and many-sided development. (John Stuart Mill, *On Liberty*, Chapter III, 1859)

Writing in the *Los Angeles Times*, former French president Valéry Giscard d'Estaing and former German Chancellor Helmut Schmidt criticised 'those in Washington who aspire to maintain some control over Europe in order to facilitate America's global geo-political aims'. The EU's 'historically unique goal', they say, is to form a country like the US. 'First priority must be given to institutional reform.' Enlarging the EU without first fortifying its institutions 'may end up diluting the union into a mere free trade area'. Deepening institutions can only be accomplished by a hard core of countries, they suggest. Britain is conspicuously absent from their list.

German Foreign Minister Joscha Fischer continued in a similar vein in a speech at Humboldt University, Berlin entitled *From Confederacy to Federation – Thoughts on the finality of European integration*:

> In the coming decade we will have to enlarge the EU to the east and south-east ... If we are to be able to meet this historic challenge, we

must put into place the last brick in the building of European integration, namely political integration.

Europe faced a stark choice, he suggested, between 'erosion or integration':

> Enlargement will render imperative a fundamental reform of the European institutions ... Clinging to a federation of states would mean a standstill with all its negative repercussions ... There is a very simple answer: the transition from a union of states to full parliamentarisation as a European Federation ... This means nothing less than a European Parliament and a European Government which really do exercise a legislative and executive power within the Federation. This Federation will have to be based on a constituent treaty.

Herr Fischer accepted the possible need to form a hard core, or in his words, 'a centre of gravity'.

> Such a group of states would conclude a new European framework treaty, the nucleus of a constitution of the Federation ... Such a centre of gravity would have to be the avant-garde, the driving force for the completion of political integration.

But he ruled out the idea of 'variable geometry' where different groups would cooperate together while retaining sovereignty and policy flexibility in some areas:

> It is of paramount importance that closer cooperation should not be misunderstood as the end of integration ... It would be critically important to ensure that the EU *acquis* is not jeopardised, that the union is not divided and the bonds holding it together are not damaged, either in political or legal terms.

In other words, alternative policies that might pose a competitive challenge to the 'centre of gravity' would not be tolerated. The outspoken fear of federalists is that the countries which stay outside the 'core' will prove to be more agile, and accelerate past them in economic performance. To prevent this, Herr Fischer calls for a unified legal system. In his view, the European Council meeting in Tampere:

marked the beginning of a new far-reaching integration project, namely the development of a common area of justice and internal security ... Common laws can be a highly integrative force.

And to ensure that the power of the hard core is not weakened by enlargement, he insisted that the current Inter-Governmental Conference must:

put in place the institutional preconditions for the next round of enlargement ... Resolving the three key questions – the composition of the Commission, the weighting of majority votes in the Council and particularly the extension of majority decisions – is indispensable.

Herr Fischer also claimed that every stage of the process of European integration 'depended essentially on the alliance of Franco-German interests'. Moreover, 'One thing at least is certain: no European project will succeed in the future without the closest Franco-German cooperation.'

And he dismisses British reservations as mere semantical quibbles:

I know that the term 'federation' irritates many Britons but to date I have been unable to come up with another word. We do not wish to irritate anyone.

Herr Fischer states bluntly that:

The introduction of the Euro was not only the crowning-point of economic integration, it was also a profoundly political act, because a currency is not just another economic factor but also symbolises the power of the sovereign who guarantees it.

Such frankness should be welcomed. It helps to clarify the debate on Europe. Romano Prodi, President of the European Commission, has also become more forthright. Addressing the European Parliament, he attacked the unanimity requirement which 'means either complete paralysis or reducing everything to the lowest common denominator'.

Britain faces a simple choice. Should we continue to argue for an end to 'ever-closer union', knowing that this has little chance of success? Or should we consider renegotiating the terms of our membership, while exploring the possibility of joining another club whose rules and members' behaviour are more congenial?

This chapter examines one such alternative club – the North American Free Trade Agreement (NAFTA) whose current members are the United States, Canada and Mexico. The analysis compares NAFTA with the 11 'founding' members of the European Monetary Union (Euroland). The US International Trade Commission has recently begun hearings on the possibility of enlarging NAFTA to include Britain and perhaps other European countries (when it could be renamed NAAFTA – the North American and Atlantic Free Trade Area).

This chapter highlights economic trends since December 1992 (i.e. the date when NAFTA was formed). Wherever available, aggregate or average data for the two groups are cited. Data for the UK and Eastern European countries show how they have been affected by their different forms of association with the EU. Information is also provided for Russia. World aggregate data are given in some cases to serve as overall reference points.

The following questions are addressed:

- Which area offers the largest markets?
- How affluent are their customers?
- Where is market demand growing fastest?
- Whose markets are most open to outsiders?
- Which group has the strongest links with the global economy?
- Whose trade expansion is the most dynamic?
- Are markets distorted by government subsidies?
- Which system creates most jobs?
- Where is labour productivity rising fastest?
- Are workers better off in NAFTA or Euroland?
- How do their 'human development records' compare?
- Where are living standards rising fastest?
- Whose fiscal policies encourage hard work and enterprise?
- Where is investment capital better mobilised?
- Which system has attracted most foreign investment?
- Where has investment grown fastest?
- What are their strengths in science and technology?
- Where are foreign workers more welcome?
- Where is economic freedom better safeguarded?

Which area offers the largest markets?

NAFTA's total population of 399 million in 1999 topped Euroland's by more than 100 million, as shown in Table 5.1.

Table 5.1 Market size, 1999

	Population		GDP	
	Millions	*%*	*$ppp billions*	*%*
US	271	4.6	9,054	21.9
Canada	31	0.5	827	2.0
Mexico	97	1.6	909	2.2
NAFTA	399	6.7	10,790	26.1
Euroland	290	4.9	6,532	15.8
UK	59	1.0	1,323	3.2
East & Central Europe	184	3.1	1,199	5.8
Russia	149	2.5	992	2.9
World	5,950	100	41,344	100

Sources: World Bank, *World Development Indicators*, Table 2.1 and IMF, *World Economic Outlook*, April 2000, Statistical Appendix Tables A and I.

Some commentators talk about British access to 370 million customers in the EU. But this includes Britain's own domestic market of 59 million consumers. Indeed, if Britain joined an enlarged NAAFTA, it would have free access to 55 per cent more customers than in Euroland.

And the value of NAAFTA's markets would be larger still. The combined purchasing power of NAFTA and the UK, measured in purchasing power parity (ppp) dollars (which take account of differences in domestic prices), amounted to more than $12 trillion in 1999. This was nearly double that of Euroland and over 29 per cent of total world GDP.

Enlargement of Euroland to include Eastern and Central European countries would add 184 million customers. Their purchasing power is substantially lower however. So even if all 18 of these countries (excluding Russia) joined overnight, they would boost Euroland demand by only $1.8 trillion, or 18 per cent.

How affluent are their customers?

Despite Mexico's relative poverty, NAFTA's average per capita GDP of $27,040 was 20 per cent higher than Euroland's in 1999.

NAFTA customers have more disposable income to spend on the sophisticated products and services on which Britain's industrial future depends. The US in particular offers rich pickings. On average, its 271 million customers each had over $33,000 to spend (including the outlays of firms and the government on their ultimate behalf) in 1999.

This was nearly 50 per cent more than in either Euroland or the UK. National incomes per head in Russia and other Eastern and Central European countries were just a fifth of the American level, and below the world average, as indicated in Table 5.2.

Where is market demand growing fastest?

NAFTA's market is more dynamic than that of Euroland. Its real GDP rose at an average annual rate of 3.6 per cent since 1992, double Euroland's rate. Total NAFTA real income was 28 per cent higher in 1999 than seven years earlier, compared with a 13 per cent increase in Euroland (see Table 5.3).

Table 5.2 GDP per head, 1999

	$ppp per head	*Index*
US	33,410	481
Canada	26,680	384
Mexico	9,370	135
NAFTA	27,040	389
Euroland	22,520	324
UK	22,420	323
East & Central Europe	6,520	94
Russia	6,660	96
World	6,950	100

Sources: World Bank, *World Development Indicators*, 2000, Table 2.1 and IMF, *World Economic Outlook*, April 2000, Statistical Appendix Tables A and I.

Table 5.3 Growth in GDP (annual percentage change, 1993–9)

	1993	*1994*	*1995*	*1996*	*1997*	*1998*	*1999*	*Average 1993–9*	*Increase 1999/2*
US	2.4	4.0	2.7	3.7	4.5	4.3	4.2	3.7	29
Canada	2.3	4.7	2.8	1.7	4.0	3.1	4.2	3.3	26
Mexico	0.7	4.5	–6.2	5.1	6.8	4.8	3.4	2.7	21
NAFTA	2.3	4.1	2.0	3.7	4.6	4.2	4.1	3.6	28
Euroland	–0.8	2.3	2.2	1.3	2.2	2.8	2.3	1.8	13
UK	2.3	4.4	2.8	2.6	3.5	2.2	2.0	2.8	22
East & Central Europe	–3.8	–2.9	1.7	1.6	2.3	1.8	1.4	0.3	2
Russia	–10.4	–11.6	–4.2	–3.4	0.9	–4.5	3.2	–2.0	–15
World	2.3	3.7	3.6	4.1	4.1	2.5	3.3	3.7	29

Sources: OECD, *Economic Outlook*, December 1999, Annex Table 1 and IMF, *World Economic Outlook*, April 2000, Appendix Table 1.

While Euroland's growth has picked up recently – the IMF projects that it will reach 3.2 per cent in 2000 – its long-term trends are far from encouraging. Since the EU began its drift to 'ever-closer union', the more its economic growth has slowed down, unemployment has soared and real wages have stagnated. Eurostat data show that the real GDP growth of the 11 present members of Euroland averaged 5.3 per cent annually during the 1960s and 3.3 per cent in the 1970s (when seven countries were not yet members of the EU), and then dropped to 2.4 per cent in the 1980s and a mere 1.8 per cent in the 1990s. Their average unemployment rate has gone in the opposite direction, rising from 2.3 per cent in the 1960s, to 4.2 per cent in the 1970s, to 9.1 per cent in the 1980s, and to 10.5 per cent over the last decade. And wage increases have become desultory: in the heady years of the 1960s, workers' real compensation soared by 5.9 per cent annually. During the 1990s they have had to be content with annual increases of just 0.7 per cent.[1]

Mexico's growth was held back by a severe recession in 1995, due to a financial crisis. But it rebounded the following year and has forged ahead at a rapid pace as the benefits of NAFTA membership became more widespread. Since 1992, its GDP has risen by 21 per cent. A blistering 7.9 per cent growth rate was achieved in the first quarter of this year. And its financial recovery is reflected in Moody's Investors Services Inc. giving Mexican bonds and notes an investment-grade rating for the first time (only three other Latin American countries are members of this exclusive club). A Moody vice-president is quoted in the *International Herald Tribune* (12 June 2000) as saying that it had based its decision on the perceived success of many initiatives of Mexican President Ernesto Zedillo: a more manageable debt load, a flexible exchange rate policy and a dynamic export sector that is 'well-integrated into the North American economy'.

In contrast, Eastern European economies have stagnated. Growth rates have averaged a mere 0.3 per cent annually since 1992. Geographical proximity to higher-income countries to the West has been of little help. Nor, apparently, have the considerable sums spent by the EU on technical assistance designed to prepare them for full membership.

UK output jumped by 22 per cent over the last seven years. It was boosted by a more flexible labour market, lower taxes and a more attractive climate for foreign investors.

Russia has remained deep in the doldrums. Its GDP has dropped by 29 per cent since 1992.

In sharp contrast, world output has risen by 29 per cent, reflecting buoyant demand in Asia in particular.

Which markets are most open to outsiders?

NAFTA markets are more accessible to exporters located outside its area, as shown in Table 5.4. Extra-NAFTA merchandise imports reached $759 billion in 1998, nearly 60 per cent of its total imports. In comparison, Euroland countries bought an estimated $637 billion of goods from outside the EU, representing around 37 per cent of their total merchandise imports.

The formation of the EU has resulted in trade diversion at the expense of other regions. For Western Europe as a whole, the share of total imports coming from the rest of the world has dropped to 31.0 per cent in 1998 from 43.8 per cent in 1963.

WTO data for the US and Canada combined show that inter-regional imports remained at a remarkably constant 72.5 per cent of total imports in 1993 and 1998, and were up from 65.7 per cent in 1963. But Mexico's exports to its North American partners rose to 8.8 per cent of their total imports, from 5.9 per cent in 1993 and 2.5 per cent in 1963.

Mexico has recently negotiated a free trade agreement with the EU which will, *inter alia*, abolish tariffs on industrial goods by the year 2003. As with NAFTA, this agreement will ease Mexico's access to the EU's markets without any loss of sovereignty or independence. In return, Mexican markets will become more open to the UK (and

Table 5.4   Merchandise imports

	Value (1998)	Share in total imports		
	$ billions	1990	1997	1998
NAFTA				
Total Imports	1,271	100.0	100.0	100.0
Intra-imports	512	34.4	39.9	40.3
Extra-imports	759	65.6	60.1	59.7
Euroland				
Total Imports	1,726	100.0	100.0	100.0
Intra-imports	1,089*	63.0*	62.9*	63.1*
Extra-imports	637*	37.1*	37.1*	36.9*

* Estimate.
Source: World Trade Organisation, *Annual Report 1999*, Tables 1.5 and 1.9.

Euroland) exporters. Their ability to take advantage of the opportunities is constrained by a growing EU regulatory burden which is estimated to cost up to 3 per cent of GDP.[2]
Were Britain to join NAFTA, our exports to this market could be expected to receive a substantial boost. Despite existing trade barriers, Americans spent $237 per head on British goods in 1998 compared with $500 by other EU members. Removal of import tariffs (currently averaging 5.2 per cent in the US, 7.5 per cent in Canada and 13 per cent in Mexico) would open up larger and wider market opportunities for British exporters, even if they were obliged to give up their duty-free access to Euroland.

Who has the strongest links to the global economy?

The growing importance of trade in the world's economies is one indication of strengthening global economic relationships. This has occurred without political integration. In fact, the number of nation states has increased markedly since the foundation of the United Nations and other multilateral institutions involved with trade, such as the World Bank, GATT/WTO, and the IMF.

Table 5.5 shows the changes between 1987 and 1997 in the relative importance of the trade in goods in relation to overall GDP. It also shows the trade in goods as a proportion of GDP derived from the production of physical goods (that is, excluding services).

Table 5.5   Links with the global economy, 1987 and 1997

	Trade in goods			
	% of ppp GDP		% of goods GDP	
	1987	1997	1987	1997
US	14.0	20.4	50.3	75.3
Canada	44.0	62.9	109.5	n.a.
Mexico	7.3	29.3	55.4	144.8
Euroland	15.7*	22.9*	49.6*	38.5*
UK	35.5	47.6	92.5	81.2
Poland	13.9	27.0	58.7	96.2
Hungary	30.1	55.2	112.1	181.4
Russia	–	21.3	–	64.4

* Extra-Euroland trade only; intra-Euroland trade is excluded because it is equivalent to trade between US states which is not recorded in international trade statistics.
Source: World Bank, *World Development Indicators 1999*, Tables 6.1 and 6.5.

It is noteworthy that Euroland has become less integrated with the rest of the world over this ten-year period. The share of goods traded (imports plus exports) with countries outside Euroland dropped to 38.5 per cent of the GDP generated in its goods sector in 1997, down from 49.6 per cent in 1987.

On the other hand, the US developed stronger links with the global economy. The value of goods traded reached 75 per cent of its goods GDP in 1997, up from 50 per cent in 1987. Britain's trade in goods dropped in relative terms, but still amounted to a hefty 81 per cent of goods GDP. But neither the US nor the UK got close to Mexican levels of outward orientation. Its trade in goods reached nearly 145 per cent of its goods GDP. But it should be pointed out that the bulk of its exports go to the US.

These trends show political integration is not a prerequisite for closer economic ties between nations, nor for effective international cooperation.

Smaller Eastern European countries like Poland and Hungary have extensive trading relationship with other countries, but much of their trade is with lower income customers and suppliers within their own region. They have lost most of their former market in Russia (which, for example, accounted for only 3 per cent of Hungary's exports in 1998). They seem to have focused their energies on trying to meet the legislative demands of the EU, hoping to become members. But because of numerous tariff and non-tariff barriers, they have been unable to increase their penetration of Western European markets substantially.

The value of merchandise exports from the whole of the former Soviet bloc fell by 5 per cent in 1998 and represented only 4 per cent of world exports. Their combined share of Western European imports dropped to 4.7 per cent in 1998 from 5.4 per cent in 1983.[3]

Whose trade is most dynamic?

NAFTA's merchandise imports are growing faster than the EU's. They increased by over 8 per cent annually from 1990 to 1999, double the EU rate. By 1999, NAFTA imports accounted for 31.8 per cent of world imports, more than twice Euroland's share (excluding intra-Euroland imports for the reason given above). Mexico provides the most buoyant market for foreign suppliers. Table 5.6 shows that its merchandise imports rose by nearly 16 per cent annually during the 1990s.

Table 5.6   Value and growth of merchandise imports

	Value ($ billions) 1999	Share %	Annual percentage change		
			1990–7	1998	1999
US & Canada	1,281	28.5	8	4	11
Mexico	148	3.3	16	15	15
NAFT[A]	1,429	31.8	8	5	11
Euroland[ab]	678	15.1	4	6	3
UK[ab]	121	2.7	5	2	2
East & Central Europe	129	2.9	12	11	–2
Russia	41	0.9	–	–20	–30
World[b]	4,494	100.0	7	–1	4

Notes: [a] Excluding intra-Euroland imports.
[b] Estimate.
Sources: WTO, *Annual Report 2000*, Table 11.3 and Appendix Tables 1 and 2; WTO, *Annual Report 1999*, Table 1.6 and A14; and WTO, *Annual Report 1998*, Table 11.4.

Table 5.7   Imports of commercial services

	Value ($ billions) 1999	Share %	Annual percentage change		
			1990–7	1998	1999
US & Canada	219	16.5	7	1	3
Mexico	14	1.0	n.a	7	9
NAFTA	233	17.5	n.a	n.a	n.a
Euroland[a]	430	32.2	6	7	2
UK[b]	81	6.1	6	11	4
East & Central Europe	30	2.2	n.a	1	–8
Russia	12	0.9	n.a	–14	–27
World	1,335	100.0	7	1	2

Notes: [a] Estimates, including intra-Euroland imports.
[b] Including intra-Euroland imports.
Sources: WTO, *Annual Report 2000*, Table 11.4 and Appendix Table 3; and WTO, *Annual Report 1998*, Table 11.8.

Trade in commercial services is less dynamic than trade in goods. The data reproduced in Table 5.7 show that imports of services grew at a similar pace in North America, Mexico, and Euroland – around 7 per cent annually during the 1990s. Note that the figures for Euroland overstate its share of world trade in services because they include trade between members. Separate data for extra-Euroland imports are not available.

The share of Eastern Europe in world imports of services is similar to that for merchandise, around 2 to 3 per cent. But its market has been depressed recently. Imports fell by 8 per cent in 1999. Russia's share of world trade in services is small (0.9 per cent) and contracting (down 27 per cent in 1999).

Whose markets are most distorted by subsidies?

Government subsidies distort free trade. They allow firms to undercut their competitors by selling their products and services at prices below their economic costs.

Table 5.8 shows the relative magnitude of various subsidies used by the EU and the US during the latest year for which comparative data are available (1997). Some of the figures are actual values given in the sources cited. Others are estimates derived from average ratios reported by the same organisations.

Reported subsidies to enterprises in the form of cash grants, soft loans, equity participation and guarantees from the government amounted to $203 billion in the whole of the EU in 1997(2.1 per cent of GDP). It is assumed that these subsidies are of proportionate benefit to exporters, suggesting that exporters from the EU receive reported subsidies of $22 billion. The figures for the US were just $33 billion and 0.4 per cent respectively for the economy as a whole – just $4 billion for exporters.

In addition to reported subsidies, there are various disguised subsidies. EU governments spend more than six times as much as the US on training and other so-called 'active' labour market programmes. The costs of similar activities in the US are largely borne by private employers and employees.

R&D activities are also subsidised more extensively in the EU. Government appropriations for non-defence R&D were worth an estimated $7 billion to EU exporters, $3 billion more than received by US exporters.

Although EU treaties are supposed to put a cap on subsidies, there are so many grounds for exemptions that many Euroland countries continue to obtain an unfair edge in global markets in this way. Table 5.9 shows the extent of this distortion in the field of agriculture.

Combining various forms of protection including tariffs and direct subsidies, the WTO estimates that the producer subsidy equivalent (PSE) for farmers amounted to 16 per cent of the value of agricultural production in the US in 1997, down from 30 per cent in 1986–8. The

Table 5.8 Who subsidises most? (1997)

	European Union GDP		European Union Exports		United States GDP		United States Exports	
	$ billions	*%*	*$ billions*	*%*	*$ billions*	*%*	*$ billions*	*%*
Total	9,461	100.0	1,030*	100.0	7,824	100.0	946	100.0
Reported Subsidies	203	2.1	22	2.1	33	0.4	4	0.4
Disguised Subsidies:								
– labour programmes	104	1.1	11	1.1	16	0.2	2	0.2
– social security	1,930	20.4	210	20.4	1,025	13.1	124	13.1
– non-defence R&D	66	0.7	7	0.7	31	0.4	4	0.4

* Extra-EU exports only.

Sources: OECD, *National Accounts 1999*; OECD, *Government Revenue Statistics 1999*; OECD, *Employment Outlook 1999*; OECD, *Historical Statistics 1998*; OECD, *OECD in Figures, 2000*; WTO, *Annual Report 1998*; and WTO, *Trade Policy Review: United States 1999*.

Table 5.9   Agricultural subsidies

	1986–8		1996/7	
	PSE ($ billions)*	% of agricultural production	PSE ($ billions)*	% of agricultural production
US	32.5	30	22.8	16
EU	70.8	48	85.0	43

* PSE = producer subsidy equivalent.
Sources: WTO, *Trade Policy Review, The European Union*, 1997, Table IV.2, and *Trade Policy Review, The United States*, 1999, Table III.2.3.

total value of the PSE was $22.8 billion in 1997. EU agricultural subsidies have stayed nearly four times higher, with transfers costing $85 billion in 1996, 43 per cent of the value of output.

Subsidies are not only unfair to competitors. They also prop up inefficient enterprises and they delay the transfer of capital and labour to more productive uses. And, ultimately, consumers end up paying more.

Who creates most jobs?

NAFTA's employment record is significantly better than that in Euroland, as shown in Table 5.10.

Since 1992, the number of jobs has risen by 38 per cent in Mexico and 13 per cent in Canada and the US, compared with only 3 per cent in Euroland and 6 per cent in the UK.

A substantially higher proportion of the working age population was actually employed in NAFTA in 1998 – 74 per cent in the US, 69 per cent in Canada, and 62 per cent in Mexico (see Table 5.11). The ratios

Table 5.10   Growth in employment (annual percentage change, 1993–9)

	1993	1994	1995	1996	1997	1998	1999	Average 1993–9	Increase 1999/2
US	1.5	2.3	1.5	1.4	2.2	1.5	1.5	1.7	13
Canada	1.4	2.1	1.6	1.2	1.9	1.5	2.8	1.8	13
Mexico	4.1	0.9	1.9	5.0	13.3	4.9	2.9	4.7	38
Euroland	–2.1	–0.3	0.5	0.4	0.8	1.6	1.7	0.4	3
UK	–0.7	0.8	0.8	1.1	1.8	1.4	0.5	0.8	6

Sources: IMF, *World Economic Outlook*, April 2000, Appendix Table 2; OECD, *Economic Outlook*, December 1999, Annex Table 20 (for Mexico).

Table 5.11 Employment ratios and levels

	Level 1998 (millions)	Employment ratio[a] 1998 (%)	Unemployment rate[b] 2000
US	130	74	4.1
Canada	14	69	5.8
Mexico	18[c]	62	2.4
NAFTA	162	72	4.0
Euroland	111	58	9.2
Germany	34	64	9.3
France	22	59	9.8
Italy	20	51	11.2
UK	27	71	3.9[d]

Notes: [a] Defined as the percentage of persons aged 15–64 in employment.
[b] April–May 2000.
[c] Urban areas.
[d] Claimant count.
Sources: OECD, *Employment Outlook*, June 1999, Tables 1.2 and Annex B; *The Economist*, June 10, 2000; OECD, *Economic Outlook*, June 2000, Table 21.

for the largest Euroland countries were 64 per cent in Germany, 59 per cent in France, and 51 per cent in Italy and Spain in 1998, and an estimated 58 per cent for the whole of Euroland.

NAFTA's unemployment rate is currently less than half that of Euroland. Mexico has brought its rate down to 2.4 per cent, thanks largely to booming exports to its North American partners. Britain's less regulated labour market has resulted in a much lower unemployment rate (3.9 per cent) than in Euroland (9.2 per cent).

Where is productivity rising fastest?

The ability of economic unions and associations to raise the incomes of their citizens depends not only on harnessing their labour resources as fully as possible, but also on lifting labour productivity. Data on economy-wide changes in productivity are given in Table 5.12.

There are no great differences in the performances of most NAFTA and Euroland members. The US and the UK top the league with a 15 per cent improvement over the last seven years, 4 percentage points higher than the Euroland average. But the most striking finding is the 12 per cent decline in Mexican labour productivity. This result can be explained by the rapid growth of employment in labour-intensive export industries and related services. This has changed the balance of

Table 5.12 Growth of labour productivity (annual percentage change, 1993–9)

	1993	*1994*	*1995*	*1996*	*1997*	*1998*	*1999*	*Average 1993–9*	*Increase 1999/2*
US	1.2	1.7	1.2	2.2	2.0	2.8	2.7	2.0	15
Canada	1.1	2.6	1.2	0.5	2.1	2.6	1.4	1.6	12
Mexico	–3.4	2.2	–4.3	0.1	–6.5	–0.1	0.5	–1.6	–12
Euroland	1.3	2.7	1.8	1.1	1.8	1.2	0.6	1.5	11
UK	3.0	3.6	2.0	1.5	1.7	0.8	1.5	2.0	15

Sources: IMF, *World Economic Outlook*, April 2000, Appendix Tables 1 & 2; and OECD, *Economic Outlook*, December 1999, Annex Tables 1 and 20 (for Mexico).

Mexico's urban employment away from import-substituting heavy industry. This structural shift has provided a better base for GDP growth, as already shown in Table 5.3.

Are workers better off in NAFTA or Euroland?

It is often alleged that NAFTA's strong export and job performances have been achieved by the payment of sweat-shop wages. OECD data reproduced in Table 5.12 reject this claim. Average annual gross earnings (measured in $ppp) for production workers in the manufacturing sector were $27,482 in the US and $27,214 in Canada in 1996. These levels compared with $21,908 in Italy, $18,451 in France and $10,573 in Portugal.

The US and Canada appear even better off if net income – i.e. income after social security contributions, income tax and other transfers – is taken into account. Table 5.13 shows that a US single worker on average wages kept $20,388 in his or her pockets after tax in 1996. This was 23 per cent more than the German equivalent. Single workers in Britain, which has also been accused of 'social dumping', received 53 per cent and 29 per cent more than their French and Italian counterparts respectively after tax.

The net average wage ($6,421) of a single worker in Mexico was lower than in all Euroland members, but was not much below Portugal's ($8,661). Mexican wages were on a par with Poland's $6,482, and exceeded Hungary's $4,727.

Table 5.13 also shows differences in the net income of families with two children and two adult earners – one paid the average wage of production workers, the other receiving two-thirds of the average. Once

Table 5.13   Annual gross wages and net income after taxes* in manufacturing, 1996

| | Single earner, no children on average production wage | | Married family, two earners, one on average production wage, one on 67% of average production wage | |
	Gross income ($ppp)	Net income ($ppp)	Gross income ($ppp)	Net income ($ppp)
US	27,482	20,388	45,803	35,151
Canada	27,214	19,690	45,356	34,242
Mexico	7,142	6,421	11,903	10,925
Germany	28,227	16,577	47,045	31,199
France	18,451	13,315	30,751	24,650
Italy	21,908	15,767	36,513	27,205
UK	23,650	17,555	39,417	31,815
Portugal	10,573	8,661	17,621	15,404
Poland	7,902	6,481	13,169	11,328
Hungary	6,716	4,727	11,193	9,361

* After social security contributions, personal income and transfer payments.
Source: OECD, *The Tax/Benefit Position of Employees 1998*, Tables 16 and 17.

again, North American families come out on top. They received $3,000–$4,000 more annually than their best-rewarded Euroland equivalents (Germans), and more than double their counterparts in Portugal. The same category of working family in Mexico gained $10,925 net, 17 per cent more than its counterpart in Hungary.

How do their living standards compare?

Some critics of the United States claim that country's unequal income distribution and lower government expenditure on social services result in poorer levels of attainment in overall human development. The United Nations Development Programme (UNDP) reports on various indicators to measure the relative performance of over 170 countries. It has also devised a composite Human Development Index (HDI) to encompass achievements in the most basic human capabilities – leading to a longer life, being educated and enjoying a decent income. The measures chosen are life expectancy at birth, adult literacy and combined educational enrolment rates, and adjusted per capita income in $ppp.

Table 5.14 gives UNDP's latest HDI rankings for some members of NAFTA and Euroland and other comparator countries, together with

Table 5.14   Human development indicators

	Human Development Index		Tertiary education enrolment rate	Private consumption
	Value, 1997	Ranking, 1997	1997 (%)	Per head ($ppp. 1997)
Canada	0.932	1	90	15,643
US	0.927	3	81	21,515
UK	0.918	10	52	14,804
France	0.918	11	51	14,115
Germany	0.906	14	47	15,577
Italy	0.900	19	44	13,415
Czech Republic	0.833	36	24	7,592
Poland	0.802	44	24	5,532
Mexico	0.786	50	16	5,453
Russia	0.747	71	41	4,324
Latvia	0.744	74	33	4,099

Sources: UNDP, *Human Development Report 1999*, Table 1 and World Bank, *World Development Indicators 2000*, Tables 2.10 and 4.11.

tertiary education rates and levels of private consumption per head. This last indicator is a better measure of living standards than GDP per head, which includes investment and government spending on defence and public administration.

The UNDP's findings rank Canada and the US well above the three largest Euroland countries in its composite HDI and on the percentage of the relevant age group enrolled at tertiary (higher) education institutions. The US is well ahead in the level of real private consumption, while Canada is roughly on a par with Germany, France, and the UK.

Mexico's HDI ranking lies in between Poland and the Czech Republic on the one hand and Latvia and Russia on the other. But it has some way to go before matching them in higher education.

Where is private consumption rising fastest?

Table 5.15 compares changes in private consumption levels since 1992. NAFTA citizens benefited from faster economic growth. Americans were able to increase their real private spending, where they alone determined the kinds of goods and services bought, by 30 per cent over the seven-year period. This rise was two and a half times greater than the consumption increase obtained by Euroland citizens.

Table 5.15   Growth of real private consumption (annual percentage change, 1993–9)

	1993	1994	1995	1996	1997	1998	1999	*Average 1993–9*	*Increase 1999/2*
US	3.0	3.8	3.1	3.3	3.4	4.9	5.3	3.8	30
Canada	1.8	3.1	2.1	2.5	4.2	2.8	3.2	2.8	21
Mexico	0.2	4.6	–9.5	2.2	6.5	5.4	4.3	2.0	15
Euroland	2.0	–1.0	1.2	1.8	1.5	3.0	2.5	1.6	12
UK	2.9	2.9	1.7	3.6	3.9	3.2	3.9	3.2	25

Sources: OECD, *Economic Outlook*, December 1999 and June 2000, Annex Table 3.

UK inhabitants also enjoyed more rapid growth in disposable incomes. Their consumption jumped by 25 per cent, double that of people living in Euroland. Britons also depend less on government hand-outs. Euroland governments spent 48 per cent of national income in 1999, compared with 40 per cent in the UK and 30 per cent in the US.[4]

Real private consumption rose by 20 per cent in Mexico, and at a particularly rapid rate over the last four years as the stimulus of NAFTA took full effect, and more people were drawn into the modern export economy and its related services. Thus Mexican workers have benefited from a free trade area that has not insisted on uniform labour standards as a prerequisite of membership.

Comparable data for Eastern Europe and Russia are not available, but they are likely to have experienced stagnation and contraction in their average living standards respectively. The EU's trade barriers, and its insistence that applicant countries must first adopt its innumerable *acquis* and regulations before admission, have prevented its neighbours from using their labour resources rationally. Imports from Russia, Central and Eastern Europe and the Baltic states (with a total population four times Mexico's) amounted to only 4.6 per cent of total EU imports in 1998, up from 3.4 per cent in 1990. Mexico's share of US imports jumped to 10.2 per cent from 5.9 per cent over the same period.

Who encourages hard work and enterprise?

In 1999, the state took a substantially smaller slice of national income in the US (31.0 per cent) than in Euroland (46 per cent). Estimates for Mexico indicate a tax take of just 15 per cent of GNP (see Table 5.16). The levels in Eastern Europe and Russia are similar to Britain's, around 40 per cent.

Table 5.16   General government receipts as % of GDP

	1993	1994	1995	1996	1997	1998	1999	Average 1993–9
US	29.2	29.4	29.8	30.2	30.5	30.9	31.0	30.1
Canada	42.4	41.9	42.0	42.6	43.2	42.8	42.8	42.6
Mexico	n.a.	n.a.	n.a.	n.a.	15.1*	n.a.	n.a.	15.1*
Euroland	45.5	45.0	44.7	45.7	45.9	45.9	45.9	45.5
UK	37.4	37.9	38.6	38.6	38.9	40.3	40.3	38.8
Czech Republic	42.3	42.1	41.5	39.8	38.9	38.2	39.6	40.3
Hungary	47.0	44.9	42.8	40.7	39.7	39.7	39.7	42.1
Russia	n.a.	n.a.	n.a.	n.a.	40.6	35.8	n.a.	38.2*

* Estimate.
Sources: OECD, *Economic Outlook*, December 1999, Annex Table 29. Data for Mexico from World Bank, *World Development Indicators 1999*, Table 5.5 and *World Development Report 2000*, Table A.1. Data for Russia from ECE, *Economic Survey of Europe 2000* No. 1, Table 3.2.7.

Top marginal tax rates on individuals are significantly lower in NAFTA and the UK than in Euroland. Top rates in Eastern Europe and Russia kick in at low levels of income.

By leaving workers and entrepreneurs more money in their own pockets, NAFTA governments have encouraged hard work and innovation.

Table 5.17   Highest marginal tax rates

	Tax rate (%) 1999	Charged on income over ($) 1999	Corporate rate 1999 (%)
US	40	283,150	35
Canada	29	38,604	38
Mexico	40	200,000	35
Germany	53	66,690	30
France	n.a.	n.a.	33
Belgium	55	69,993	39
Italy	46	81,665	37
Spain	40	71,398	35
UK	40	46,589	31
Poland	40	15,192	34
Russia	35	8,587	35

Source: World Bank, *World Development Indicators 2000*, Table 5.5.

Where is capital better mobilised?

Households and enterprises save and invest independently. The financial system's role is to mediate between them and to recycle funds. Savers invest in financial institutions, which pass these funds to their final users. As an economy develops, this indirect lending by savers to borrowers becomes more efficient: financial assets increase gradually relative to GDP. This wealth allows increased saving and investment, facilitating and enhancing economic growth. The level of credit available to the private sector is therefore an important development indicator.

Table 5.18 shows that credit to the private sector had reached 138 per cent of GDP in the US in 1998, 52 per cent higher than the Euroland level. The strength of Britain's financial sector brought its credit availability to a level well above the average for its continental rivals. However Mexico and Eastern European countries have a long way to go before closing the gap.

Venture capitalists are a key source of funds for the 'new economy', particularly for high-tech start-ups. NAFTA is well ahead of the game in this field also. A recent PricewaterhouseCoopers study revealed that venture capital investment in US technology firms reached $18 billion in 1999, compared with $2.2 billion in the UK, $1.4 billion in Germany and $1.0 billion in France.

As economies grow, specialised financial intermediaries and equity markets develop. Stock market size can be measured in a number of ways. Market capitalisation is the share price times the number of

Table 5.18   Capital mobilisation

	Credit to private sector, % of GDP 1998	Market capitalisation		Listed domestic companies, number 1999
		$ billions 1999	% of GDP 1999	
US	138	13,451	144	8,450
Canada	92	543	94	1,384
Mexico	20	154	23	188
Euroland	91	4,223	65	3,106
UK	124	2,374	175	2,399
Poland	20	30	13	221
Hungary	22	16	29	66
Russia	13	72	7	207

Source: World Bank, *World Development Indicators 2000*, Table 5.5.

shares outstanding. The figures in Table 5.18 under this heading show the overall size of a country's or group's stock market in billions of US dollars and as a percentage of GDP.

Market capitalisation totalled over $14 trillion in NAFTA in 1999. That of Euroland was $10 trillion less. There were more than three times as many companies listed on NAFTA stock exchanges as in Euroland. The value of the UK's stock market alone was 56 per cent of the total for the 11 members of Euroland. As a percentage of GDP, Britain's market capitalisation was nearly three times higher than Euroland's.

Equity markets are still in their relative infancy in Eastern Europe. But they are growing rapidly in Mexico; its market value increased fivefold from 1990 to 1999.

Who has attracted most foreign investment?

Inflows of foreign direct investment (FDI) into NAFTA grew twice as fast as flows into Euroland between 1993 and 1998. By 1998 the NAFTA levels were 53 per cent higher than those in Euroland.

Note that the data for Euroland exaggerate its attractions to investors outside the region as they include intra-EU transfers. These amounted to an estimated 60 per cent of the total. Similarly, the data for NAFTA countries include investments made by one NAFTA country in another NAFTA country. The same remarks apply to the figures for the accumulated stocks of inward and outward FDI given in Table 5.20. Intra-Euroland transfers are equivalent to US inter-State transfers which are not included in the US's FDI data.

Table 5.19 FDI inflows (US$ billions)

	1993	1994	1995	1996	1997	1998
US	44	45	59	76	109	193
Canada	5	8	9	9	11	16
Mexico	7	12	10	9	13	10
NAFTA[a]	56	65	78	94	133	229
Euroland[b]	55[a]	56[a]	76[a]	76[a]	74[a]	140[a]
UK	15	9	20	26	37	63
Central & East Europe	6	5	12	10	13	16
Russia	1	1	2	2	6	2

Notes: a Includes intra-NAFTA investment.
b Includes intra-Euroland investment.
Source: UN, *World Investment Report 1999*, Annex Table B.1 and Figure 11.7.

Table 5.20 **Stock of foreign direct investment**

	Inward investment		Outward investment		Total FDI[b]
	1990	*1998*	*1990*	*1998*	*1998*
	$ billions	*$ billions*	*$ billions*	*$ billions*	*% of $ppp GDP*
US	395	875	435	994	4.6
Canada	113	142	85	157	6.3
Mexico	22	61	1	6	1.4
NAFTA	530	1078	521	1157	4.7
Euroland	484[a]	1052[a]	501[a]	1327[a]	6.1[a]
UK	219	327	233	499	18.5
Central & East Europe	3	70	–	6	5.8
Russia	–	13	–	7	0.4

Notes: [a] Includes intra-Euroland investment.
[b] Sum of absolute values of inward and outward flows.
Source: UN, *World Investment Report 1999*, Annex Table B.3 and B.4; and World Bank, *World Development Indicators 2000*, Table 6.1.

Britain's lower-tax, less-regulated economy has accumulated FDI valued at 18.5 per cent of its GDP in 1998, easily the highest level among the groups covered. But pressure for 'harmonisation' of EU taxes towards higher Euroland levels is increasing, and calls for abolition of the national veto in this field are becoming more strident. Both EU and foreign investors may be induced to seek more hospitable environments elsewhere, including NAFTA. Portfolio investors in the city of London could be similarly motivated, affecting one of the most vibrant parts of the British economy.

FDI inflows to Eastern and Central Europe have been quite substantial, and the value of its FDI stock has reached 5.8 per cent of its ppp GDP. However, much of it has taken the form of acquisitions of existing plants producing for domestic markets, and has not succeeded in boosting total national output or exports. This is in sharp contrast to Mexico, where in response to changes in the foreign investment regime and a strengthening of intellectual property rights, investment and marketing links with foreign (especially US) firms have contributed considerably to the surge in its Mexican exports, which rose by 14 per cent annually from 1990 to 1998.[5]

Where has total investment grown fastest?

NAFTA's success in mobilising savings and attracting FDI has been translated into faster growth of total fixed capital investment.

Last year, in the US, its level was 67 per cent higher than in 1992. In Euroland, it went up by only 12 per cent, well below the UK's 42 per cent increase over the same period. Mexican investment growth has also been much more vigorous than Euroland's, especially since its 1995 recession (see Table 5.21).

What are their strengths in science and technology?

Rapid development in science and technology is changing the global economy. It is also driving rapid shifts in comparative advantage between countries. Table 5.22 shows some of the key indicators that

Table 5.21   Growth of real investment* (annual percentage change, 1993–9)

	1993	1994	1995	1996	1997	1998	1999	Average 1993–9	Increase 1999/3
US	5.7	7.3	5.3	8.3	7.5	10.6	8.2	7.6	67
Canada	−2.7	7.4	−1.9	6.5	13.9	3.6	9.3	5.2	43
Mexico	−1.2	8.4	−29.0	16.4	21.0	10.7	5.8	4.6	37
Euroland	−6.6	2.6	2.6	0.9	2.2	4.8	4.9	1.6	12
UK	0.8	3.6	2.9	4.9	7.5	11.0	5.2	5.1	42

* Total gross fixed capital formation.
Sources: OECD, *Economic Outlook*, December 1999, Annex Table 5.

Table 5.22   Science and technology strengths

	Scientists & engineers in R&D per million people 1987–97	Expenditure on R&D 1998 (% of GDP)	High-tech exports % of exports (manufacturing) 1998	Royalty & licence fees Receipts $ millions 1998	Patents filed by residents, Number 1997
US	3,676	2.6	33	36,808	125,808
Canada	2,719	1.7	15	574	4,192
Mexico	214	0.3	19	139	429
Euroland	2,126	2.2	15	9,808	101,037
Germany	2,831	2.4	14	3,252	62,052
France	2,659	2.2	23	2,336	18,669
Italy	1,318	2.2	20	477	2,574
UK	2,448	2.0	28	6,724	26,591
Poland	1,358	0.8	3	22	2,401
Hungary	1,099	0.7	21	46	774
Russia	3,587	0.9	12	28	15,277

Source: World Bank, *World Development Indicators 2000*, Table 5.12.

provide a partial picture of the 'technological base': availability of skilled human resources, the competitive edge countries enjoy in high-technology exports, sales of technology through royalties and licences, and the number of patent applications filed.

Among the largest industrial economies, there is little difference in the number of scientists and engineers per million people, although Italy is less well staffed than its neighbours. As a percentage of GDP, US spending on R&D averaged 0.4 points higher than Euroland's over the ten-year period from 1987 to 1997. But expenditure in Mexico was only 12 per cent of the US level, while Eastern Europe and Russia were in the 27–35 per cent range.

Big disparities exist in the ability to sell R&D results to foreigners. High technology exports accounted for a third of total US exports in 1997, and 28 per cent in the UK. These proportions easily topped the Euroland average of 15 per cent. Similarly, US receipts from royalties and licence fees were far higher than in other countries, and NAFTA's total was nearly four times greater than Euroland's. Britain earned more than twice as much as Germany, the highest individual Euroland recipient.

Russia has a high proportion of scientists and technologists. It also files plenty of patents. Political instability and the parlous state of its economy have prevented it from exploiting these resources adequately. However, some Eastern European countries, such as Hungary, are beginning to penetrate export markets for high-tech products, mainly through partnerships with foreign firms.

Where are foreign workers more welcome?

In most high-income countries, the natural growth of the population has been the main source of additional manpower needed to maintain their dynamism. But in many of these countries, population expansion has recently slowed to a trickle, and the proportion of retired persons is expanding rapidly. The World Bank projects that Euroland's population will decline by 0.1 per cent per year between 1997 and 2015 while the percentage of over-65s will rise to 19.4 per cent in 2015, from 15.6 per cent in 1997.

In the future, could differences in the degree of openness to immigrants be a factor in economic performance? Table 5.23 shows that Canada and the US have substantially higher proportions of foreign workers in their labour forces than most Euroland economies. Note

Table 5.23   Openness to foreign immigrants

	Foreign population		Foreign labour force		Inflows of foreign population	
	% of total population		% of total population		Total, 000s	
	1990	1997	1990	1997	1990	1997
US	7.9[a]	9.7[a]	9.4[a]	11.6[a]	1537[a]	798[a]
Canada	15.6[a]	21.1[a]	18.4[a]	24.8	214[a]	216[a]
Germany	8.4	9.0	8.4	9.11[b]	842	615
France	6.3	6.3[b]	6.4	6.1	102	102
Italy	1.4	2.0[b]	n.a.	1.7[b]	n.a.	n.a.
Spain	0.7	1.5	n.a.	1.1	n.a.	n.a.
UK	3.2	3.6	3.5	3.6	52	237

Notes: [a] Foreign-born only.
[b] 1996.
Source: World Bank, *World Development Indicators 1999* and *2000*, Table 6.13.

that the figures probably underestimate the gap because European countries generally define foreigners by nationality of descent, whereas the US and Canada use place of birth, which is closer to the concept of the immigrant stock as defined by the United Nations. Furthermore, the figures for EU members include internal migrants (especially from Spain, Portugal and Italy). From the point of view of the impact on total labour resources, such intra-EU migration merely 'robs Peter to pay Paul'. The US and Canada, on the other hand, have highly effective visa programmes to attract skilled manpower and entrepreneurs from all over the world.

Data for inward migration to Mexico and Eastern European countries are not readily available. There has been substantial migration (both legal and illegal) from Mexico to the southern states of the US, particularly California and Texas. This immigration has helped to fill job vacancies in a wide range of occupations, and contributed to the well-known dynamism of these states.

Where is economic freedom better safeguarded?

Underlying the differences in performance identified earlier are significant differences in the degree of economic freedom extended to people and enterprises. A *Wall Street Journal*/Heritage Foundation study ranks countries on the basis of ten indicators. These include the extent of government intervention in the economy, wage/price controls, property rights, regulation, trade, and level of taxation. The US was ranked 5th overall, Britain 7th and Canada 15th out of 153 countries covered in 1997. The average score for Euroland members put them in the 23rd slot. But 44 countries were found to have less government intervention than France and Germany.

Among Eastern European countries, the Czech Republic was found to allow greater economic freedom, with an overall ranking of 11th. But Hungary was only on a par with Uganda and Peru at 64th. Poland was ranked 85th, and Russia 115th. Greater exposure to North American policies through trade and other contacts should help Mexico to move up the scale from its 94th ranking in 1997.

An annual study by the Geneva-based World Economic Forum also measures various forms of economic freedom and evaluates their impact on countries' competitiveness. Its *Global Competitiveness Report 1999* ranks France 57th and Germany 53rd (out of 59 countries covered) in the extent and rigidity of their labour regulations. They also come close to the bottom of the league in the extent of administrative regulations and taxes on labour. The overall competitiveness rankings of France (23rd) and Germany (25th) are well below the US's 2nd, Canada's 5th and the UK's 8th.

Conclusions

On this evidence, a bureaucratic, over-centralised Euroland has performed less well and delivered fewer benefits than a more flexible NAFTA. Free trade promotes economic integration more effectively than regulation. Competition should be seen as an instrument to enhance welfare, not as a means of establishing control by one bloc over another. Harmonisation may sound attractive, but if enforced by directives rather than induced by markets, it can prevent countries from realising their potential, and exclude too many people from the fruits of their labour.

If Euroland's political leaders insist on deepening central institutions at the expense of entrepreneurship, individual liberties and local autonomy, Britain could seriously consider joining NAFTA. With an independent voice in the WTO restored, the UK could join forces with other like-minded countries (such as the Cairns Group) to further a free trade agenda. And with membership of the UN Security Council and the Group of Seven (G7) industrial powers secure, combined with its leadership of the Commonwealth, Britain could continue to play a central role on the world stage as an advocate of freedom, democracy and healthy competition.

Participation in flexible trading agreements like NAFTA would not preclude continued cooperation with Britain's continental European neighbours in many areas of mutual interest. And they, in turn, have no good reasons to cut themselves off from lucrative UK markets. Short of a radical change of heart and direction by Euroland leaders, Eastern European countries should also forge alliances with other trading partners before their competitive advantages become too eroded.

This chapter began with a quotation from J. S. Mill. Another great liberal philosopher and economist, Adam Smith, also has sound advice for present-day protectionists:

> To give the monopoly of the home market to the produce of domestic industry ... is in some measure to direct private people in what manner they ought to employ their capitals, and must, in almost all cases, be either a useless or a hurtful regulation. If the produce of domestic industry can be bought there as cheap as that of foreign industry, the regulation is evidently useless. If it cannot, it must generally be hurtful. It is the maxim of every prudent master of a family never to attempt to make at home what it will cost him more to make than to buy. (Adam Smith, *The Wealth of Nations*, Book 4, Chapter 2, 1776)

He was also far ahead of his time in supporting the voluntary separation of Britain from its American colonies and in advocating a free trade treaty between Britain and America:

> Great Britain would not only be immediately freed from the whole annual expense of the peace establishment of the colonies, but might settle with them such a treaty of commerce as would effectively secure to her a free trade, more advantageous to the great body of the people, though less so the merchants, than the monopoly which she at present enjoys. By thus parting good friends, the natural affection of the colonies to the mother country which, perhaps, our late dissentions have well nigh extinguished, would quickly revive. It might dispose them not only to respect, for whole centuries together, that treaty of commerce which they had concluded with us at parting, but to favour us in war as well as in trade, and instead of turbulent and factious subjects to become our most faithful, affectionate and generous allies. (ibid.)

Over the last century, Canada and the US have certainly proved to be Britain's most generous allies. Might not the time have come to conclude a free trade agreement with NAFTA along the lines first imagined by Adam Smith two and a quarter centuries ago?

Notes

1. See Eurostat, *Economic Data Pocket Book*, 31 May 2000, Tables 1, 7 and 11.
2. See *The Mexico–EU Free Trade Agreement*, Global Britain Briefing Note No. 8, June 2000.
3. WTO, *Annual Report 1999*, Tables I.3 and II.4.
4. See OECD, *Economic Outlook*, December 1999, Annex Table 29.
5. See WTO, *Annual Report 1999*, Table III. v23.

6
The Bank that Rules Europe: The ECB and Central Bank Independence

Mark Baimbridge, Brian Burkitt and Philip Whyman

Introduction

The idea that central banks should be independent from political influence has deep historical roots and featured in the discussions leading to the establishment of many twentieth-century central banks (Toniolo, 1988). The historical desire to impose limits upon the government's ability to fund itself through seignorage merges with the orthodox contemporary argument that politicians manipulate monetary policy to win elections; thus policy tends to exhibit a stop–go nature, reflecting an excessive concentration upon short-term macroeconomic fine tuning (Swinburne and Castello-Branco, 1991). Consequently it is argued that long-term economic efficiency requires the removal of monetary policy from the sphere of democratically accountable politics, and its delegation to an independent central bank with an effectively designed constitution and internal reward system that imposes price stability as the overriding policy objective.

Few institutional reforms recommended by economists have gained such rapid, widespread acceptance as the demand to grant central banks independence from political control. Countries of the North and the South, the post-communist nations of Eastern and Central Europe as well as established capitalist states have all been affected by the debate on the appropriate role and status of the central bank (Posen, 1993). Thus the notion of central bank independence has taken on the character of a panacea, a quick institutional fix, producing desirable macroeconomic results in a wide variety of national contexts. The search for such a beneficial institutional framework has taken shape within the European Union (EU) through the position accorded by the

Maastricht Treaty to the European Central Bank (ECB) and the European System of Central Banks (ESCB) at the heart of Economic and Monetary Union (EMU).

There is, however, an interesting division of views between the EU, where an internal integrated monetary order is frequently perceived as a necessary complement, perhaps even a prerequisite, for the successful completion of the single internal market, and the North American Free Trade Area (NAFTA) where there has been no call for, nor consideration of, any agreement on monetary inter-relationships to support free trade. The difference is in objectives; the EU saw the single internal market as a stepping stone to a single currency, and thence to political integration. By contrast, NAFTA is focused solely upon the economic advantages derived from a free trade area.

Of the economic consequences flowing from the single currency, the attainment of the Maastricht convergence criteria and the Stability and Growth Pact have received considerable attention. However, the crucial role to be played by the ECB within the euro zone is becoming increasingly apparent to politicians and citizens alike. Therefore this chapter examines the EU's preoccupation with establishing a new monetary authority for Euroland.

The meaning of independence

The concept of 'independence' is generally perceived to be obvious; it means simply that the government possesses no formal mechanism to influence central bank decisions over monetary policy (Wood, 1993). However, one of the earliest analyses of the various possible dimensions covered by such a concept was made by Friedman (1962), whose broad definition of independence was that monetary policy is entrusted to some separate organisation which is subject to the head of that agency. In that sense the Bank of England was always independent. Alternatively, on a more rigorous definition, the Bank of England was not independent of the government during the post-war period, except in regard to those functions where the Treasury explicitly or implicitly granted it discretion. Section 4(1) of the Bank of England Act 1946 provided the Treasury with the power to give directions to the Bank on any aspect of policy, whilst the Crown, in effect the Prime Minister, appointed the Governor and the members of the Court. This practice still occurs even under the more 'independent' Bank of England created in May 1997, demonstrating that government retains the desire and ability to influence Bank policy, albeit on a long-term rather than a short-term operational basis.

In practice, however, the Bank traditionally possessed considerable managerial freedom and exercised a degree of discretion in deploying its resources to support the banking system when it comes under threat. Moreover, it has tacitly been allowed considerable scope in the field of banking supervision, which was given statutory form in the Banking Acts of 1979 and 1987 (Hopkin and Wass, 1993). However, whilst the Bank of England always enjoyed substantial freedom of manoeuvre, these links between government and the central bank imposed severe limits on its potential independence. For example, it does not influence the exchange rate for sterling, nor long-term interest rates, whose levels are affected by fiscal policy and by market expectations as well as by short-term rates. Neither does it control either the liquidity or the maturity of government debt, which significantly influence the degree to which such debt can be monetised by being placed in the banking system. Moreover, the appointment of the Governor and senior members of the Court will presumably remain under any institutional reform, in the hands of the Prime Minister. The power of appointment normally carries with it the power to dismiss. Therefore governors could find their position untenable, if they pursued policies that the government disapproved, even when they enjoyed the statutory freedom to do so.

It should be noted that some commentators prefer to use alternative expressions to that of 'independence'. Hetzel (1990), for example, adopted a terminology of central bank 'autonomy' or 'autonomy with discretion' because of the risk that 'independence' could be taken to imply a lack of constraints. Similarly Fair (1979) referred to 'independence within government' rather than 'independence from government', even equating this preferred definition to the provision of independent, professional advice by the central bank, possibly combined with the ability to publicise or at least signal a policy disagreement with government. Such a position could be seen as the minimum level of central bank independence.

Models of independence

Alternative forms of central bank independence are as numerous as the number of 'independent' central banks; the memoranda submitted by 19 OECD central banks to the Treasury and Civil Service Committee

(1993) provide abundant evidence. Consequently, this section concentrates upon a limited number of blueprints. These are the German Bundesbank, the Federal Reserve of the United States of America and the Reserve Bank of New Zealand, which are often cited as models for an independent Bank of England, whilst they influenced the ECB framework outlined in the Maastricht Treaty.

Until recently, most discussion of central bank independence centred on the German Bundesbank, which was widely regarded as being successful in delivering consistently low inflation, with its objectives defined in statutes which insulate it from governmental interference. Moreover, it was not formally accountable, either to the Federal Government or to the Bundestag, for the discharge of its statutory functions (Marsh, 1992). The Bundesbank Act of 1957 required it to 'regulate the quantity of money in circulation and of credit supplied to the economy with the aim of safeguarding the currency' and also to 'support the general economic policy of the federal Government, but only insofar as it can do so without prejudice to the performance of its own functions'. While it is sometimes argued that these objectives may result in conflict, a hierarchy of goals was established in its statutes where price stability was clearly stated as the priority.

In contrast, the United States of America's Federal Reserve maintains its independence 'within' government, regarding itself as an integral component in the interlocking federal structure. The Federal Reserve's integration into government is secured by its regular accountability, whilst its Chairman and Board are appointees of the President, subject to the consent of the Senate. Furthermore, the objectives of the Federal Reserve are more widely defined than those of the Bundesbank, with no single objective, such as price stability, specifically laid down.

Another model of central bank independence is that instituted by the 1989 Reserve Bank of New Zealand Act. It assigned the Reserve Bank a general responsibility 'to formulate and implement monetary policy directed to the economic objective of achieving and maintaining stability in the general level of prices'. A second, unique feature of the Act required the Minister of Finance and the Bank's Governor to establish 'precise and agreed policy targets consistent with the Act, and to publish these without delay'. Such arrangements have been described as devolving 'operational autonomy', rather than independence to the Reserve Bank, because the government retains the power to authorise a departure from the statutory objective of price stability.

An alternative framework for central bank independence is provided by the Maastricht Treaty. The EU's view on central bank independence is defined by the provisions contained within Article 107 of the Treaty, which states that, 'when exercising the powers and carrying out the tasks and duties conferred upon them by this Treaty and the Statute of the ESCB, neither the ECB, nor a national central bank, nor any member of their decision-making bodies shall seek or take instructions from Community institutions or bodies, from any Government of a Member State or from any other body. The Community institutions and bodies and the governments of the member states undertake to respect this principle and not to seek to influence the members of the decision-making bodies of the ECB and of the national central banks in the performance of their tasks' (European Communities, 1991).

However, the legal framework, institutional arrangements and emerging operating practices of the ECB are increasingly coming under closer scrutiny and criticism (Buiter, 1999).

A central issue arising from these alternative models is the extent to which international experience is applicable to either the UK or the EU. Indeed, Eddie George, the Governor of the Bank of England, has conceded the problematical aspect of transposing overseas institutions within a different constitutional context. A fundamental difficulty is that the UK is a unitary state, so that its economy and constitutional traditions differ from those of many foreign countries, such as Germany and the US, whose federal systems of government reinforce the independence of the central bank and its board members. In contrast, Parliament is the focus of Britain's political structure with all legitimate power derived from it. Given that no Parliament is capable of binding its successors, it follows that every political decision can be reversed, which appears incompatible with the principle of an independent central bank (Busch, 1994).

Although the apparent success of the New Zealand model made it a candidate for imitation by Britain, reflected in New Labour's changed relationship to the Bank of England, a number of reasons exist for doubting its relevance. First, the New Zealand reforms were introduced in response to an inflationary crisis; second, its economy is much smaller than the UK and less prone to currency speculation; and third, the reformed arrangements have operated primarily in a period of recession, so that it is too early to evaluate their lasting effectiveness (Evans et al., 1996).

Moreover, the UK is almost unique amongst developed economies in the importance attached to variable short-term interest rates, because of its method of financing house purchases and small business operations (Miles, 1994). Additionally, the British economy is vulnerable to international developments and to associated changes in the external value of sterling (Taylor, 1995). These factors demonstrate that overseas models of central bank independence are less than wholly appropriate to the UK.

Issues in central bank independence

The conceptual case for central bank independence is primarily based on the view that arrangements which raise the credibility of monetary policy will increase its effectiveness in pursuit of price stability. Although this view has long been held, only in recent years has the concept of policy credibility been defined and analysed rigorously (Cukierman, 1986; Blackburn and Christensen, 1989).

The establishment of an independent central bank with strong anti-inflationary preferences is seen as a way for the state to bind its hands against the electoral temptation of inducing unanticipated increases in the price level. As commitment increases credibility, orthodox theory predicts that divergences between the central bank's policies and people's expectations will be smaller. Therefore lower costs and fewer delays are incurred when adjusting to monetary policy shifts. It is from this theoretical perspective of monetarism and rational expectations that the ECB was launched. However, just months after its inception, the ECB faces intense pressure from European politicians to cut interest rates. Given the levels of inflation and unemployment, the case is strong, but the ECB fears the danger of being seen as open to persuasion. It argues that an independent central bank must guard its credibility. If the financial markets suspect that the bank is susceptible to political influence, long-run inflation and the cost of controlling it would be higher.

This argument has recently been challenged. If central bank independence increases credibility, it should be associated with greater rigidity in the setting of nominal prices and money wages, reflecting the fact that the bank's promise to keep inflation low is believed. However, a study of OECD countries by Posen (1993, 1998) indicated that neither effect occurs. Indeed, independence not merely fails to reduce the cost of disinflation, but rather seems to increase it. Getting inflation down takes as long and calls for a larger short-term sacrifice of output and jobs, on average, in countries with relatively independent central banks.

Most of the contemporary support for central bank independence stems from a partial and frequently historically naïve view of West

German experience. Any one item that helped to promote rapid post-war German growth, such as the independent Bundesbank, was part of a structural totality defining its role. Accordingly it is unlikely to be effective if transferred by itself to other countries or onto the broader EU stage (Dowd, 1989, 1994). It may be more appropriate to reverse the fashionable view; the structural conditions that produced the strength of the German economy, allowing it to grow while maintaining a low inflation rate, also enabled it to afford the luxury of an independent central bank concentrating on monetary stability. For example, the wage negotiations system in Germany has generally produced a less inflationary outcome than in many other countries over the post-war period, thus not requiring intervention from the Bundesbank. Therefore it must be open to question whether the creation of a more independent central bank is significant in containing inflation, or whether the existence of an independent bank merely reflects a political economy in which price stability is a widely shared objective and where governments, as well as the central bank, regard low inflation as an overriding objective (Mitchell, 1993). Consequently, the possibility of 'reverse causality' is accepted by economists as a significant constraint when interpreting the experience of countries with independent central banks.

The theoretical case for independence is based on two analytical assumptions that have become generally accepted by economists over the last decade: (a) the 'no-trade-off' vertical long-term Phillips curve, which implies that price stability can be achieved at no long-term cost of unemployment; (b) the political business cycle. However, both rest on insecure foundations. First, the vertical Phillips curve analysis rests upon the concept of a natural rate of unemployment, about whose frequently changing determinants economists remain largely ignorant (Davidson, 1998; Karanassou and Snower, 1998; Madsen, 1998; Nickell, 1998; Phelps and Zoega, 1998). Second, repeated studies indicate that relatively little evidence exists for the occurrence of any systematic political business cycle (Kalecki, 1943; Breton, 1974; Nordhaus, 1975; MacRae, 1977; Wagner, 1977; Frey, 1978; Alesina, 1989).

These theoretical difficulties are compounded by the empirical evidence concerning central bank independence and lower-than-average inflation which again draw heavily upon the German Bundesbank, although counter-examples exist. For instance, the US with an independent central bank has not enjoyed such a phenomenon. Moreover, German experience since reunification demonstrates that an independent central bank is unable to guarantee low inflation, whilst the Bank of Japan, no more independent than the Bank of England, frequently presided over falling rates of price increase.

The dominance of monetarism led to the widespread conviction that low inflation is an essential, or at least a very important, condition for high, sustained growth, so that its achievement should be the priority for government economic policy. The importance attached to low inflation as the prerequisite for high employment and rapid growth is central to the case for an independent central bank, which pursues price stability as its major, or sole, objective. However, the belief that low or zero inflation produces sustained growth is not supported by the available evidence, with many studies indicating that no significant relationship exists between low inflation and higher rates of growth, until double-digit rates of price increase occur, which do retard economic development (Thirlwall and Barton, 1971; Brown, 1985; Stanners, 1993). Thus, the consensus of research fails to support the advantages of low inflation, so that a key element in the case for an independent central bank remains unsubstantiated.

Until the 1980s the cornerstone of British economic policy was the pursuit of four policy objectives, namely high levels of employment, stable prices, balance of payments equilibrium and an expanding economy. However, if responsibility for the second objective rests solely with an independent central bank, while the other three remain with the government, economic management potentially becomes more difficult due to the separation of monetary and fiscal policy (Blake and Weale, 1998). Hence, an advantage of a non-independent central bank is that budgetary and monetary measures can complement each other, forging a coordinated strategy of economic management. A failure of policy coordination was demonstrated by Germany's problems in the aftermath of reunification, when the failure of the Kohl administration to raise taxes for financing reunification generated a historically large budget deficit, which in turn triggered the Bundesbank into setting high interest rates. Such policy inconsistency highlights the ambiguous nature of 'independence' itself. The Bundesbank could not be seen to succumb to political pressure, which may damage its credibility, but was unable to avoid a political role; for instance, it regularly lowered interest rates before G7 meetings to avoid criticism from its trading partners. Analysis of the role of a central bank confirms that, in a world of external shocks, the case for delegating monetary policy is weak and that a coordinated approach is more likely to achieve the electorate's objectives (Rogoff, 1985a, 1985b).

Furthermore, if eliminating inflation is all-important and elected politicians cannot be trusted to give it priority, the logical conclusion is that all economic instruments, including fiscal policy, should be taken out of their hands. The assertion often made is that monetary policy is different, because it is a technical operation with a single objective and well-understood, reliable techniques. Such a belief is questionable, since monetary policy impacts upon employment and living standards, as vitally as does fiscal policy. Moreover, periods of high inflation have not occurred wholly, or even mainly, due to lax monetary expansion, whilst there is greater international evidence of fiscal, rather than monetary, policy being manipulated for electoral ends (Alesina, 1989). Despite this, few economists advocate placing fiscal policy in the hands of independent functionaries, because such a course of action would be obviously undemocratic.

Difficulties of measuring independence

When assessing the impact of central bank independence upon price stability, economists have mostly utilised imputed 'degrees of independence' to evaluate the heterogeneous character of central banks. These are based upon factors ranging from the level of political control exerted upon the bank to its operational role with the economy. A large body of literature focusing upon single or multi-country time-series studies has accumulated, with an additional series of studies attempting to rank independence for a cross-section of countries. The majority of this research draws attention to the inherent difficulty of defining, let alone measuring, the concept of independence (Mangano, 1998).

The initial method of imputing degrees of independence, based solely on legislature arrangements, found no relationship between inflation performance and independence (Bodart, 1990). The index was refined by subsequent studies, which constructed a measure of central bank independence that reflected both 'political independence' and 'economic independence' (Alesina and Grilli, 1991; Grilli et al., 1991). The former relates to the ability of the monetary authorities to choose the goals of policy, whilst economic independence is defined by their capacity to choose the instruments with which to pursue policy objectives. The main conclusion from such analyses is that the average rate of inflation, and occasionally its variability, is significantly lower in countries that possess independent central banks. However, the value of such evidence is problematic, as the authors usually acknowledge, because measurement of 'degrees of independence' possesses serious weaknesses, which cast doubt upon the validity of any purported association between central bank independence and the attainment of price stability. The main failings are:

- A limited spread of rankings inevitably restricts sensitivity across a wide number of inherently different countries, which raises difficulties concerning the index's analytical usefulness.
- Many of the studies cover overlapping time periods, opening up the possibility that they have found a result unique to that particular set of data. Therefore it becomes crucial to test a hypothesis on data sets other than those which suggested the hypothesis (Friedman and Schwartz, 1991).
- The time periods covered by some studies increase concern over the reliability of their findings; for instance, the participation of countries within the EMS could be viewed as a potentially important determinant of inflation rates. Consequently, if all countries in a pegged exchange rate system are compelled to possess the same rate of inflation over the long-run, whatever the various influences are on that rate, the status of national central banks cannot be amongst them.
- Disregard for non-economic factors that shape fiscal and monetary policy choices is a consistent feature of these studies, illustrated by their assumption that electorates always prefer low inflation to the possible trade-off of higher economic growth and employment (Muscatelli, 1998). However, even casual observation of Swedish public opinion refutes this perspective; it has consistently favoured full employment over low inflation as the central objective for economic strategy.
- Even after analysing the role of political factors, other potential sources of differences in inflation rates are often neglected. For instance, even if EU countries were subject to the same exogenous shocks in the post-war period, structural differences – labour relations systems, wage indexation mechanisms, vulnerability to raw material price changes, varying preferences for inflation versus unemployment – between them may explain their different reactions.
- The position of the government in the political spectrum and various proxies of social consensus offer some explanation of inflation rates in different countries (Hansson, 1987). Likewise, the size of the public sector appears to be another significant factor

(Alesina, 1988). Moreover, lower inflation in Germany and Switzerland could result from the presence of 'guest' workers during periods of economic growth, who absorb part of the unemployment costs of disinflationary policies by having to return to their country of origin when the work is no longer available (Burdekin and Willett, 1990).

- In an attempt to compare monetary regimes, many studies focus exclusively on institutional characteristics, disregarding behavioural indicators such as the average rate of growth of the money supply or the level and variability of interest rates.
- New research rarely possesses at first the reliable database it requires. Therefore greater attention should be devoted to improving databases and to recording any national specificity that may exist or has occurred.
- These studies suffer from the omission of indicators not identified as potential explanatory factors, so that influences other than central bank independence may be important, but as yet unidentified, determinants.

Empirical analysis of central bank independence

Here we examine the issue of central bank independence within those EU members states (excluding Luxembourg which at the time did not possess its own central bank) who were original signatories to the 1991 Maastricht Treaty. Although this reduces the number of countries in comparison to several of the previous studies, it offers a logical basis for the subsequent analysis. Little analytical precision is gained, when examining the likely impact of the ECB, by including those countries which will never enter EMU (for example, Australia, Canada, Japan, New Zealand and the US). Moreover, few previous studies offer a rationale for the countries they include: for instance, whilst focusing upon industrialised economies, they all fail to incorporate every member of such a representative grouping as the OECD.

A further aspect that differentiates this analysis is that it disaggregates central bank independence into its constituent features of political and economic independence. The approach is further developed by dividing these principal features into 16 individual components. Such a procedure enables a detailed examination of the separate elements that comprise a central bank's independence, alongside an evaluation of the aggregate level analysis pursued in previous research. Finally, in addition to the now traditional comparison of central bank independence and inflation, an additional GDP growth variable is introduced to evaluate the proposition that independence carries no detrimental consequences for output (Eijffinger et al., 1996).

Table 6.1 shows the correlation results between the series of measures of central bank independence and both the rate of inflation and growth. An association between a particular indicator of independence and either macroeconomic variable is demonstrated by the use of a reference symbol to represent alternative significance levels of 1 (††), 5 (†) and 10 (*) per cent.

Table 6.1   Correlation between central bank independence and macro-economic variables for EU member states

Indicator of central bank independence:	Rate of inflation	GDP growth
Governor not appointed by government	0.20	0.05
Governor appointed for > 5 years	−0.51	−0.20
All the board not appointed by government	0.52	0.31
Board appointed for > 5 years	−0.63†	−0.13
No mandatory participation of government representative on the board	0.07	−0.10
No government approval of monetary policy formulation is required	−0.55*	−0.23
Statutory requirements that central bank pursues monetary stability amongst its goals	−0.39	−0.01
Legal provisions that strengthen the central bank's position in conflicts with the government are present	−0.20	−0.02
Cumulative index of political independence	−0.48	−0.12
Direct credit facility – not automatic	−0.34	−0.60†
Direct credit facility – market interest rate	−0.52*	−0.57*
Direct credit facility – temporary	−0.32	−0.15
Direct credit facility – limited amount	−0.13	0.34
Central bank does not participate in primary market for public debt	−0.84††	−0.53*
Discount rate set by central bank	−0.32	−0.31
Banking supervision not entrusted to the central bank at all	−0.16	0.10
Banking supervision not entrusted to the central bank alone	−0.42	−0.35
Cumulative index of economic independence	−0.81††	−0.62†
Cumulative index of political and economic independence	−0.81††	−0.45

With regard to the relationship between central bank independence and inflation, Table 6.1 indicates that only the factors of the 'board appointed for > 5 years' and 'no government approval of monetary policy formulation is required' are significant from the series of political features, whilst 'direct credit facility at market interest rate' and 'central bank does not participate in the primary market for public debt' are the sole significant economic characteristics. Hence only four of a possible 16 features of central bank independence contribute to lowering inflation. Such results hardly support the contention that an independent central bank is an effective anti-inflationary mechanism.

Although these findings partially support the conclusions of previous studies (Alesina, 1989; Grilli et al., 1991; Alesina and Summers, 1993), there are several important caveats. First, the analysis of the individual features of political and economic independence indicates that only a limited number are statistically significant, raising difficulties concerning the necessity for all such characteristics to be present simultaneously within the ECB. Second, the index of political independence is insignificant, indicating that such criteria proved historically inconsequential to EU member states' inflation rates. Third, although the indices of economic and combined independence are inversely related to inflation, only 66 per cent of the variation of inflation is 'explained'. This surely is insufficient evidence from which to launch such a fundamental institutional reform, or to expect it to persist over the medium to long term, particularly if negative externalities are associated with greater independence.

The relationship between central bank independence and output is also examined to evaluate the orthodox hypothesis that the former constitutes 'a free lunch' (Grilli et al., 1991, p. 375), because it carries no detrimental consequences for GDP growth. The final column of Table 6.1 shows the correlation results for the individual features and the three indices of independence in relation to growth. With respect to political independence, neither the individual factors nor the index are statistically significant, whilst three of the economic independence criteria are significant: 'direct credit facility not automatic', 'direct credit facility at market interest rate' and 'central bank does not participate in the primary market for public debt'. Of particular interest, however, is the negative association between these features and GDP growth, which contradicts the previously established proposition that central bank independence has no 'costs in terms of macroeconomic performance' (ibid). The probability therefore is that independent central banks exert a negative impact on the rise in their citizens' standards of living. Such a research finding constitutes an ominous background to the actual operation of the ECB.

The ECB and contemporary political reality

The ECB, which started running the monetary policy of the 11 countries adopting the euro on 1 January 1999, is a creation of the Maastricht Treaty, which designed it to be the most independent monetary authority in the world. The Maastricht Treaty established the ECB as the only institution possessing the right to issue the single currency. Its sole aim is to pursue price stability. Article 3A makes the latter goal legally explicit, and therefore binding, whilst stating that other objectives may be pursued only 'without prejudice' to price stability. Furthermore, the ECB is forbidden by its founding charter to balance the goal of price stability against other aims such as growth and job creation.

The ECB's architects at Maastricht sought to insulate it completely from political pressures, both at the national government and at the EMU-zone level. By contrast, the US Federal Reserve, for instance, is required to take into account output and employment objectives alongside inflation targets, whilst being subject to fierce, regular scrutiny by Congressional committees with wide powers of investigation and review.

The position of the ECB under the Maastricht Treaty permits no clear accountability to any national nor EMU institution. It stipulates that the ECB Council's deliberations remain confidential, although Wim Duisenberg, the ECB's President, suggested that minutes of Council meetings could be made public after a time lag of 16 years! The only method of questioning the ECB's policies is through periodic reports to the ineffective European Parliament. Consequently, in an EU structure of decision-making widely acknowledged to be suffering from a 'democratic deficit', the powers handed to an unaccountable ECB will exacerbate the shortcoming. Charles Dumas of Lombard Street Bank recently argued, 'the ECB's "excessive" independence was the price paid for persuading German voters to give up the mark' (*The Times*, 3 March 1999).

In Britain, the US, Canada, Australia and a growing number of smaller countries, monetary policy is used to control both inflation and unemployment by managing aggregate demand. For example, the UK government and the Bank of England's Monetary Policy

Committee have recognised (as was implicit in the Chancellor's specific 2.5 per cent inflation target) that moderate inflation may generate growth and a greater number of jobs. By contrast, within Euroland any suggestion that monetary policy could be used to increase living standards and reduce unemployment is a heresy not to be contemplated. The ECB's legal responsibility is to maintain price stability, but that target has not been attained in France and Germany for the past five years. However, the ECB consistently ignores the success of the UK and the US in achieving low inflation, whilst simultaneously deploying monetary policy to reduce unemployment. The explanation of this conundrum lies in the ECB's origins and the macroeconomic theory it has adopted.

From its monetarist background, the ECB argues that the majority of Euroland's historically high unemployment (currently around 17 million) originates from structural deficiencies on the supply side of its member states economies. Consequently it denies responsibility for increasing aggregate demand to lower unemployment, believing that there is no further room for expansion in the Euro-II economies. In support of this thesis, another impeccably orthodox economic institution, the OECD, has published estimates for the natural rate of unemployment, below which inflation is believed to accelerate, for all industrialised economies. The estimated weighted average for Euroland is 11 per cent, where the actual average was 10.6 per cent in January 1999. On this reasoning, no scope exists to reduce unemployment without accelerating inflation. Such a view emphasises the grip that the natural rate of unemployment hypothesis exerts over ECB policy-makers.

Contemporary EMU monetary policy is dominated by the view that inflation inevitably increases once unemployment falls below a critical level (the non-accelerating rate of unemployment). Therefore the focus of monetary policy becomes to ensure, in practice, that unemployment is sufficiently high to reduce price and wage increases. This theory is the clue to ECB strategy. However, if the sole objective of policy is to maintain a constant rate of inflation, wide variations in output and employment may be required. In so far as a potential conflict exists between steady inflation and full employment, the latter should enjoy priority, because the consequences of fluctuation in employment are more serious than those in the rate of inflation. Apart from the human costs of lower income, job insecurity, loss of skills, poorer mental and physical health, and higher crime rates, the industrial cost is enormous, since lost capacity cannot subsequently be made good when demand recovers.

These problems do not deflect Europe's establishment from its objectives. As Strauss-Kahn, the French Finance Minister, said in a speech to the Centre for Economic Policy Research on 9 November 1998: 'We have made the choice of having an independent central bank. Its autonomy vis-à-vis national governments and the EU institutions, which results from an international treaty, is more soundly guaranteed than anywhere else in the world ... We have clearly enshrined in our treaty a fiscal policy that emphasises the need for fiscal responsibility and we have drafted secondary legislation that will make sure that member states will deliver on this commitment.' On the change from an international economy dominated by the fear of inflation, when the Maastricht Treaty was signed in 1991, to today's deflationary climate, Strauss-Kahn remarked: 'Our task is to make this system work in a context which is clearly different from the one the architects of Maastricht had in mind when they drafted the Treaty.' The more effective alternative of changing the policy decision-making framework as circumstances change is self-evidently not on the agenda.

Strauss-Kahn does, however, accept the 'need for institutions that can deliver effective co-ordination between the eleven governments of the euro-zone, and between them and the independent ECB', because 'in the absence of effective co-ordination, doubts about the other players might well lead the euro-zone to adopt a less than optimal policy-mix'. However, difficulties arise when Strauss-Kahn claims that 'the efforts made since the late 1980s have created conditions for a long EU cycle of growth'. Such a claim flies in the face of all the evidence; the EU was a low growth area over the last decade, when these 'efforts' were undertaken, expanding at 1.7 per cent per annum between 1991 and 1997 compared to 3.5 per cent for the rest of the world. Consequently unemployment in the EU was 5 million in 1979, 14 million in 1992 and is now nearly 19 million. Similar increases have not occurred in other OECD countries.

Nonetheless the ECB's monthly bulletin of February 1999 asserted that monetary and fiscal conditions 'are favourable for sustained output and employment growth in the euro-zone in line with price-stability' (ECB, 1999). The ECB has consistently said that it would have to see clear signs of deflation before reducing interest rates. However, Robin Aspinall, chief European economist at National Australia Bank, argued on 16 February 1991 that

> the ECB will have to cut rates eventually because there is no sign of any inflationary danger. However, the ECB is resisting a cut because it distrusts the fiscal discipline of Europe's politicians. The ECB deli-

berately keeps its inflation target vague, at simply below 2 per cent, so that it would not be beholden to the bidding of politicians once it meets its objective. The ECB also thinks that interest rates will not have much effect on unemployment. It favours structural reform to reduce unemployment. (*The Times*, 17 February 1999)

However, the attainment of a 2 per cent inflation target has not been achieved by any major economy in recent times; the US figure over the last decade was 3.3 per cent and that of Germany 2.8 per cent. Therefore an unaccountable institution has assigned itself an exacting inflationary goal, with ramifications for other dimensions of economic policy. Furthermore, the ECB argues that Germany's current troubles are structural not cyclical, but even if correct, embarking upon structural change and realising its results, is a lengthy process. However, distancing itself from democratic demands to emphasise its independence is a crucial tactic for building ECB credibility.

Following World War II, British economic policy was directed to the simultaneous attainment of four policy objectives: high levels of employment, stable prices, balance of payments equilibrium and an expanding economy. Within Euroland, responsibility for the second lies solely with the ECB, whilst the other three remain with national governments. An obvious danger is that economic management will become more difficult through the separation of budgetary and monetary policy. It was demonstrated by the shortcomings of the Reagan–Volcker era in the US and Germany's problems following reunification; in both cases lax fiscal policy resulted in high interest rates. By contrast, with a non-independent central bank, budgetary and monetary management can complement each other, forging a coordinated strategy of economic management.

Since the EU Heads of Government met at Maastricht in 1991 to finalise the blueprint for EMU, their political complexion has changed beyond recognition. The centre-left now controls or shares power in 13 of the 15 EU governments, Ireland and Spain being the exceptions. The majority won elections by promising job creation. Therefore a new European consensus is emerging which prioritises the need to reduce unemployment.

Consequently the theoretical possibility of a division between the conduct of budgetary and monetary policy has become a reality within months of the launch of the euro, far more rapidly than even sceptics anticipated. A crevasse has opened up between centre-left governments focusing upon unemployment and the ECB operating from a monetarist, natural rate of unemployment perspective. Moreover, the bankers insisted in advance, via the Stability and Growth Pact, that governments should be deprived of the ability to spend their way out of recessions. The battle between the ECB and European politicians was thrown into sharp focus by the resignation of Oskar Lafontaine. However, the underlying structural conflicts within Euroland lie deeper than the career of any individual, so that the danger of divisions between fiscal and monetary policies remains. Moreover, the gloomy economic prospects for the EMU zone ensure that such pressures will intensify; for instance, the German economy contracted by 0.5 per cent in the last three months of 1998, whilst in France industrial output declined by 1.6 per cent in December 1998.

The Euro-II countries, even without the UK, do not constitute an optimum currency area (see Baimbridge et al., 1998). Consequently for many years to come, persistent national divergences in growth and unemployment are likely to recur. This nightmare scenario has not taken long to unfold; Wim Duisenberg felt obliged to concede on 4 March 1999 that the economies so painfully corseted together by meeting the convergence criteria are already diverging (*The Times*, 6 March 1999). While Ireland appears likely to overheat due to large reductions in interest rates at a time of unprecedented high growth, Germany appears to be drifting ineluctably into recession. Whatever happens in the future, it is plain that one key argument of the eurosceptics is correct; no single interest rate is suitable for the euro zone. Therefore any action of the ECB will cause trouble for some parts of Euroland, whose economies are destined to diverge over the foreseeable future. Thus, in the last quarter of 1998, Germany's GDP fell by 0.5 per cent, yet Spain's rose by 0.8 per cent, whilst Ireland's increased by 8.0 per cent over the whole year. Such sharp divergences in economic performance will make the ECB's stewardship a difficult task.

Conclusion

The weight of theoretical and empirical evidence surveyed in this chapter suggests that the creation of an independent central bank in an established national economy, is an enterprise with certain costs and with only dubious prospects of the anti-inflationary benefits so frequently claimed. To transpose such a hazardous undertaking to a supranational framework such as the EU, whose constituent national economies experience varying economic cycles and possess divergent economic structures, is fraught with difficulties.

The decisions taken by the ECB are amongst the most sensitive actions deployed in a modern economy. Determining interest rates influences the growth of living standards, the level of unemployment and the amount that people pay for their credit and their mortgages. However, nobody votes for the ECB, which is unaccountable for its actions. It does not publish its forecasts nor the minutes of its deliberations. ECB members cannot be removed from office by the European Parliament, by the Council of Ministers nor even by the European Court. Therefore the move to ECB control reduces the amount of democracy, increasing disillusionment and grievance with democratic institutions.

The ECB's problems arise from its lack of democratic accountability, its arbitrary objectives, its outdated economic philosophy, and its potential for intermittent conflict with the national governments whose destinies it possesses considerable influence over. Therefore the ECB as currently constituted is an anti-democratic, economically inept institution. Its lack of accountability, transparency and democratic legitimacy makes clear that no British government concerned for the efficiency of the UK economy and capacity for self-governance could submit to the ECB's monetary authority. Therefore it is crucial that the British people, if and when consulted, steer clear of this ill-defined, bureaucratic nightmare.

References

Alesina, A. (1988) *Macroeconomics and Politics*, NBER Macroeconomic Annual 1988, NBER, Cambridge MA.

Alesina, A. (1989) 'Politics and business cycles in industrial democracies', *Economic Policy*, 8, 58–98.

Alesina, A. and Grilli, V. (1991) *The European Central Bank: Reshaping monetary policies in Europe*, Discussion paper 563, CEPR, London.

Alesina, A. and Summers, L. H. (1993) 'Central bank independence and macroeconomic performance: some comparative evidence', *Journal of Money Credit and Banking*, 25 (2), 151–62.

Baimbridge, M., Burkitt, B. and Whyman, P. (1998) *Is Europe Ready for EMU? Theory, evidence and consequences*, Occasional Paper 31, the Bruges Group, London.

Blackburn, K. and Christensen, M. (1989) 'Monetary policy and policy credibility', *Journal of Economic Literature*, 27 (1), 1–45.

Blake, A. P. and Weale, M. (1998) 'Costs of separating budgetary policy from control of inflation: a neglected aspect of central bank independence', *Oxford Economic Papers*, 50 (3), 449–67.

Bodart, V. (1990) *Central Bank Independence and the Effectiveness of Monetary Policy: A comparative analysis*, International Monetary Fund, Central Banking Department, IMF, Washington DC.

Breton, A. (1974) *The Economic Theory of Representative Government*, Macmillan, now Palgrave, London.

Brown, A. J. (1985) *World Inflation since 1950*, Cambridge University Press, Cambridge.

Buiter, W. H. (1999) *Alice in Euroland*, CEPR Policy Paper no. 1, Centre for Economic Policy Research, London.

Burdekin, R. C. K., and Willett, T. D. (1990) 'Central bank reform: the Federal Reserve in international perspective', paper prepared for the special issue of *Public Budgeting and Financial Management*.

Busch, A. (1994) 'Central bank independence and the Westminster model', *West European Politics*, 17 (1), 53–72.

Cukierman, A. (1986) 'Central bank behaviour and credibility: some recent theoretical developments', *Federal Reserve Bank of St Louis Review*, 68 (5), 5–17.

Davidson, P. (1998) 'Post Keynesian employment analysis and the macroeconomics of OECD unemployment', *Economic Journal*, 108 (448), 817–31.

Dowd, K. (1989) 'The case against a European Central Bank', *World Economy*, 12 (3), 361–72.

Dowd, K. (1994) 'The political economy of central banking', *Critical Review*, 8 (1), 49–60.

Eijffinger, S. and Schaling, E. (1993) 'Central bank independence in twelve industrial countries', *Banca Nazionale del Lavoro – Quarterly Review*, 184, 49–89.

European Central Bank (1999) *Monthly Bulletin – February 1999*, ECB, Frankfurt.

European Communities (1991) *Amendments to the EEC Treaty – Economic and monetary union*, Conference of the Representatives of the Governments of the Member States – Economic and Monetary Union, CONF–UEM 16 21/91.

Evans, L., Grimes, A. and Wilkinson, B. (1996) 'Economic reform in New Zealand 1984–95: the pursuit of efficiency', *Journal of Economic Literature*, 34 (4), 1856–902.

Fair, D. (1979) 'The independence of central banks', *The Banker*, October.

Frey, B. S. (1978) *Modern Political Economy*, Martin Robertson, Oxford.

Friedman, M. (1962) 'Should there be an independent monetary authority?', in L. B. Yeager (ed.), *In Search of a Monetary Constitution*, Harvard University Press, Boston.

Friedman, M. and Schwartz, A. J. (1991) 'Alternative approaches to analysing economic data', *American Economic Review*, 81 (1), 39–49.

Grilli, V., Masciandoro, D. and Tabellini, G. (1991) 'Political and monetary institutions and public financial policies in the industrial countries', *Economic Policy*, 13, 341–92.

Hansson, A. (1987) 'Politics, institutions and cross-country inflation differentials', unpublished.

Hetzel, R. L. (1990) 'Central banks' independence in historical perspective: a review essay', *Journal of Monetary Economics*, 25 (1), 165–76.

Hopkin, B. and Wass, D. (1993) 'Independence of the Bank of England', in Treasury and Civil Service Committee, *The Role of the Bank of England*, Volume II, Appendix 28, House of Commons, HMSO, London.

Kalecki, M. (1943) 'Political aspects of full employment', *Political Quarterly*, October–December, 322–31.

Karanassou, M. and Snower, D. (1998) 'How labour market flexibility affects unemployment: long-term implications of the chain reaction theory', *Economic Journal*, 108 (448), 832–49.

MacRae, C. D. (1977) 'A political model of the business cycle', *Journal of Political Economy*, 85, 239–63.

Madson, J. B. (1998) 'General equlibrium macroeconomic models of unemployment: can they explain the unemployment path in the OECD?', *The Economic Journal*, 108 (448), 850–69.

Mangano, G. (1998) 'Measuring central bank independence: a tale of sujectivity and of its consequences', *Oxford Economic Papers*, 50 (3), 468–92.

Marsh, D. (1992) *The Bundesbank – The bank that rules Europe*, Heinemann, London.

Miles, D. (1994) *Bank of England Quarterly Bulletin*, February.

Mitchell, A. (1993) *Democracy and Monetary Policy*, Memorandum submitted to the Treasury and Civil Service Commence.

Muscatelli, V. A. (1998) 'Political consensus, uncertain preferences, and central bank independence', *Oxford Economic Papers*, 50 (3), 412–30.

Nickell, S. (1998) 'Unemployment: questions and some answers', *The Economic Journal*, 108 (448), 802–16.

Nordhaus, W. D. (1975) 'The political business cycle', *Review of Economic Studies*, 42, 169–90.

Phelps, E. S. and Zoega, G. (1998) 'Natural-rate theory and OECD unemployment', *The Economic Journal*, 108 (448), 782–801.

Posen, A. (1993) 'Why central bank independence does not cause low inflation: there is no institutional fix politics'; in O'Brien, R. (ed.) *Finance and the International Economy*; 7, Oxford University Press, Oxford.

Posen, A. (1998) 'Central bank independence and disinflationary credibility: a missing link', *Oxford Economic Papers*, 50 (3), 335–59.

Rogoff, K. (1985a) 'The optimal degree of commitment to an intermediate monetary target', *Quarterly Journal of Economics*, 100, 1169–90.

Rogoff, K. (1985b) 'Can international monetary policy coordination be counterproductive?', *Journal of International Economics*, 18, 199–217.

Stanners, W. (1993) 'Is low inflation an important condition for high growth?', *Cambridge Journal of Economics*, 17 (1), 79–107.

Strauss-Kahn, D. (1998) *European Economic Perspectives*, Centre of Economic Policy Research, 9 November.

Swinburne, M. and Castello–Branco, M. (1991) *Central Bank Independence: Issues and experience*, International Monetary Fund Working Paper no.91/58, IMF, Washington DC.

Taylor, M. (1995) *A Single Currency – Implications for the UK economy*, Institute of Directors, London.

Thirlwall, A. P. and Barton, C. A. (1971) 'Inflation and growth: the international evidence', *Banca Nazionale del Lavovo – Quarterly Review*, 98, 682–95.

Toniolo, G. (1988) *Central Banks' Independence in Historical Perspective*, Walter de Gruyter, Berlin.

Treasury and Civil Service Committee (1993) *The Role of the Bank of England*, Volume I and II, House of Commons, HMSO, London.

Wagner, R. E. (1977) 'Economic manipulation for political profit: macroeconomic consequences and constitutional implications', *Kyklos*, 30, 395–410.

Wood, A. (1993) 'Memorandum to Treasury and Civil Service Select Committee', in Treasury and Civil Service Committee, *The Role of the Bank of England*, Volume II, House of Commons, HMSO, London.

7
Has the Euro Lived Up to Expectations?*

Wilhelm Nölling

Preparations to introduce a new European currency began in the early 1970s. The so-called Werner Report of October 1970 spelt out the numerous conditions required for success, but the difficulties involved meant that the idea was temporarily put to rest. Following the publication of the Delors Report in April 1989, which included detailed plans for Economic and Monetary Union, one of its principal contributors, the then President of the Bundesbank Karl Otto Pöhl, commented during a Central Bank Meeting: 'In my life-time we will not see a common currency.'

However, only two and a half years later the Maastricht Treaty was signed – kick-starting the process towards EMU. Its strict timetable was supposed to lead to common efforts to establish the preconditions for the greatest currency experiment in the history of mankind. As it turned out, basic prerequisites such as political unity, real progress in productivity, the harmonisation of fiscal policy, the removal of important legal restrictions and the completion of the internal market were not met. The euro was launched regardless on 1 January 1999. The adventure had begun in earnest a little earlier, in the summer of 1998, with three countries, Great Britain, Sweden and Denmark opting out of Stage III and Norway remaining outside of the EU.

The sheer magnitude of the project was bound to elicit strong feelings. Politicians, economists and numerous citizens all across Europe began to debate the pros and cons of a single currency. Two sets of expectations evolved: category one I like to call 'positive expectations' – hope, wishes, goals, promises and advantages. The second category, 'negative expectations' is that of fear, risk, disadvantages, dangers to

* First published in the *European Journal*, January 2001.

individuals, businesses, sectors of the economy, nation states and Europe as a whole.

An Official Propaganda Exercise was started to talk up the benefits of EMU. The single currency would result in more solidarity, they said, as well as more political cooperation and unity, making the EU a stronger participant in world affairs. EMU would also serve as an instrument to bring about institutional reforms in Europe. Economic advantages would include the removal of transactions costs, enhanced cross-border price transparency, more competition and increased economic growth, productivity and employment. In addition, the enlargement of financial markets would mean easier access to a larger pool of capital at lower prices and the reduction of risk premiums. In order not to sow the seeds of doubt and endanger its acceptability, especially among Germans, advocates of EMU shied away from encouraging public debate and played down its real and perceived risks.

Negative expectations with regard to political and economic developments centred on the fact that even though EMU's critics accepted that the project could bring major economic advantages, they strongly disagreed that EMU was a suitable instrument to bring political progress to Europe. They denounced the undertaking as irresponsible, not least because an 'emergency exit' (of the type discussed by the philosopher Sir Karl Popper) was ruled out in the strongest possible words.

These critics maintained, based on historical experience, that a currency union would founder unless backed up by political union. Newly born and lacking in experience, the ECB would easily succumb to political pressure and would experience great difficulties in establishing efficiency, a good reputation and credibility. Since some of the major prerequisites for success were missing, the bank's leadership would be like a swimmer diving into an empty pool. The clash of a centrally administered monetary policy with first 11, now 12 and eventually many more still predominantly sovereign nation states would permanently weaken the new monetary order and, in its wake, Europe's economy and political system. In all these respects critics such as myself assumed that the birth defects of the euro would turn out to be incorrigible and would not disappear in the course of time.

I and others of my persuasion argued and continue to argue today that the risks and dangers involved would lead to reduced economic growth, more inflation, capital flight, insecurity and social and political unrest. Instead of becoming a truly respected world power, Europe's standing would decline. Member states would constantly discuss leaving the union, thereby making a mockery of the concept of irreversibility.

In the end, as we all know, the proponents of the euro were victorious. In Germany, an alliance of a broad spectrum of political parties, unions, employer associations, banks and industry supported the destruction of the Bundesbank and the launch of the new currency. This was despite the persistent and strong opposition of the majority of ordinary Germans who were, unfortunately, incapable of being organised into a coherent resistance movement. Hence it was hardly surprising that EMU in Germany was pushed through without bothering to hold a referendum, reinforcing even further the lack of democracy inherent in the project.

So far we have had a trial period of two and a half years since mid-1998 (when it was finally decided who would go on to Stage III on 1 January 1999). I would like to deliver a short and preliminary assessment of EMU's performance to date.

It is only fair to begin by examining its positive aspects so far. If you believe Mr Prodi, the euro is already one big success story. I think we need to distinguish between wishful thinking and self-serving assertions on the one hand and facts on the other.

Since many people did not really believe that Europe's politicians would be able to muster the strength to embark on EMU, I am willing to consider this a political success. As a consequence the Eurosystem is growing, especially banks and insurance companies. The number of employees at the ECB is also growing very rapidly and stood at over 1000 at the end of 2000. Europe-wide statistics are slowly becoming more accurate and reliable as well as more readily available (which by the way makes them entirely useless for the purpose of comparison over time). Despite signs of strain caused by widening inflation differentials, the mutually agreed fixed exchange rates have survived two and a half years. Finally, preparations for the changeover of national currencies into euro notes and coins are in full swing – although the logistical and other costs involved are staggering.

The peripheral countries of the Mediterranean have benefited most from unusually low interest rates, which on the whole they did not deserve. This is the main reason why public deficits everywhere have been kept from rising – the interest governments have to pay on public debt is lower. Overall price developments have followed the tendencies in all industrial countries since the mid-1980s. However, Great Britain and Sweden have actually done better and average price increases in Euroland are on their way up. Soon they will exceed by at least 50 per cent the 2 per cent inflation benchmark set by the ECB. To try to camouflage this, there have already been suggestions that the benchmark be changed by eliminating the effect of oil price increases. I wouldn't be surprised if they also start to contemplate eliminating the impact of the weak euro (it has pushed up the price of imports and hence led to an increase in the consumer price index). It is a bit like enlarging the goal of a rival soccer team by 50 per cent or 100 per cent to ensure success.

Although the increase in public deficits has slowed considerably, at the end of 1999, more than eight years after the Maastricht Treaty came into force, six out of the then 11 Euroland countries still exceeded the 60 per cent public debt limit; the zones' overall debt to GDP ratio stood at more than 72 per cent.

The euro has many undisputable shortcomings.

The first major failure took place in May 1998 during the launch of the ECB. This important phase was overshadowed by a breach of the ECB's constitution. The French wanted to extract a binding promise from the newly appointed President Wim Duisenberg to step down after no more than four years. What really happened during more than 15 hours of bickering and manoeuvring behind the scenes is still not fully known. However, a recent report in *Der Spiegel* revealed that most of the important documents relating to the events are missing; and there were many contradictory statements about what happened. The question 'Who is lying?' could not be answered.

The shenanigans of the ECB are merely symptomatic of a wider problem. While I was preparing this article it was reported in the press that the European Parliament had refused – for the sixth time in a row – to approve the Commission's budget. Negligence when handling European taxpayers' money, corruption, ineptitude and nepotism all seem to be ingrained features of the Commission.

The ECB has modified its behaviour and its approach to explaining policy in ways that are hard to understand. Beyond that, its effectiveness and credibility are harmed by the theory it has adopted to explain the decline in the external value of the euro. When the euro was first launched, most officials boasted of its terrific potential as a new and strong contender in world markets. Therefore, steady appreciation was to be expected whereas depreciation was definitely ruled out. After decline became the trademark of the euro, the blame was laid on the unexpectedly good and long-lasting state of the US economy and on its higher rates of return on capital. All of a sudden, the lack of basic reforms – the many unfulfilled prerequisites – were discovered and widely blamed for the depreciation of the currency. However, European decision-makers should have known that Euroland would have no hope of qualifying as an optimal currency area and that remedies would never be ready on time – certainly not within Mr Duisenberg's eight-year term. The rationalisation given is flawed because it fails to explain why the euro has declined so heavily against the yen, the currency of a country that has been economically depressed for more than ten years. What about Britain's impressive performance? The UK's success can largely be explained by its withdrawal from the shackles of the EMS.

What is missing in Euroland is that its political and monetary authorities are not the same. This leads to permanent quarrels and to major inconsistencies in policies, and violates what I consider to be the first prerequisite for a central bank to gain and maintain credibility. When Sir Edward George, the governor of the Bank of England, asked himself publicly in October 2000: 'Why then has the euro weakness persisted?', he answered revealingly 'Frankly, I am not at all sure that anyone really knows the answer to that question.' I suggest that he should acquaint himself with my attempt to identify as the main reason the various birth defects referred to above.

I am struck by the audacity of the euro's defenders in claiming success on the inflation front. In December 1998 a concerted action led by the Bundesbank brought the Central Bank's money market rates down from 3.3 per cent to 3 per cent, thus in effect establishing the rate for Euroland as a whole. A little later, the Bundesbank Annual Report of April 1999 argued: 'The price climate remained remarkably quiet. No particular risks of inflation in the near future are recognisable.' The ECB's first action took place that very April. In the face of all kinds of disturbances (with the exception of inflation), the rate was lowered again, to 2.5%. There were no problems with inflation until oil prices began to feed their way through the consumer price index at the turn of the century. More than seven rather timid rate increases have been pushed through since November 1999, supposedly enough to deal with inflationary dangers. The facts are clear: inflation is on the rise all across Euroland. The German CPI is a case in point. It increased by 1.7 per cent in 1995, 1.4 per cent in 1996, 1.9 per cent in 1997, 1.0 per cent in 1998 and 0.6 per cent in 1999. German inflation is now four times higher than it was in 1999. In September 2000, the prices of German imports were up by nearly 14 per cent. The comparative figures are –3.2 per cent for 1998 and –0.5 per cent for 1999. Inflation in late 2000 stood at 6 per cent in Ireland and around 3.5 per cent in

Spain and Portugal; and the Euroland average of 2.8 per cent is rather higher than the 2 per cent allowed for by the ECB. I am not blaming the ECB for this inflationary resurgence. But I take issue with their propaganda that a major achievement of the new bank was to maintain domestic price stability.

Advocates of the euro in Germany are guilty of falsifying monetary history. The argument, used especially by the former Chancellor Helmut Schmidt and the leading managers of what is left of the Bundesbank, is that in the past the DM was also susceptible to bouts of weakness with regard to the dollar. Of course, we all remember the DM's ups and downs. However, unlike the euro, the DM actually remained strong with regard to all other currencies and the credibility and reputation of the Bundesbank remained unshaken. The euro has weakened not only against the dollar, pound and yen but also against no fewer than 48 other currencies including the Zimbabwe Dollar, the Indian Rupee and the Iranian Rial.

The ECB started fighting market forces in September 2000. The Central Bank Council unashamedly enlisted the help of the dollar, the currency Euroleaders had wanted to dethrone and – in the long term at least – to relegate to second place. When the euro's dramatic decline continued, the ECB believed it would improve its performance by going it alone. The results show that intervention can make a difference if the conditions are right. However, the euro's basic weakness cannot be remedied by selling a strong currency to prop up a continuously weak one. Intervention means that the ECB has admitted to its fundamental weakness and that the authorities are continuously attempting to gamble this weakness away. The attempt to induce the markets around the world to believe at last in the tremendous potential of the euro to appreciate has failed so far. It takes more to convince or outwit markets than what the partially disabled leadership of Europe is at present in a position to muster.

I believe that the external weakness of the euro reflects its structural deficiencies. Euroland's centralised monetary policy is on a permanent collision course with the uncoordinated economic and social policies of 12 and soon 10 or 15 more member states. It has to cope with widely diverging rates of growth and inflation among the member states. I believe that a 'one-size-fits-all' monetary policy for a continent that will remain highly diverse for decades to come is bound to fail. It almost certainly will win neither the trust of international investors nor that of most of the people in Euroland itself.

Euroland's political elite seems determined to continue the experiment. They are deliberately shutting their eyes and are refusing to admit that the euro has seriously flopped. It does not bother them at all to be responsible for a totally unacceptable, un-European and asymmetrical division of the continent. It hardly helps that while major countries such as Great Britain, Norway, Sweden and Denmark remain outside the euro, the EU has embarked on extending itself into the unchartered waters of the East. Even Russia and the Ukraine are now among potential applicants.

It may well be that, for political reasons, we cannot ignore the challenge to integrate up to 20 countries from Eastern Europe. It may also be that the conditions of entry cannot be watered down to the point of meaninglessness. To my understanding, however, it was a mistake to promise full membership to all. We would have been wiser to offer step-by-step tailor-made offers to applicants.

The combination of deepening integration on the one hand and the uncertain outcome of enlargement on the other is not conducive to the euro establishing its credentials as a currency sought after by investors.

On the last day of September 2000 we – the 'Four Professors' who tried to delay the euro by appealing to the Constitutional Court – conducted a symposium in Hamburg. We asked high-level participants to help us to find an answer to the question 'What remains to be done to save EMU?'

Our conclusion was that a prolongation by five to ten years of the trial period still under way would be a good idea. It would mean a temporary return to the EMS disbanded in 1999. The delay would give us time to reconsider the state of monetary and political affairs in Europe in order to find ways and means to build more stable foundations for a European currency. The response by most of the leaders to whom we sent our manifesto was downright cynical: with the exception of Prime Minister Biedenkopf from Saxony, a well-known sceptic, the respondents told us to keep quiet. We should realise at long last that the euro is here to stay, they said, and that it is a success already. What nonsense. Not only has the performance of the euro to date confirmed my very critical predictions, I actually believe that the years ahead will be really stormy for the euro.

Part II
Political Euroscepticism

8
The Myth of Europe
Russell Lewis

Some of my best friends are Europhiles. Like many of their persuasion, while on most matters they have sensible views, at the very mention of the word 'Europe' their critical faculties seem to go on strike. How otherwise can one account for their indifference to four undeniable defects in the EU which, if proven about any other political project, would make them condemn it out of hand? These are its lack of democracy, its excessive regulation, its corruption and its structural bias against British interests.

Undemocratic

Why are these upholders of parliamentary government so unconcerned about the European Union's present oligarchic structure? Why aren't they angry (especially the MPs among them) at the prospect, under federalism, of unelected bankers and bureaucrats becoming our masters and our general elections becoming a farce? What made Tony Blair endorse so fulsomely as new President of the European Commission the Italian Romano Prodi, who, once appointed, announced that his first aim was to destroy the nation state? Why can't they see that the sort of centralised unitary European state we shall be ruled by if the federalists have their way is such a threat to our right to govern ourselves that membership of it is not even worth considering?

It is not as if these Europhiles are under any illusion about the EU's lack of democracy. One of the most prominent, Michael Heseltine, for example, in his book *The Challenge of Europe: Can Britain win* readily acknowledges its undemocratic character. As he says, 'The ... notable characteristic of present political arrangements is that they are about as ineffective and as unaccountable as they could be ... the institutions themselves are totally incapable of adjusting to that change. We have federalism by stealth, whether because national electorates cannot be told the truth or are not trusted to understand it, or because their elected leaders have failed to comprehend what they have assented to.'[1]

Overregulation

Again, the Europhiles know what everybody knows – that economic controls, with which Brussels is increasingly identified, promote inefficiency. It is astonishing to recall today, after the tragi-farce of beef and butter mountains, wine lakes and olive production subsidies claimed for double the acreage planted, that the Common Agricultural Policy (CAP) was once the showpiece of the Community. Yet this white, or rather green elephant, which the council of Ministers has only made the feeblest efforts to reform, is a flop on virtually every count. It uses up nearly half the Community budget, adds £20 a week to the average family food bill, reduces the income of more efficient producers abroad including some of the world's poorest peoples, is an ecological disaster (fostering overproduction of grain on unsuitable soils through excessive use of chemicals), is notoriously riddled with Mafia and other scams and has recently, over the hormones-in-beef issue in which the Commission is clearly in the wrong, become a serious bone of contention with the United States, threatening to undermine world free trade.

In industry and services too Brussels' regulation and protectionism raise producer, consumer and welfare costs, in this respect reflecting the deadweight bureaucratic culture of our continental partners which is today making mainland Europe the G7's unemployment blackspot. In these circumstances the Brussels harmonisation programme becomes not, as it claims to be, the route to a level playing field but a device for raising British costs to make us less competitive. Tony Blair knows this full well, otherwise why does he keep preaching to his continental partners that deregulating and tax-cutting are the only sure way to create jobs?

Professor Patrick Minford has calculated that if Britain harmonised completely with the rest of the EU, the combination of minimum wages, the rise of union power and the higher social costs burden could increase UK unemployment by as much as 3 million.

Corruption

Regulation is moreover the seedbed of fraud and after the recent devastating report of the European Parliament which led to the sacking of Jacques Santer and his team, there is no need to quote chapter and verse to show that the European Commission is riddled with corruption. The excuse offered by Madame Cresson, the worst offender – that she was guilty of no behaviour that is not standard in French administrative culture – is beyond satire. It also illustrates the grossly irresponsible attitudes towards public duty among many members of the continental political and bureaucratic elite, attitudes too deep-rooted to be removed by reformist tinkering. Romano Prodi, the new President appointed with the express task of cleaning up the Commission, has since been revealed as deeply suspect himself and lucky not to be in jail for jobbery in Italy.

Hostile to British interests

Finally, Ministers and Foreign Office officials know very well that the EU is run by the Franco-German axis on an agenda routinely agreed between the two nations on the eve of each and every EU summit meeting. Why, then, do they surrender one British interest after another on the grounds, constantly belied by experience, that this will generate goodwill and prompt similar concessions from Germany and France? Even as recently as the eve of the February summit, top FO officials produced a position paper blithely proposing, contrary to the Prime Minister's emphatically declared position, that we should offer a reduction of our budget rebate in the hope of prompting equivalent climbdowns by our partners. The historical evidence points to the conclusion that the European Union is congenitally unfriendly if not blatantly hostile to British interests and no amount of diplomacy can change that melancholy fact.

When normally reasonable people sincerely support a policy and won't let go despite apparently overwhelming objections to it,

either
They have lost their marbles
or
They think they have no choice because it is inevitable
or
They calculate that the benefits of that policy outweigh the costs.

Not bonkers but out of date

Take these possibilities in turn. First, though I think that the Euro-integrationists are wrong-headed, I don't think that they are crazy. The one element of irrationality which may afflict some of them is a reluctance to admit that they are mistaken, or even more to admit that circumstances have changed so that a policy that was right in the past is wrong today because the situation has changed. Many, like the author, were enthusiastic supporters of greater European unity during the Cold War because they saw it as a part of strengthening the West against the threat of military conquest or political subversion from the Soviet Union. It then seemed sensible for the Common Market to be the right institution for improving the economies of the member states and allowing them to shoulder a bigger share of the burden of self-defence. (I did however warn, in a pamphlet I wrote for the Institute of Economic Affairs, 'Rome or Brussels' that, though, as I hoped, the Common Market would continue broadly on the lines of the Rome Treaty to promote free movement of goods, capital services and people within its borders and global free trade, it might follow the Brussels model and become more bureaucratic, more regulated and protectionist.) Some, believing that the Cold War division of the world would extend far into the future, even wondered whether the time might come when the Americans, tired of footing most of the bill for protecting the not too grateful Europeans, might elect an isolationist president and leave us in the lurch. Greater unity in Europe, with provision for our own defence capability, thus appeared to many of us as the way we would have to survive. To those few who were worried about the dangers of centralisation of power in Brussels it must be remembered that, up until the appointment of Jacques Delors as President of the Commission, the prospect of a European federal state trampling on the rights and interests of the sovereign member states seemed remote. A more economically integrated Europe did however appeal not only as a contribution to stiffening the West's defence against the Soviets but also as a way of keeping the Germans on side, and, by making them feel fully included in the fraternity of Western nations, reducing the temptation for them to do a deal with the Russians, go neutral and defect from NATO in exchange for ending the division of Germany.

Needless to say, for those who thought like this, the double collapse of the Soviet Union and the Berlin wall removed the two main props of the argument for Britain's positive role in the European Community. Alas, for many politicians it was and remains embarrassing to change tack on a policy which they have espoused for decades. Few now recall how long it took many Tories to stop shouting the odds for Empire and Commonwealth, even when, as a power structure, it had disappeared.

Europe as economic pace-setter

Many British EU fans cling to the belief that the other senior members have an economic vitality that we lack and that, if we become more like them, their higher productivity and living standards will rub off on us. This view made sense in the 1960s and 1970s when Germany, France and Italy were enjoying economic miracles and we were suffering from inflation, stagnation and strikes. What most of them do not realise is that, meantime, the situation has not only changed but actually reversed. These former role models have diluted their dynamism in a mass of regulations, taxes and social contributions. OECD statistics show that, today, while our wage costs are lower than in Germany, France and Italy, our living standards are substantially higher. On present trends Britain in GDP terms will soon resume its place as number four in the world economic league. And that is how it looks like continuing. As Anatole Kaletsky put it (*The Times*, 8 June 1999) 'Britain is almost certain to remain the world's fourth- fifth- or sixth-largest economy for the rest of our lifetimes. The idea that such a country is too small to operate as an independent entity is therefore manifestly absurd.'

Historical inevitability

So some Europhilia is no more than a post-Cold War and post-Wirtschaftswunder hangover, but most of it is not. For many a much more compelling theme of the euro rhetoric is the idea that federalism

Table 8.1 Relative competitiveness and living standards

	Wage living	
	Cost[a]	Standards[b]
US	100	100
Japan	100	103
UK	83	86
Germany	145	81
France	98	65
Italy	85	77

Notes: [a] Feb 1998 estimate based on US Bureau of Statistics Series.
[b] Single man on average earnings – OECD at purchasing power parity 1996.

is part of history's irresistible tide. Sovereign national states, it is claimed, reflect the age of steam, railways and the Morse code. Now outmoded by the global revolution in transport, telecommunications and information technology, they are having to make way for the superpowers of which Europe must either unite and join or shrink into insignificance. The most insidious propaganda ploy in favour of European Monetary Union is the claim that it is inevitable, so we might as well accept it. Many clever people are captivated by the thought of surfing the wave of the future – witness the crop of idealistic intellectuals who became Communists and even willing Soviet spies in Britain in the 1930s. They were not perturbed at betraying their own country and succouring a totalitarian regime because they thought they were marching with history. For them the prestige of contributing to the unstoppable progress of mankind made such temporary embarrassments seem trivial. If evidence did surface of brutality and murder by the Soviet regime it was brushed aside with such pearls of wisdom as 'You can't make omelettes without breaking eggs.' This notion of events moving of their own accord and dragging us along, leaving us no other option than to give them a little push, is very appealing to those who yearn to walk with destiny. In the case of the Euro-federalists it is less a case of walking than riding, shown by their constant allusions to the European bus or boat that must not be missed. Yet this notion that history is a self-propelled vehicle which we can hop on to but cannot control is piffle. History is what we make it, no more no less. All too often, indeed, it is, as Gibbon described it, 'a register of the crime, the vice and folly of mankind', though it does not have to be. The European bus has no pre-programmed destination – it may ascend the sunlit uplands, or, like the Gadarene swine, rush over the cliff. Either way we are free to choose whether or not to jump aboard.

Evidence against

In any case the facts don't support the theory of a global drift from nation states to federal superstates. For one thing there are today roughly twice as many states in the United Nations as there were at the time it was founded, most of them with under 5 million people. For another, far from national loyalties being on the wane, many of these new countries, both large and small, are giving top priority to nation building. Moreover, post-war history is littered with examples of federal failure, including Pakistan (with the loss of Bangladesh), the

Central African Federation, the Soviet Union, Yugoslavia and Czechoslovakia, to name but a few.

Euro mythology

Related to this vision of history as an irresistible urge towards ever bigger units of government culminating in the superstate (and eventually world government, the most super superstate of all) is the belief that our continent, the cradle of civilization, forfeited its rightful place as world leader and fell, the exhausted casualty of rival nationalisms. The most benign expression of this view was put by Winston Churchill: 'If only Europe were united, there is no limit to the happiness, the prosperity or the glory which its three or four hundred million people would enjoy' – though the Europe he was talking about was one to which, he assumed, Britain would never belong.

Federalist ideology

Thus emerges the core Euro-federalist interpretation of history and the action programme which logically follows for those who believe in it:

1. Nationalist divisions brought about Europe's decline.
2. The European peoples can only be restored to their rightful (leading) role in the world through the liquidation of nationalism and the abolition of the political and cultural institutions which underpin it.
3. National loyalties must be replaced by adherence to, on the one hand, the European Union and its array of supranational institutions, and on the other, regional governments which devitalise national organisation and help to erase national consciousness.

Former European supremacy

This interpretation of past and present has an appealing simplicity, comparable with Marx's 'All history is the history of class struggles' and like his is all the more plausible because it contains an element of truth. The major theme of the history of the last four centuries was indeed the Europeanisation of the world. From the fifteenth century onwards, European mariners explored the oceans, traded with distant lands and were followed by soldiers, priests and colonists. Their supporting military technology and the explosive growth of their manufacturing made them irresistible. Europe's pioneering of power-driven machinery, its sophisticated capitalist enterprise, and the population

explosion fostered by the industrial revolution, gave its peoples dominion, either directly by conquest or indirectly by economic penetration,
over most of the world. At the time of Queen Victoria's Diamond
Jubilee, European-led progress seemed like a law of nature. As the poet
Swinburne put it: 'Let the great world spin for ever down the ringing
grooves of change.'

Then disaster struck. Two world wars in the first half of the twentieth
century left Europe devastated and the world divided between the two
outside superpowers of America and the Soviet Union. Western Europe
at least recovered behind the NATO shield, though as a dependency of
a benign US, but the European empires disappeared.

Nationalism in the dock

But was Europe's downfall really due to the follies of its numerous
nationalisms, and was disaster due to what some have called 'Europe's
civil wars'? It would be more accurate to attribute them to the folly of
German nationalism. There is now a consensus among professional
historians, including German historians, that both world wars began as
German wars of conquest. The programme of the federalists to prevent
future European wars by marginalising nationhood is thus founded on
the false premiss that the wars are the product of rival nationalisms.
Even if this were so (and the fact that wars occurred long before
nationalism existed makes it look a bit silly) it is not true, as federalists
claim, that the peace of Europe since World War II has been kept by
the Common Market stopping the nations of Europe from being at
each other's throats. The only threat to peace in Europe in the post-war
period has come from the Soviet Union. That was contained by the
Atlantic Alliance, the backbone of which was provided by America,
until the Soviet collapse. Within Western Europe nationalist feelings
have not disappeared but they have not led to war because the countries of which it consists (apart from Serbia, the exception which
proves the rule) are democracies, and experience so far shows that
democracies do not tend to go to war with each other. This argument
applies with special force to Germany which, today, is a stable democracy. The military clique which once ruled the roost there has disappeared and German militarism is dead. A further point, underlined by
the post-war experience of Europe's democracies, is that you don't
need an empire and you don't need to grab other countries' land in

order to prosper. Wars to gain territory have therefore lost their appeal. Indeed the countries with the highest standards of living in Europe – Switzerland, the Scandinavian countries and Luxembourg – have never had empires (apart from Sweden, briefly, in the seventeenth century).

Glory in diversity

Yet this belief that the great tragedy of Europe is its political divisions and that it would have been wonderful if it had long ago been united is a myth. On the contrary, the source of the glory and greatness of Europe has been its political diversity. This is not only true of the splendour and variety of its national cultures but also of the material power which it was able for centuries to project across the world. As mentioned above, Europe's global dominance was based on its techno-logical and economic prowess. Of first importance was military and naval technology, which rested on scientific advance. But science does not progress very far without freedom of inquiry and experiment. It is pertinent to note that in the ancient world the greatest scientific thinkers were found not in the great empires of Egypt and Rome but in the small, independent (and usually warring) cities of Greece. The modern scientific first took shape not in the great territorial states like Spain but in the little city republics of Renaissance Italy, whose citizens were also – it was no accident – the wealthiest people in Europe. Freedom of thought, both political and scientific, flourishes where power is dispersed. If it is dispersed geographically, intellectuals whose ideas are not politically or religiously correct in one country can emig-rate to another where the authorities are more tolerant or at least find their ideas more congenial.

Fortune failure

If the various attempts by the Germans at creating an efficient empire on the Roman model during the middle ages had succeeded, or if the Papacy had won supremacy over the secular powers, scientific inquiry would have withered on the vine. Not that the Protestants of the six-teenth-century Reformation were necessarily more tolerant of new ideas than the Catholics (Calvin punished what he regarded as heresy with great severity, while the great humanist thinker, Erasmus, was a Catholic). However the Protestant emphasis on people reading the

Bible for themselves did encourage individualism. Catholic intolerance was more extreme than it would otherwise have been because, at an early stage, the Spaniards assumed leadership of the Catholic cause. For the Spaniards, unlike the other European peoples, had never stopped fighting the crusades. In their case it was waged against the Moorish Kingdoms for seven centuries until the final triumph over the Kingdom of Granada in 1492. Had Philip II of Spain succeeded in conquering the English, the Reformation would have been suppressed and political and intellectual freedom would have been eclipsed. He failed with the scattering of the Armada. Again, had Europe been united half a century later by the Catholic side winning the Thirty Years War – with Spain still making the running and the Counter-Reformation in full swing spearheaded by the Jesuits (founded by the Spaniard Ignatius Loyola) and enforced by the Spanish Inquisition – there would have been no scientific revolution in the seventeenth century. Newton's apple would have dropped unobserved.

Scientists persecuted

Anyone who doubts that should look at the fate of the great scientific genius Galileo, who, in 1633, in Spanish-controlled Italy at the height of the Thirty Years War, was forced on pain of death to recant his view that the earth went round the sun. This was because it was held, rather absurdly, to be contrary to scripture. After that he was put under house arrest and his career as a scientific thinker terminated. Yet he was lucky compared with Giordano Bruno whose ideas about the universe – billions of burning stars, matter composed of atoms, infinite space, rotating earth revolving round the sun – were rather close to what we think today. In February 1600 he was burnt for heresy in Rome.

The next attempt to unite Europe after the Spanish attempts at hegemony was under the France of Louis XIV, a more enlightened country than Spain. Even there, however, the great French philosopher Descartes, whose career overlapped that of Galileo, had found the Jesuitical atmosphere too stifling and moved to Protestant Holland. In his later years Louis XIV became increasingly authoritarian and finally expelled the Protestant Huguenots, to the great detriment of the French economy. It took the French intellectuals, who were possibly even more blinkered in their chauvinism than they are today, several decades to accept the ideas of Newton simply because he was a product of England, the traditional enemy.

So, had Europe united under Spanish or French absolutism, freedom of scientific inquiry would have been snuffed out. There would have been no 'century of genius' as the era of scientific breakthrough associated with the names of Galileo, Newton, Leibnitz and Descartes has been called. The economic cost would have been dire. The spate of technological innovation spurred by the new thinking and which culminated in the industrial revolution would not have occurred. Those many whose idea of Louis XIV's rule in France is based on *The Three Musketeers* may be surprised to learn that it was during his reign that numerous artisans were executed, broken on the wheel, or sent to the galleys for not observing the outdated, anti-innovatory, textile regulation of Louis' chief minister Colbert.

Unity versus capitalism

Moreover, had Europe been united under Spanish or French absolutism, that would have put paid to the rise of the enterprise culture of modern capitalism. For that too requires freedom (both economic and political), the rule of law and respect for individual property rights. It was the pathbreaking sociologist Max Weber who first attributed the rise of capitalism to the virtues of honesty, thrift, sobriety and hard work inculcated by the Protestant religion, especially the Calvinist version. That, he believed, explained the Catholic south of Europe's economic decline and the rise of the Protestant north from the late sixteenth century until recent times. More convincingly, however, Hugh Trevor-Roper has shown it was more a case of the Catholic response to Protestantism in the form of the Counter-Reformation that was to blame for suppressing intellectual freedom. As a result it drove out the creative and individualistic people who created wealth. Thus Italy, which had been the cradle of progressive ideas as well as the richest country in Europe in the fifteenth century, lost its intellectual edge and its prosperity during the sixteenth century after it fell under the heel of Spain and the Inquisition. Spain impoverished itself not only by endless wars and what Professor Paul Kennedy has dubbed 'imperialist overstretch' but also by the bigoted and wanton expulsion of the economically productive Jews and Moors. Spain's neighbour Portugal, once in the van of advance in commerce, exploration and navigational science, fell so far into the trough of superstition and ignorance that, by the eighteenth century, as Voltaire's Candide discovered, the response of the citizens of Lisbon to a catastrophic earthquake was to hold an *auto-da-fé*, to burn the heretics, whom they stupidly presumed to be responsible for the visitation of God's wrath. Later on, as already mentioned, France dealt its own manufactures a serious blow by expelling the industrious (Protestant) Huguenots who took their skills to Britain and Holland.

The general truth which these examples illustrate is that the worst enemy of scientific and economic progress is oppressive government. You don't get good science when research results have to conform to the bigotry of politicians or priests. You don't get sustained economic progress where regulation is stifling, taxation is ruinous and private property can be confiscated at the ruler's whim.

Unity hinders progress

This view may seem obvious enough to us today, but for centuries, indeed for millennia, it was far from apparent to regimes and cultures outside Europe, which, if wealth and sophistication were all that mattered, would have 'taken off' into self-sustaining growth many centuries ago, but in fact either stagnated or declined.

The main reason why our continent left the others trailing was that, since the Roman Empire, uniquely among civilisations, that of Europe was never united under a single authority. So dissenters from the orthodoxy in one country could usually in the last resort up sticks and emigrate to another. This diversity of political authority was partly due to geography. Europe's mountain ranges, river and dense forests made it relatively easy for different peoples to live separate lives. That was not the case with the great riverine civilisations elsewhere. Egypt, the saying goes, is the gift of the Nile and the same went for the other old civilisations. Babylon, China and India were oriental despotisms under the thumb of whoever held the rivers and the canals they fed and thereby controlled the food supply. Despotism made all the difference. Apart from that, these other civilisations had most of the elements which should have enabled them to take off into self-sustaining growth.

Why not China?

The Chinese produced a large number of important inventions including the wheelbarrow, the stirrup, the rigid horse collar (to prevent the horse from choking and the lack of which meant that the Romans used up horses ten times as fast as they should have done), paper, printing, gunpowder and porcelain. They had a water-driven machine for spinning hemp as early as the twelfth century – 500 years ahead of England. They were smelting iron, by using coal and coke in blast furnaces and producing 125,000 tons a year back in the eleventh century, an output it took Britain 700 years to equal. In the fifteenth century the Chinese government sent out fleets of hundreds of ships including some 400 feet long and 160 feet wide (far larger than the Europeans were building even a century later) on seven expeditions to explore the Indian Ocean and the Indonesian archipelago.

Meddling mandarins

Yet despite these early advances, which should have given the Chinese a head start in economic development, the impetus waned. In Europe paper and printing provided the means to universal literacy and an explosive spread of knowledge to whole populations. In China they remained a preserve of the mandarins who wanted to hang on to their knowledge monopoly. Gunpowder transformed warfare in Europe and hastened the end of feudal privilege. In China it was very little developed for war, because the Emperor and his mandarins didn't need it to keep out the nomads on the frontier, who were the only enemy, and they feared that firearms might fall into subversive hands. For, like all despots, they doubted the loyalty of their subjects. The hemp-spinning machine, another early Chinese invention, was never adapted for cotton and cotton manufacture and was never mechanised. Iron smelting fell into disuse. Clocks were the only things in which the Chinese acknowledged that the Europeans were far ahead – the Chinese only had water clocks which were quickly clogged with impurities and became inaccurate. In Europe mechanical clocks wrought a social revolution, imposing a new discipline and precision into economic life, and inculcating the notion of 'time is money'. With the development of the chronometer it became possible to measure longitude exactly for the first time and to navigate with great accuracy. In China, clocks were treated as toys for the Emperor and his court. As for maritime exploration, this was stopped by a faction at the imperial court who favoured a policy of isolation, like true Confucians abhorring commercial success, and eventually made it a capital crime to go to sea in a multimasted ship.

So China, despite huge initial advantages in wealth and technology, lost out, and almost, during the nineteenth century, became a vassal of Europe. Why did it fall? Because it was united under a powerful dictatorial government interfering with and regulating everything and strangling enterprise. Its economy was run by a centralised bureaucracy not a free market and development was stifled by lack of institutionalised property rights.

Why not India?

When the English arrived in India three and a half centuries ago, it was a populous empire where the ruling Moguls were fabulously rich. The revenue of the Mogul Emperor Aurangzeb is said to have amounted to ten times that of his contemporary, France's Louis XIV, the richest, most powerful monarch in Europe. India had a very productive agriculture and made the world's finest cotton yarn and textiles. Yet, though many businessmen made a fortune, they could never be sure that it would not be confiscated by a predatory government. Therefore, instead of ploughing their profits into the business, they bought gold and jewels and hid them. Similarly the peasant did not try to improve his lot by investing in tools or better methods of production for fear of seizure by extortionate tax collectors. The Emperor and his court had no idea of improving their domains: if they wanted more money they just squeezed the peasant a bit harder. In other words the conditions of capitalist development and technological progress – legally guaranteed, private property rights and free markets – did not exist. It was a country of the opulent few and the impoverished many who had no reason to love their masters. No wonder it fell like a ripe plum into the English lap.

Why not the Arabs?

Between 750 and 1100 Islamic science and technology far surpassed those of Christian Europe. Muslims gave us algebra, adopted paper and introduced coffee and sugar. Even the Ottoman Turks, who eventually became a byword for obscurantism, were, to start with, eager to use cannon and clocks. Unfortunately for them, though happily for their Christian foes, the religious zealots soon got the upper hand. As a result, for centuries many Muslim countries were opposed to printing, particularly of the Koran. There were no printing presses in Istanbul until the nineteenth century. The Muslim ideal appears to be a theocracy. The distinction between the religious and the secular authority, embedded in the European mind by the long medieval struggle between the Empire and the Papacy, was not recognised by the Muslim world. Is it even today? In any case we only have to look at the recent history of Iran to see that economic backwardness is assured when the fundamentalists take charge.[2]

Soviet arthritis

A more modern example of the weakness of societies which exercise thought control was the Soviet Union. Scientists there had to toe the party line. Charlatans, like the agronomist Lysenko, who claimed to grow blue tomatoes in the Ukraine but who faked his results, flourished. (A biologist friend of mine at Cambridge went to one of his lectures and managed to grab one of the so-called blue tomatoes that was on the lectern and found that it was made of wax.) Lysenko was able to ensure that only his ideas were taught in the schools. He believed in the discredited Lamarckian theory that acquired characteristics could be inherited (blacksmiths father sons with big muscles), which fitted in nicely with Marxist ideas about the new Soviet man. He outlawed the Mendelian theory of genetic inheritance, which rested on solid research and was and is universally accepted elsewhere. Interestingly enough it was the military leaders who (after they saw the air defence system they had given to the Syrians easily taken out by the Israelis with the help of far superior American weaponry) were the first to recognise that, in a high-tech world, Soviet-blinkered science and technology could not provide the sophisticated weapons needed to compete with those developed by the nerds of Silicon Valley and Seattle – particularly when President Reagan initiated the Star Wars challenge. They concluded that the only hope was to modernise their whole society which meant making it more free. That was the real beginning of glasnost and the collapse of the regime.

Unconvincing

That, as they say, is history. Yet today's protagonists of a united Europe will argue that, though past would-be unifiers of our continent might have undermined the very qualities that gave Europe the edge over the rest, that would not be the case today. They will say is because Europe now consists of democracies in which intellectual liberty is guaranteed. Alas this argument does not convince. As mentioned above, though the member states are democracies, the EU is not. Although its institutions resemble those of the US with their apparent division of powers between executive, legislative and judicial functions, in practice they reinforce the European old boy network and Brussels-style 'democratic centralism'.

Legal serfdom

The European Commission's scheme to unify by stealth the legal structure of the EU in the so-called *corpus juris* is especially alarming. In Britain the legal pillars of personal liberty are habeas corpus, trial by jury and the presumption of the courts that the accused is innocent until proved guilty. All these are threatened by the so-called *corpus juris* scheme of unifying EU law at present in the drafting stage. In Britain we take for granted habeas corpus – the right of an individual not be held in prison without charge. On most of the European mainland where the Napoleonic code is the norm, there is no such right. In France two-fifths of the prison population is held on remand, that is on the order of a judge on suspicion of having committed a crime, most of them without being formally charged. Their average length of stay in prison is four months, but some languish for years without being brought to trial. M. Jospin's government, to its credit, is trying to reform this situation, though far from radically. In Italy and Belgium the situation is worse. Indeed in Italy those held in preventive detention without trial amount to half the total. Do we really want to harmonise into a system of law which tramples thus on rights we in this country have known for centuries?

Totalitarian democracy

Those who have lived through decades of the Cold War and watched the wholesale faking of popular government in the so-called 'peoples democracies', have no excuse for forgetting that there is such a thing as totalitarian democracy and that possession of the vote is no guarantee of freedom. Nobody voted more often than the citizens of the

Soviet Union and much good it did them since they had no genuine choice! In Europe, however, it might be thought that elections should at least ensure that an unpopular government can be removed. Yet the general drift towards proportional representation, even in Britain – it is being used in EU elections and elections for the Assembly and Parliament of Wales and Scotland – works towards party not popular rule. In the worst scenario, numerous parties emerge and governments are formed out of coalitions which make deals about policies which bear absolutely no relation to what people thought they were voting for. In the party fixers' politically correct equivalent of smoke-filled rooms, all policies are negotiable. Also, unless there is a universal revulsion against the traditional parties, as happened in Italy in the early 1990s, elections produce only slight changes in representation with 80 per cent or more of the MPs remaining in their seats – and in some cases in power as well – permanently (remember that until his arrest for his Mafia connections, Signor Andreotti had been in every Italian government since World War II). With the list system, this means that senior figures in the parties are irremovable. In that situation why should the elected representatives care a fig about the electors? This is the position within many countries in mainland Europe already. Since the EU authorities are far more divorced from the electors than they are in the national governments, the more that power comes to be centralised in Brussels the more dictatorial the regime under which we shall be living. Of course figureheads like the bumbling and discredited M. Jacques Santer do not seem very threatening, but he is only a front for a bureaucracy and Europolitical clique which is increasingly in the saddle and out of control.

Subsidiarity a fraud

Europhiles argue that the dangers of centralisation in the EU are kept at bay by the principle of subsidiarity – according to which a 'higher' level of government should only act when its action is more 'effective' than that at the lower level would be. This claim is a cynical fraud. The obligation in Article C of the Treaty of European Union to respect in full the *acquis communautaire* (the accumulated body of policies which have been transferred to the EU level) comprehensively contradicts the devolutionary principle. Meanwhile there is no natural limit to the blatant and unconcealed desire of the Brussels politico/bureaucratic complex to add to its existing powers. All the numerous proposals for

further integration, notably in defence, foreign policy and social harmonisation, are strongly centralist, with not a whiff of subsidiarity
about them. Already libertarians have sounded the alarm about the
trend within Europe's national states towards growing concentration of
political and economic power. Laws and regulations have multiplied
exponentially while the government's share of the national income
has grown stupendously. The EU institutions only magnify this
ominous trend.

Freedom day comes late

The Adam Smith Institute has popularised the idea of freedom day –
the day each year that people stop working for the government and
start working for themselves. In Britain it is in late May, on the
European mainland mostly it is well into August. Government has traditionally been bigger on the continent than in Britain. Indeed at the
start of this century Britain's freedom day came in mid-February,
despite the heavy cost of the naval arms race. This is no place to trace
how this huge growth in leviathan occurred. Suffice it to say that the
biggest component of this growth has been in welfare provision which
is a bad joke because it mostly consists of taking the citizen's money
from one pocket and putting much the same amount back in the
other, minus what the bureaucracy creams off. State welfare is not even
an exercise in so-called social justice because, as has been proved, the
poor do worse out of it than the middle class. Mrs Thatcher sought
zealously to reverse this Big Brother trend with wholesale unloading of
state assets and the repeal of swathes of price-fixing regulations, but
recoiled at tackling the welfare state. In mainland Europe, there has
also been modest progress in privatisation but welfare liabilities, particularly pensions have spun out of control.

Don't harmonise, repatriate

For Britain, harmonisation into an EU system in which we have to pay
for lavish German, Italian, French and Belgian pensions would be a
nightmare. One thing is for sure: the more public spending is done by
Brussels the less accountable and more extravagant it will be. The way
forward for Europe is not through imposing uniformity which can
only stifle its peoples' creative energies, but through restoring the
diversity which has been the key to its past achievements. This will
only happen if it unburdens itself of the deadweight state which

represses incentive and devalues effort. It is ironic that, since 1989 when the Berlin Wall fell and the cause of political and economic freedom has been sweeping the world, the European Union has been moving in the opposite direction. The latest research[3] has shown that it is the countries with the most economic and political freedom – that is where there is the least state interference – where the people prosper most and also where there is the greatest degree of economic equality. So there is not even a case for government intervention to further so-called 'social justice'. The task for Europe in the next few decades is to reduce the huge state burden which has grown up in this century and today threatens to engulf it. It cannot be tackled by Brussels whose control freaks will merely aggravate the problem. Only the national governments of the EU member states can lighten the loads which they themselves have heaped on their peoples and which have since been gratuitously added to by the EU. It is time to institute cut-throat rivalry between the EU member states, rivalry in downsizing government. Otherwise Europe will wilt under pressure not only from high-tech America but from the low cost, emerging world and the liberated but still impoverished countries of the former Communist bloc.

There is no Third Way compromise of free economy production financing socialist largesse. There is no Rhineland corporatist or social market alternative. These are failed politico-economic models out of the same stable as the discredited European myth. If our continent is to flourish again there must indeed be cooperation between its sovereign member states, but cooperation which is largely driven by competition. The force will only be with them if they bulldoze the debris of overgovernment and restore the civic society of free peoples on which Europe's past glories were built.

Notes

1. He does admittedly suggest a way to meet the problem by institutional reform. Yet his proposal to reassert control by national parliaments over the EU by sending contingents from them to a new Euroland upper house, though superficially plausible, would raise once again the problem of dual membership which (in the old European Assembly) proved insoluble before. I mean the problem of political schizophrenia – of loyalties divided between two different bodies and, through lack of full commitment to either, correspondingly ineffective. Besides, as there is no such thing as a coherent European public opinion for it to reflect, Europe-wide democratic representation in the European Parliament is incapable of assuming coherent form. The new body would be nothing more than a Tower of Babel (despite the availability of instantaneous interpretation).

2. I am deeply indebted for the above examples of the relative failure of non-European peoples, at least until recent times, to develop modern scientific, technological and economic advance to the masterful study by David S. Landes, *The Wealth and Poverty of Nations*, Little Brown, 1998.
3. Johnson, Holmes and Kirkpatrick, '1999 Index of Economic Freedom', Heritage Foundation *Wall Street Journal*.

9

Britain, Europe and the United States: Reflections of an Anti-Maastricht Europhile*

Oliver Wright

I am honoured, delighted and flattered to be invited to give this inaugural Harry Allen Memorial Lecture, for I have had the good fortune to be associated with the Institute of United States Studies for many years and know the high reputation which it enjoys in the academic world and more widely. I am honoured to have a hand in helping the Institute celebrate its founder Director and delighted by so doing to emphasise the importance to our country of serious academic study of our friendly superpower. That study has never been so important as at the present time, when the ties that bind need to be re-evaluated, and re-invigorated. I am flattered to be asked to mount the lecture platform again to contribute my mite – as in 'widow's mite' – when I thought my role in life had been relegated to that of tribal memory, chatting away merrily into the cassettes of delightful PhD candidates about what I had seen and done, which, of course, to them was history.

Nothing wrong with history; we forget it at our peril. For what that great historian, Sir John Plumb, has called 'the Dominion of History' shapes our lives and fortunes whether we like it or not. Nothing wrong with tribal memory, either. The tribe needs to know how and why it got into the mess it is in if it is to plot the way out of it with as much good sense as it can muster. On a May afternoon we all need to remember that the leaves would not be on the trees if the roots had not been alive and healthy beneath the soil all winter. As the Bard puts it:

> In December I no more desire a rose
> Than wish a snow in May's new-fangled shows.

*The inaugural Harry Allen Memorial Lecture, Institute of United States Studies, 1999.

May 1999 seems to be especially rich in 'new-fangled shows' and I shall be discussing some of them.

I did not know Harry Allen. I wish I had. But I have spoken to many who did and am grateful to them for their insights into his work and character. We were near contemporaries and in many ways our lives moved in parallel, never meeting. Our most favourite years were during World War II, when he was in the Army and I was in the Navy. He, a soldier, wore and kept a moustache; I, a sailor, wore a beard and shaved it off on return to civvy street at my wife's urgent request. Serving alongside American troops, Allen was impressed by the sheer magnitude of the American contribution. He wondered how it was possible that a nation of such size and power could have been virtually ignored by the British educational establishment.

The war over, he took up a Commonwealth Fellowship at Harvard; unbeknownst to him, I was down the road in New York City in my first job in the Diplomatic Service as Vice-Consul. Back in Oxford, he embarked on what is still the only comprehensive overview of Anglo-American relations to have appeared this century – *Great Britain and the United States*, published by Macmillan in 1954. Allen belonged to a small group of scholars who led and shaped the rapid growth of American studies in Britain after World War II. If he needs a monument, look around you at American studies in this country, led in turn by his distinguished successors as directors of this Institute, Esmond Wright, Peter Parish and Gary McDowell, and by many other scholars too numerous to mention, with a plenitude of enthusiastic students at their feet.

I have a reason to be personally grateful to Harry Allen. When this lecture was announced, Macmillan got on to me, said that they had published Harry Allen and would be glad to publish me if I was minded to turn this lecture into a book. Let not your hearts be troubled. While it was nice to be asked, I have declined. Macmillan's judgement of Harry Allen, echoed by all I have spoken to, was: 'he was a fine scholar and a particularly nice man'. One could hardly wish for a nicer tribute than that.

The title of this lecture is: 'Britain, Europe and the United States: Reflections of an Anti-Maastricht Europhile'. The theme of the lecture is the quadruple danger we face: of the dismemberment of the United Kingdom and the disenfranchisement of the electorate, the reduction of the remains to little more than a province of Europe and the consequential destruction of the relationship, special, unique or whatever you would like to call it, with the United States. The message of the lecture is: 'Wake up, England.' When I was a lad in the late 1930s there was a splendid lady with a yacht who sailed from port to port around our island with that message blazoned in lights on its rigging. You will know why. She was thought to be a tad eccentric by some, downright barmy by others. She was merely right.

In my life-time, I believe our country has undergone two 'existential' experiences. The first was in 1940 when, after the disasters of Norway and Dunkirk, we called, just in time, upon Winston Churchill to imbue us with the spirit which led us eventually to victory, after a year on our own, and with a little help from our friends, temporary in the case of the Soviet Union and permanent in the case of the United States. Not much help from the continent: Churchill wrote that one of the heaviest crosses he had to bear in war was the Cross of Lorraine.

The second 'existential' experience was during the 'Winter of Discontent' of 1978–9, when the public service workers refused to perform their public services, when the garbage collectors refused to collect the garbage, the gravediggers refused to dig the graves, the hospital porters refused to move the patients. They destroyed the government they were supposed to support. Fortunately we had then, just in time, Margaret Thatcher, to stop the nation from going down the tube, to take us by the scruff of our necks and tell us to be sensible. We obeyed. The rest is history.

I believe our country may be approaching its third 'existential' experience if constitutional reform and the abandonment of the Maastricht opt-outs are allowed to proceed unchecked. We British are an easy-going lot and tend between disasters to tend our gardens. As a nation, we seem to have introduced the 'just in time' concept into our politics long before the technique was adopted by manufacturing industry. What we do have, to ensure that we avoid the third existential experience, is the vote, an existential vote if you like, in the referendum we are promised, allegedly on whether we join the euro, but in fact on whether we submerge our identity, eventually, in a United States of Europe. We are now engaged in what has rightly been called the second Battle of Britain.

I must justify my theme. First is the danger of the dismemberment of Britain and the progressive disenfranchisement of the electorate. It is a great tribute to Mr Blair that he has accepted the Thatcher economic revolution as the cornerstone of his economic policies: indeed, it was a precondition of his success at the polls. He has after all inherited the best economic legacy of any government in living memory. But it is a pity that he has entered uncharted waters by going on a constitutional binge: a Parliament for Scotland, an Assembly for Wales, the introduction of proportional representation for Scotland, Wales and Europe, the reform of the House of Lords. I leave Northern Ireland on one side except to note that if Mo Mowlam's preferred solution – 'united by consent' – comes about, that will automatically mean the end of the United Kingdom. I also leave on one side the reform of the House of Lords as not strictly germane to my theme, except as an aspect of the general urge to reform everything constitutional on sight.

In Scotland there will be the first parliament for nearly 300 years. Nothing necessarily wrong with that, but what about the consequentials? What about the West Lothian question, raised by Gladstone 100 years ago and by Mr Tam Dalyell at the time? If the English have no say in the governance of Scotland, why should the Scots have a say in the governance of England? And still without an answer. What about the Barnett formula, whereby the English taxpayer remits vast sums of money north of the border with little or no say in how they are spent? The Scots seem to be having a whale of a time, for in addition to governing Scotland, they seem to be governing England as well. And they seem to have a monopoly of representing Britain abroad; Blair, Cook and Robertson – Bravehearts to a man – are directing the war in Kosovo on our behalf. We English need to keep an eye on these Scots, with their historical connections with Europe. We should do well to remember the trouble Elizabeth I had with Mary. We have only John Prescott and Jack Straw in the great offices of state to hold high the banner of St George for us. When will they start demanding our money back? Europe offers a useful precedent: Grantham is not far from Hull. Prescott could ask Lady Thatcher how it is done.

At the moment those who favour the Union are in a majority in Scotland. Thank goodness for that. But will devolution satisfy the Scottish desire for self-government; or will the appetite grow by what it feeds on? The Scottish National Party are now the main party of opposition. In democracies it is in the nature of things that the electorate eventually gets fed up with the government, especially if expectations are not fulfilled and then the opposition becomes the government. Then, heigh-ho, independence for Scotland and the end of Great Britain. Mr Blair seems to have gone for the top line without thinking through to the bottom line.

Perhaps the best example of reforming zeal run riot was the referendum and election for a Welsh Assembly: 50 per cent of the Welsh people were not sufficiently interested in what was on offer to bother to turn out and vote: of those who did bother, 25.1 per cent voted for an Assembly, 24.9 per cent voted against. All the counties bordering on England, plus Pembrokeshire, little England, voted against. Wales was trebly split: geographically down the middle, North to South; half voted and half stayed at home; half voted for and half against. Just in case there was any doubt about who was in charge, the Welsh Labour party was not allowed to have the leader they wanted but had a man imposed upon them from London. Blair giveth and Blair taketh away: blessed be the name of Blair.

If events in Ireland and Scotland threaten to dismember the realm – and remember there may be more to come if we get a whole clutch of regional assemblies for England – the Scots setting the dismemberment of England in train to ready it for the Europe of the regions: now that's a thought for you – the last bit of this intemperate haste to change everything at once is proportional representation. On the face of it – and many of this government's actions are 'on the face of it', that is superficial – reasonable and fair. It does seem reasonable and fair that parliament should reflect more precisely how the people vote. That is the upside. The downside is less obvious and more dangerous. Proportional representation lessens the direct relationship between the Member of Parliament and the constituents he represents. The party-list people owe more to their party and less directly to the electorate. Party lists drawn up at party headquarters ensure that only those of proven docility get high enough on the list to get a seat. The late Derek Fatchett, Labour MP for Leeds Central, got it right when he said: 'you would not have government by the ballot box but government by the smoke-filled room'. Donald Dewar and Jim Wallace will know what he meant. Proportional representation means that the electorate are marginalised.

It has been interesting for a tribal elder to observe in three of the constitutional reforms – Scotland, Wales and proportional representation – the law of unintended consequences working itself out. It always does, and particularly when measures are taken which have not been properly thought through.

It cannot have been the intention that the Scots and the Welsh should have greeted elections to their legislatures with even less enthusiasm and lower turnouts than to their referendums setting them up. It cannot have been intended that Labour should have failed to get by proportional representation the overall majorities it would have obtained by first-past-the-post, or that the two nationalist parties should have made such inroads into Labour's heartlands and become the major opposition parties. The idea, I thought, was to draw the sting of national sentiment, not strengthen it. It cannot have been the intention that Mr Dennis Canavan, deselected by Labour, should have trounced the official Labour candidate in Falkirk. Or that Mr Alun Michael, Mr Blair's emissary from London, should have won his seat on the party list only because Labour had done so badly on the constituency lists. These are merely some of the immediate unintended consequences of policies designed for immediate effect and inadequately thought through. No wonder our sorcerer's apprentice looked a sadder and perhaps a wiser man – only time will tell – the day after, as he contemplated the television cameras and the results of his innovative constitutional handiwork in the garden of No. 10 Downing Street.

We have been spared proportional representation for Westminster, doubtless because focus groups, which now determine policy, have revealed that the English are not ready for it and that that election pledge is best put on one side, at least for the time being. Thank goodness for that. No doubt that is why the beautiful political friendship between Tony Blair and Paddy Ashdown, and Mr Ashdown's political career, have come to premature ends. Sad, for Paddy, in many ways; but he has had a good innings.

But we still, each one of us, have a vote, an effective vote, an existential vote, in the referendum we are promised on the euro. We must use it. Wake up, England! The price of our liberties is still eternal vigilance.

What about Europe and the clear and present danger of Britain's being reduced to a province of it?

On 1 January the euro was launched in Frankfurt with champagne, fireworks and hype, the triumph of political will over economic sense. The shenanigans brought to mind Walpole's remark on the outbreak of war with Spain: 'They now ring the bells; but they will soon wring their hands.' I am not an economist, so I will spare you my economic analysis. But Milton Friedman, who is an economist of some repute, has written: 'for a monetary union to work, a common language, a common culture, a common loyalty are necessary: and these do not prevail in the EU'. Both the President of the Bundesbank and the Governor of the Bank of England have said that having EMU before political union is putting the cart before the horse. One-size-fits-all interest rates seems crazy to me: Germany, sluggish, may need a reduction: Ireland, in the midst of a boom, needs one like it needs a hole in the head.

In any case, the economic arguments have never been decisive. Tribal memory recalls that in the debates in the early 1960s, in both Houses, it was generally admitted that the economic pluses and minuses about cancelled each other out. Things have, of course, moved on quite a bit since then, 35 years on. The world has changed. The economic case for proceeding with this business has shifted. The European market is still a very important one; but it is mature and one with which we are in permanent deficit. The rest of the world is equally important, and we are in surplus with it. Investment, in and out, is very much a rest-of-the-world matter. Whatever the big boys of the Confederation of British Industry may say, the figures show that they do not put their money where their mouths are. BP takes over Amoco for $60 billion, HKSB takes over Republic New York Corp for $10 billion. For them it is still 'Westward, look, the land is bright.' Foreign direct investment into Britain shows no sign of declining despite John Major's opt-out, and perhaps because of it. The fact is that finance has already become globalised and trade is rapidly becoming globalised. The *world* should once again be Britain's oyster, not a backward-looking, regulated, protective part of it.

Today, the politics have moved on too. The main objections of the anti-Maastricht Europhile are political. It was the wrong treaty at the wrong time; yesterday's treaty; yesterday's answer to yesterday's problem – the ancient enmity between France and Germany. It was being negotiated before communism collapsed and Germany was reunited – quite important events, don't you think? – and signed *after* they had been completed as if the world in which we live had not changed. Europe's priority *should* have been to support the nations of Eastern Europe, doubly liberated, from the Soviet Union and from communism, just as it did when Spain, Portugal and Greece got rid of their dictators. Ten years later, ten years lost, we are at last coming round to it. But the impediments to their entry are now greater than they were ten years ago. No wonder the President of Estonia, one of the applicants, has remarked rather ruefully: 'Europe has a tendency to build a fence round it.' One big fence is, of course, the Common Agricultural Policy. It needs to be, but apparently cannot be, reformed. The *acquis* is sacred.

But for this anti-Maastricht Europhile, the benefit in the 1 January celebrations was the number of cats let out of the bag. There can be no excuse now for not knowing that for our continental partners the euro is but one stop on the road to political union, a United States of europe. I was going to quote Jacques Santer, but was rudely interrupted by his resignation. Fortunately, no sooner had Santer gone, than Mr Blair's choice – I hope due diligence was done – gave my lecture a raft of equally apposite quotations in lieu. Thus Mr Prodi: 'The Single Market was the theme of the '80s. The Single Currency was the theme of the '90s. We must now face the task of moving towards a single economy, a single political unity.' Clearly I should have thought it, as Stalin used to say. He went on: 'Amsterdam and Maastricht need to be followed by a treaty which will give us our own defence capabilities.' On the BBC's *On The Record* programme he spelled out what he meant when he suggested that the creation of a single army, in which British soldiers fight under an EU flag and take orders from a European commander, was the logical next step. It seems we have yet another sorcerer's apprentice in our midst. I was glad to see that No. 10 said that this was not an idea we favoured. Thank goodness for that. But at least our continental partners are honest about their intentions. The only government which is not levelling with its people is the British Government. For example, the Chancellor of the Exchequer has stated that if Britain joins the euro, that would have no constitutional significance. The *Daily Telegraph* has stated editorially that politicians who say that are lying. Mr Brown is not, so far as I am aware, suing. There is an all-party motion in the House of Commons, with over 100 signatures, which reads: 'This House calls on HMG to publish a White Paper on the constitutional, economic and political consequences of the UK joining the European single currency.' So far, no response. I should have thought that any straightforward government – I suppose, alas, that that is an oxymoron – with an existential decision for the country ahead, would want to have what it clearly wants to do, to be supported by the clear and informed view of the British people. But no; the preferred technique in politics today is apparently to operate by stealth.

Of course, the fundamental objection to the single currency is, like its origin, political. The European Union lacks political legitimacy and the forthcoming elections to the Strasbourg parliament will not remedy that defect. It is a Union of elites, of political classes and enarques, an oligarchy inadequately responsive and responsible to public opinion. Indeed I have heard it suggested, in all seriousness, that this is one of its strengths. I happened to tune in some time ago to a late-night discussion on television chaired by Jon Snow on public opinion and the euro. He asked one of his panel, a German MEP, how it was that the German government intended to sign up to the euro when clearly a majority of Germans did not want to give up the Deutschmark. His reply is scorched in pokerwork on my brain: 'if the German political classes had listened to public opinion in the past, Germany would not have been the success it has been'. *The Economist* made much the same point in its survey of Germany in February: 'All the most existential decisions German governments have made since the war have been taken against the wishes of a majority of the people: re-arming the Bundeswehr, joining NATO, setting up the EMS, joining the euro.' Well, the Germans are perfectly entitled to do things their way. Our political cultures are just different. *Vive la différence*, perhaps. I like to think that Brits take the democratic deficit seriously.

In fact, one of the charms, for politicians and officials alike, of going to Brussels to meet their fellow Prime Ministers, Foreign Ministers or whatever is that they are able to enjoy strutting and fretting their hour upon the larger stage without a legislature at their heels. This is known as *la déformation professionelle*. I know. I have watched it happen. Tribal memory recalls only one politician who did not succumb to this deformity and she was not popular east of Calais.

The so-called sharing of sovereignty is so much clap-trap if it does not provide a tried and tested mechanism for removing our governors from office. EMU adds to the democratic deficit. The new European Central Bank is a case in point. It is quite different in nature from the Bank of England. New Labour has given the Bank of England back the independence which Old Labour took away 50 years ago. But at least the Old Lady of Threadneedle Street publishes its minutes fairly soon after its meetings and this answers to the public as well as to Parliament. So, by the way, does the Federal Reserve Bank in the United States. In contrast, it took the unanimous vote of the 11 Euroland members to set up the ECB and it needs the unanimous vote of all of them to abolish it if things do not turn out as hoped. You can see that happening as well as I can. And the President of the ECB has made it clear on more than one occasion that he does not intend to justify his actions by publishing the minutes of his Board – at least not for 16 years. His little joke? Or a whiff of hubris in the air? If so, nemesis will ineluctably follow.

So if Mr Blair's choice for President of the Commission gets his way, more and more competencies and powers will be transferred to Brussels and Parliament at Westminster will be hollowed out. Jacques Delors once claimed that 80 per cent of all government decisions would eventually be taken in Brussels. He did not exaggerate. Westminster would be reduced to the status of the Scottish Parliament or the Welsh Assembly. England will be reduced to a province of Europe as it was of Rome 2000 years ago. Churchill's dictum is being reversed: our liberties are being *narrowed* down from precedent to precedent. The time to stop it is now, before it is too late. Wake up, England!

Does it not strike you as odd, to say the least, that the 15 nations of the former Soviet empire, after 70 years of union, reclaimed as soon as

they could their separate national identities, and that most of the component nations of Yugoslavia did likewise? Does it not strike you as
odd, that, when all the evidence is that people want to govern themselves, Europe should have embarked on the dangerous experiment of
forcing many ancient nations with languages, cultures and loyalties of
their own into being governed by other people? Nearer to home, does
it not seem odd to you, to say the least, that our government's chief
contribution to the gaiety of nations is to do the political splits, by
being integrationist in Europe and devolutionist at home? These Scots
really are getting their own back. If that is what the political class east
of Calais want, let them have it. There is no reason why we English,
like sheep, should follow them. I await the working out of the law of
unintended consequences with some interest.

What does this mean for our relations with our friendly superpower,
the United States? Let me say at once that I do not buy the idea, sometimes expressed, that our influence in Washington will be proportional to
our influence in Europe. I recognise there a State Department view. But
the State Department, while important, is not, constitutionally or in practice, decisive. The White House is. The reason is simple. The President is
the sole *elected* member of the Executive. I leave aside the Vice-President,
who is there for the heartbeat and the chores. All the members of his
administration are appointed. They have no independent source of
power, for example by being elected. The State Department has of course
a duty to keep the many and varied interests of the United States in
balance. A famous recent example was the Falklands, when the department, as my predecessor would testify, sought under Secretary of State Al
Haig to maintain a balance between America's closest democratic ally and
the Argentina of the disappeared and the military junta.

All British Ambassadors in Washington naturally value the best possible relations with the State Department. But they never forget where
power lies: in the White House. And if one needed friends, one sought
and found them in the Pentagon. Concerning the Falklands, while the
State Department was busy keeping the balance, the Defence
Department from the start was letting us have all the logistic support
we needed – unlike one of our European allies which would not sell us
the arms we needed, not even for ready money.

Tribal memory yields a few corroborative details to lend artistic
verisimilitude to an otherwise bald and unconvincing narrative. After
the disaster of Suez, France and Britain went their separate ways.
Macmillan gave priority to the restoration of British relations with the
United States, greatly facilitated by his personal wartime relationship

with Eisenhower. The first fruit of this relationship was the repeal of the MacMahon Act, which enabled the resumption of nuclear collaboration between Britain and America, interrupted since the end of World War II. Second, when John Kennedy became President, Macmillan got Polaris at Nassau, when the President decided, against the advice of all his advisers, in favour of the Prime Minister. Third, when Harold Wilson paid his first visit to Washington to meet Lyndon Johnson, the main topic of discussion was the MLNF, a mixed-manned warship with nuclear weapons, designed by the State Department to satisfy an alleged German desire for a seat at the top nuclear table. We thought it was a load of codswallop and Wilson deployed the case against it very effectively. The President and his team withdrew to the Oval Office. The Prime Minister and his team remained in the Cabinet Room. A wag amongst us, I think it was Denis Healey, quipped 'Ball's last stand', George Ball being, of course, Under Secretary of State. The President decided in favour of Wilson. The MLNF was sunk without trace.

A fourth and more recent example was the way we obtained the successor to Polaris, Trident. The State Department was making difficulties, mesmerised as always by the importance of Germany. I was instructed to take the matter up with the White House. Suffice it to say that we got Trident: Margaret Thatcher's influence with President Reagan was decisive.

My own judgement is that so long as we remain strong and reliable, so long as we maintain the Thatcher revolution and keep our economy robust, so long as we do not have too many more defence reviews to emasculate still further our defence capabilities, just so long will our voice be heard where it matters: in the White House. America, for all its faults, and we all have our faults, is still, in President Bill Clinton's words, the one indispensable nation: it is the only superpower; it is indisputably the greatest democracy around. Today, it is the sole motor of the world economy, having re-invented itself in the last ten years to place itself at the cutting edge of the technological revolution for the twenty-first century. (It is astonishing to think that only 15 years ago it was concerned about Japanese competition.) But it is still reluctant to be the world's policeman; it needs reliable allies. The Prime Minister, all prime ministers, are right to seek to be on the best of terms with the President, with all presidents. I very much doubt whether a dismembered Britain which had become a mere province of Europe would have anything like the sort of clout with the United States that I am sure we all want.

Indeed, I very much doubt that a *United States of Europe* would have the sort of relationship with the United States of America we should want. In commerce, there are protectionist forces at work on both sides of the Atlantic, but they are worse on this. The banana row was a case in point; a trivial case, perhaps, but indicative. It is worth remembering that the World Trade Organisation found against Europe, with us in it. More important to my mind are the political incompatibilities. France makes no secret of its anti-Americanism: the dominion of history is at work there. Germany has twice rejected the offer of 'partnership in leadership' – a State Department wheeze, if ever there was one – under both George Bush and Bill Clinton, because it gives priority to its relations with France over its relations with the United States. Again, the dominion of history is at work. Since we do not share their history, we do not share their priorities. I am firmly of the conviction, having tasted both, that our political and economic cultures are more akin to those of the United States than to those of Europe; that the Channel is, in these respects, wider than the Atlantic.

So what do we do about it? Fortunately we still have that crucial vote and I hope we still have the will-power to use it. It is to vote 'No' in any referendum on whether to join the euro. For we shall not only be voting on a single currency, but on harmonisation of taxation, a common foreign policy, a common defence policy and a single armed force in a United States of Europe. I do not exaggerate. That is what our continental friends say they want and I see no reason to doubt their sincerity. The only government which is refusing to say what it has in mind for the future of the nation is our own. So far, as I have suggested, it has apparently shelved its proposals for proportional representation for Westminster because it has presumably found out from its focus groups that the Brits collectively are not ready for it. What we have to do is to get the same message across to the present government about the euro and the referendum. The best thing would be not to have one. But if we do have one, then we have to get the vote out against it. Maybe we shall have to march, as the advocates of the countryside did with salutary effect. I shall be there if we do, with my zimmer frame if need be.

On the whole, 1999 has been quite a good year so far for anti-Maastricht Europhiles like Harry Allen and myself, who want maximum cooperation with our continental friends but minimum further integration with them. Let us walk and talk with them; let us buy and sell with them. But let us *not* be governed by them. Let us keep the single market; they cannot throw us out if we don't want to go. Let us continue to govern *ourselves*. To paraphrase Lyndon B. Johnson: our governments, of whatever complexion, may be sons of bitches, but they are *our* sons of bitches. And we can, if enough of us want to, 'turn the rascals out'.

It has been quite a good year because the euro, despite the champagne and fireworks and hype on 1 January, has been quietly subsiding against both the dollar and the pound. It is early days yet, but it has still to exhibit the characteristics of a safe haven. It has been quite a good year because all 20 commissioners have been forced to resign. Tribal memory recalls General de Gaulle's description of the Commission to Harold Wilson when he was in London for Churchill's funeral – *cet aréopage inélu*, that unelected areopagitica. You should have heard the disdain in his voice. That was 36 years ago. It is still an unelected areopagitica, but grown monstrous in power and arrogance. Some of the 20 ousted commissioners may be back, but the culture of irresponsibility has been exposed for all to see. The phrase is not mine, but that of the committee set up to investigate the Santer-led Commission.

It has been quite a good year so far because a poll of economists in *The Economist* registered a 65 per cent 'Yes' vote to the question as to whether it would be in Britain's interest to join the euro within the next five years. *The Economist*, no Eurosceptic rag, headlined its story, 'A Setback for the Euro.' The sub-heading was 'Two-thirds of Britain's Economists Cannot Be Right.' Tribal memory delights to recall the 364 economists who took a full-page advertisement in *The Times* in early 1981 to record their considered opinion that the Thatcher–Howe policies for the recovery of our country from the Winter of Discontent were wrong. As every schoolboy knows, from the moment Britain started into growth, and except for two disastrous years' membership of the Exchange Rate Mechanism, from which George Soros mercifully rescued us, it has never looked back since.

Best of all, as I said, the cats have been let out of the bag. There is now no excuse for our fellow countrymen and women not knowing what is afoot and even less excuse for our government refusing to come clean about what, by 'stepping up a gear' in preparation for the euro, they are letting us in for. Mr Prodi's European army under a European commander may be, in his own words, 'years and years away', but as the Chinese saying goes, a journey of a thousand miles starts with the first step. If you do not want to get to the destination, do not get on the bus that is going there. All we have to do now is wake up to reality. Then, to finish, as I started, with the Bard:

> Nought shall make us rue
> If England to itself do rest but true.

I rest my case.

10

Can Self-Government Survive? Britain and the European Union

Nevil Johnson

Introduction

The European Union may well be approaching a decisive stage in its development. Or again, it may not be. As always in the affairs of the EU, it is hard to discern where it is going, who is generating decisive impulses, who is putting on the brakes, what kind of bargains on this matter or that may be feasible and so on. So prophecy remains a hazardous business.

Nevertheless, certain objective circumstances suggest that the current Inter-Governmental Conference which is intended to reach conclusions on treaty revisions before the end of 2000 may take some far-reaching decisions; and that the effects of these will push the EU decisively towards seeing itself more like an emergent state and less like an association of sovereign nation states cooperating for mutual advantage. For example, a reduction in the veto rights of member states and a realignment of qualified majority voting rules is held by many to be required both to facilitate decisions in the EU as it now exists and to accommodate a wider membership after prospective enlargement.

There is also a clear need, ahead of any enlargement, to reconsider the membership, structure and size of the European Commission. Additionally there are strong pressures for the proclamation of a new code of human rights which some see as the first step towards the achievement of a genuine constitution for the EU. And on top of that, there is pressure for a further development of social policies which would be binding across the board. Finally, in the eyes of the present members of the Economic and Monetary Union, there is an urgent need to devise more effective methods of formulating and carrying out common economic policies to back up the monetary union they have joined and, if possible, to consolidate and strengthen the common currency launched at the beginning of 1999.

Progress on any or all of these matters would constitute a watershed and would offer proof that the European Union was at last irrevocably launched on the road to effective statehood. For this reason alone there is ample justification for looking again at the peculiar challenges that the evolution of the EU presents to a nation like Britain which remains for the most part doubtful about the onward march to 'ever closer union'.[1] This is what this chapter proposes to do.

A short history lesson

Ever since Britain committed itself in 1972 to membership of the European Economic Community – known more familiarly at that time as the Common Market – its relationship with the Community (or to be more exact, the 'Communities') has been an uneasy one. Sometimes it seemed that Britain was concerned only with getting out of the Community what it regarded as its due, most famously when Mrs Thatcher argued vehemently for, and eventually secured, a rebate on our budgetary payments.

But there have also been times when Britain has given strong support to important policy developments, notably in putting through the measures called for to complete the single market provided for by the Single European Act in 1986. Even when the relationship with the European Communities was at its most tense and difficult, for example during the run-up to the Maastricht Treaty in 1992 and in the course of its subsequent passage through Parliament, politicians continued to talk optimistically of 'Britain's place in Europe' and of their desire to see Britain taking a lead in the development of the European project. With the arrival of the Blair Government, the desire to be 'at the heart of Europe' became even more explicit. Mr Blair professed his determination to show that by adopting a more conciliatory approach to policy issues in the EU than his predecessors had done – an approach which *inter alia* resulted in adherence to the Social Chapter agreed at Maastricht and from which Britain had secured an opt-out – it would be possible to assume a comfortable position on the bridge of the good ship European Union. Britain would, it was hoped, have a hand on the policy tiller.

Yet despite Mr Blair's well-publicised efforts to persuade his European partners to take over his 'modernising' agenda, he has continued to have awkward moments with them. He remains worried about loss of powers over taxation and appears to be resolutely non-committal about joining the Economic and Monetary Union. This makes it hard to discern many convincing signs of Britain gravitating to the centre of the policy initiatives which, so it is widely asserted, must be taken and decided before the end of the current year.

In reality, reluctance to rush ahead and caution remain the hall-marks of the British approach to the great adventure of building in Europe 'an ever closer union'. Politicians of various parties continue to assert that we must get closer to the heart of Europe, yet it remains an inescapable fact that such demands continue to be at odds with the evidence of what happens day by day. There is no sign that Britain is comfortably at the centre of policy-making in the EU: it continues to be either a brake or a dissenter most of the time, and a reluctant partner nearly always. One of the aims of this chapter is to review some of the underlying reasons why this has been so.[2]

A glance to the future

While it remains important in respect of nearly all political problems to have some grasp of the past circumstances and experiences in which they are rooted, we are bound also to be concerned with the future and the question of whether there are likely to be serious opportunities for changing the situation and prospects. In relation to the future evolu-tion of the European Union and Britain's place within it, this means considering whether it is realistic to believe that the EU can be changed or is likely to change of its own accord on any terms likely to be acceptable to a majority of voters in Britain. Francis Maude, the Shadow Foreign Secretary, put the choice very explicitly in a letter to the press in which he wrote:

> It is now high time for the Commission to discard the old dogmas of ever closer integration and centralisation. Instead it should adapt to the realities of globalisation ... by proposing a more outward-looking, flexible and free-enterprise future for Europe.[3]

These remarks highlight a fundamental policy issue facing not only the present Government, but also any alternative Government in the future: if a majority of member states of the EU continue to insist, as they have done since at least 1990, on pressing on ever further down the road of 'ever closer union', and are ready to accept the greater degree of political and economic integration entailed by such steps, what is to be done about it? Indeed, can anything at all be done about it?

It is highly likely that the majority of the British people will continue to oppose moving ever further down the road sign-posted 'ever closer union'. They can see that whatever might be the ultimate character of 'ever closer union', it is bound to entail a continuing loss of their rights of self-government. Moreover, there is some evidence for the belief that they would not wish to follow this path, even though it may be claimed that the economic benefits of so doing are overwhelming. If these conditions hold good, then two further questions have to be faced up to. One is whether there is any realistic prospect of persuading our partners in the EU – or at least a significant number of them – that there are reasonable and viable alternatives to the inexorable pursuit of 'ever closer union'. And if the answer to this question looks like being in the negative, then it becomes necessary to ask whether it would be more honest towards the British people to consider how we might modify in perhaps fundamental ways our position and obligations within the EU with the minimum of damage both to ourselves and other member states.

No questions please

Any effort to think critically about the future shape of the EU and Britain's relationships within it runs the risk of being regarded as simply another exercise in euro-scepticism. This happens in part because so much discussion of the whole subject both in Britain and on the continent has become dominated both by ideological commitments ('no turning back now') and by the dictates of political expediency ('never admit that we made a mistake'). Indeed in many parts of the continent of Europe it has become virtually impossible to raise serious practical questions about the methods, aims and limits of the integration process. To do so is seen as calling into question the validity of the whole enterprise. While it is acceptable to indulge in colourful rhetoric offering visions for the future, there is very little space for asking critical questions about specific changes that might be made to improve the functioning of EU institutions and the effectiveness of its policy implementation.

The deep fear of any plain-speaking about the condition of the EU and where it might be going found vivid expression in the recent contretemps between France and Germany over the speech by the German Foreign Minister, Joschka Fischer. He offered the world his thoughts as a private individual about the desirability of the EU evolving into a federation of some sort or another. When the former French Interior Minister, Jean-Pierre Chevènement, voiced his doubts about such a federal vision, he was indelicate enough to suggest that perhaps the German desire to confer the benefits of their kind of federation on the rest of Europe reflected several aspects of their earlier history, including a deep mistrust of the national state inherited from the Nazi epoch. Shocked voices of protest were heard in both countries.

Yet what this French politician was saying is fairly familiar to anyone who has studied post-war German foreign policy in general and European policy in particular, and thought carefully about its underlying motivations. Nevertheless, such critical comments had to be firmly disavowed and their author (who happens to be very well-informed about German history and culture) persuaded to offer a semi-retraction. After all, nothing must be allowed to disturb the harmony of the two Governments which like to see themselves as the twin motor of European integration and the privileged source of policy initiatives to take it further forward.

There can be no question that this climate of conformity and artificial optimism makes the task of constructive criticism exceedingly difficult.

Most of the problems and arguments to be discussed in what follows are political rather than economic. In Britain, sensible and rational consideration of the EU, what it is, and where it is going, has long been hampered by a failure to recognise that the politics and economics of membership are indissolubly tied together. To take the most obvious current example of this, the decision whether or not to join the euro zone is inextricably political and economic. The two aspects of the issue cannot be separated, which is why the Chancellor of the Exchequer's claim that adopting the euro would have no constitutional implications is either hopelessly naive or dishonest. However, it is not surprising that many people would like to persuade themselves that such a separation can be made. Many of those in Britain who endorse the EU in a broad sense defend their position by arguing that future economic survival depends almost exclusively on continued membership: they see the EU as a 'zone of prosperity' to which we must belong. The advocates of this view then tend to push the political side of the equation under the carpet or into a distant future.

In contrast, those who dislike the EU chiefly on political grounds (and these political grounds can be diverse) tend to discount its possible economic benefits. Some critics also do not want to recognise that the national interest demands that Britain should maintain good relations with the EU even if by some means or other major changes were to be made in the terms on which the EU is constituted, or on which Britain works within it. Indeed, even the most radical policy option of all – a decision to try to negotiate an orderly withdrawal from the EU – would still call for a determined effort to retain as many of the economic benefits of membership as possible. So in whatever direction we look in the future, the economics and politics of the terms of membership must be seen as indissolubly linked.

There are few dedicated eurosceptics in Britain in the sense of people who are actively hostile to our continental neighbours. Equally, there are very few euro-faithful who are so dedicated to the cause of European union that they do not care about its political character and are ready to follow wherever the Pied Piper leads. But what we can be sure about is that there are many in Britain who want to cooperate as fruitfully as possible with the EU and its member states, to safeguard British prospects of economic prosperity, and yet to retain their traditional rights of self-government to the maximum practicable extent. If a serious consideration of the available evidence suggests that it may not be possible to satisfy all these requirements to a similar degree, then decisions will, some day, have to be made. These decisions will involve the judgement of political values as well as of material advantages. That day seems to be getting closer. And such a decision might make it clear that British interests call for a radical reappraisal of the shape and purposes of the European Union.

The historical heritage

It is well known that Britain moved reluctantly towards membership of what was then the Common Market or European Economic Community. After two abortive attempts to enter the Community, Edward Heath's Government finally signed up to accession in 1972. After passage of the necessary legislation through Parliament, Britain took up membership at the beginning of 1973.[4] After a somewhat specious show of renegotiating some aspects of the terms of accession by the Wilson Government, approval to Britain remaining in the Community was given in a referendum held in 1975. All this happened at a time when the perception in the country of relative economic decline was strong and there was a widespread hope that in some way or other membership would stimulate economic growth. The political aspects of accession to the Treaty of Rome were for the most part played down. Indeed, several assurances were given by Mr Heath's Government that membership would involve no serious derogation from the sovereignty of the British Parliament. In short, it was essentially a common market that we were joining.

A divergence of economic policy

Ironically, the economic revival which a few years later got under way in Britain owed little or nothing to membership of the EEC. Far more important was the return to market economics and the liberalisation of the British internal economy pioneered by Margaret Thatcher after she took office in 1979. Inevitably this tended to open up ever-widening differences between the approach to economic policy favoured in Britain and that preferred by most member states of the EEC (and to a considerable extent by the European Commission also).

In the early years of British membership, these differences had not been so significant. Then, there was a widespread commitment in most European states to the notion that the state should play a major role in 'managing the economy'. Indeed, in some respects, roles were gradually reversed: until the arrival of the Social Democrat/Free Democrat coalition in 1969, West Germany stood for a much more market-orientated line in economic policy than both Britain and the other members of the EEC. But during the 1980s, the radical nature of the Thatcher Government's policies in relation to the role of government in the economy, together with the great success of the privatisation programme, meant that large differences of approach were established.

The willingness of the British Government to give its support to the 1986 agreements converting the Common Market into a Single Market rested on a serious misunderstanding. Most of the other member states in the European Community and the then President of the Commission, Jacques Delors, hoped to secure something far more ambitious. Without doubt, the British were thinking almost entirely in terms of a single market freed from internal barriers to trade of all kinds. Others, including M. Delors, saw the single market as the basis for further achievements on the road to closer integration. Indeed, hardly was the ink dry on the agreements establishing the single market when preparations began to be made for a much more ambitious plan, the introduction of a common currency.[5] After all, there was some plausibility in the argument that this would be a logical and compelling step to take in the completion of the single market.

Thus, the economic remit of what was once the Common Market has steadily widened as the single market began to be implemented. It soon became apparent that the notion of a Single Market lent itself to very wide interpretation and so could be used to open the door to more or less unlimited harmonisation. Thus, for example, the 1992 Single Market Programme embraced areas like veterinary controls, food and drugs standards, aspects of the travel industry and many others. Indeed, there is virtually no limit to what can be treated as ancillary to the achievement of a single market and, therefore, subject to Community regulation.

A widening remit

Then, just as the Common Market became a Single Market with a concomitant increase in Community powers and competences, so the European Union superseded the European Communities as a result of the Maastricht treaty signed by the member states in 1992.[6] It was, of course, this treaty which set the seal on the commitment to establish by the beginning of 1999 a common currency, a development from which Britain (and others) secured an opt-out. But the Maastricht treaty was by no means concerned only with a major step forward in the process of economic integration. In addition to providing for the highly symbolic introduction of EU citizenship, it contained numerous conditions which have since functioned as markers in the integrationist effort. The range of policy areas within which the EU would be able to intervene has widened significantly. Social affairs, including at a later stage employment policy, was one such area; justice and home affairs were signalled as other areas within which there was potential for EU cooperation and harmonisation. And it has become clear that the political ambitions of the EU were to be strengthened to embrace at least some aspects of foreign and defence policy. The movement towards allowing the EU to develop an active role in defence and foreign policy was confirmed and given further impetus by the Amsterdam treaty of 1997. As is so often the case in EU negotiations, this was held to be little more than the tidying-up of loose ends left unresolved and unagreed at the preceding Maastricht negotiations.

By these and many other steps, a Community which had started off almost exclusively focused on economic objectives became an overtly political association. It has been empowered to supplant the discretion of democratically elected national governments in a complex, loosely-defined and potentially unlimited range of affairs. All these developments have been justified by its supporters on the continent on the grounds that they represent decisive progress towards the goal enshrined in the Treaty of Rome of 'an ever closer union of peoples'.

Meanwhile, the scope for its members to reach their own decisions even in areas strictly speaking outside EU competence has narrowed steadily. In foreign affairs, for example, even the larger member states of the EU display more and more hesitation about taking up any stance at all on numerous issues. No doubt this is because they fear that they might get out of line with their partners or pre-empt some initiative that might be taken formally in an EU framework. Meanwhile, preparations are being made for further treaty revisions and additional protocols or declarations which would accelerate the movement towards political consolidation of the Union. Regardless of the outcome of the Inter-Governmental Conference, it is already impossible to overlook the fact that the crucial questions facing all member states are primarily political: they bear directly on the continued survival of the nation state and its capacity to provide opportunities for its citizens to engage in the practices of self-government.

The view from Britain

In Britain, a degree of tension between the economic and political objectives of the European project has always existed. In earlier years, and perhaps even down to about 1990, it was usual in Britain to treat the commitment to political union as largely theoretical, something for a distant future. This is no longer plausible. Large strides have been made during the past decade or so, and especially since the Maastricht treaty, to bring to the forefront of attention within the EU the all-embracing political character it has assumed. It has acquired functions which take it far beyond even a generous interpretation of what is germane to the effective operation of a single market. At the same time, the claim that it has become at least a quasi-state is heard far more frequently.

British Governments have nearly always been reluctant to acknowledge these profound political issues openly (although, especially towards the end of her time in office, Margaret Thatcher was an exception to this).[7] This reticence on the part of most politicians of all parties can no doubt be attributed chiefly to the fact that they know more or less instinctively that a majority of the British people remain deeply suspicious of European union as a political project and opposed to the loss of their rights of self-government by a stealthy process of erosion. So Labour and Conservative Governments have always tended to focus on the economic benefits of membership and to play down political issues – especially if they concern the values of self-government and democratic politics.

Ever since 1973 the relationship has been difficult because of the underlying tension between a British desire to confine the EEC/EU to economic affairs and a continental European desire of fluctuating intensity to transcend economics and push ahead with harmonised social policies and full political union. But broadly speaking, in the endless bargaining that constitutes the routine of keeping the European Union show on the road, it is the Europeanists who have got their way. That has meant that Britain, along with some other hesitant member states, has had to accept large slices of the 'ever closer union' agenda. Yet there has never been any act of 'whole-hearted consent' to all this by the British electorate, many of whom feel that they are being led by the nose and subjected to what is seen by them as a form of 'alien rule'.

The traditions of a self-governing nation

The difficulties of the relationship with the EU cannot, however, be explained solely by reference to what has happened over the past 25 years. It is not just the transition from a primarily economic project to an attempt to weld a large part of Europe into some kind of political union, nor frequent disagreements about particular policies and how best to pursue them, which account for a strained and uncomfortable relationship. The problems lie much deeper, in differences in attitudes and in the approach to social and political cooperation. It should be obvious – though many politicians and commentators nowadays apparently do not find it so – that Britain has had a radically different history from that of our continental neighbours. As a result, a significantly different view of political community and institutions evolved.

Divergent concepts of the 'State'

In this context it is crucial that Britain has had no notion of the state in the European sense. Rather, it evolved and has retained a different view of law and of the judicial function from that which has generally prevailed on the continent. Its approach to institutions is also substantially different.

The concept of the state, often presented as 'the State', has played a large – and some would say inflated – part in the continental European theory and practice of government since the eighteenth century.[8] For the French, the concept has been primarily legal and political, with the emphasis on the state as a coherent and autonomous structure of powers expressive in some mysterious way of the general will of the people. This view of the matter can at one extreme degenerate into legal formalism, at another into a species of political mysticism of the kind expressed by General de Gaulle. Nevertheless, this account of the state has the virtue of being comprehensible and on the whole workable. Its influence has been greatest in the Latin societies of Europe, though none of them has applied it with the sophistication of the French.

The German view of the state also sees it as a legal unity, a coherent structure of legal norms, held together and developed since 1949 by judicial interpretation of the highest norms – that is, those in the constitution. But there has been another element in the state as understood in the German political tradition. This is perhaps best defined as the state as a sense of moral unity and a commitment to the realisation of the values on which it claims to be founded. This was in some degree the heritage of German philosophical idealism, particularly as formulated by Hegel in the early nineteenth century (i.e. well before the formation of a German nation state). The fact that ideas of this sort were later harnessed to the cause of German nationalism and then perverted in disastrous ways by the Nazi regime served to discredit them.

Yet in a curious way they have experienced a respectable revival under the aegis of the constitution of modern Germany. For one of the consequences of the success of the Basic Law of 1949 has been to put enormous emphasis on the moral values implicit and explicit in it, especially those which were expressed in its opening catalogue of basic human rights. These rights are not only justiciable before the Federal Constitutional Court whose decisions now fill upwards of one hundred volumes. They are also declared to be beyond substantive amendment, though new rights can be added to the list.

The sanctity of basic rights has in turn encouraged the notion that the constitution represents a 'commitment' (usually referred to in German as an *Auftrag*) which all should help to fulfil. Particularly on the part of the numerous cohort of public lawyers in Germany, it has also encouraged a return to the regular use of the language of the state in place of the far more concrete terminology of government and politics, functions and institutions. This German view of the state is largely shared by Austria, and has had some modest influence in both Spain and Italy, again chiefly amongst lawyers and intellectuals.

There are many reasons why this continental preoccupation with the state has never been congenial in Britain. Paradoxically at first sight, one of the main reasons has been that England achieved political unity and became, therefore, a 'strong state' much earlier than any society on the continent. As a result, the focus in political argument was on established and strong institutions – the Crown, Parliament and the courts of law. The outcome of the political conflicts of the seventeenth century barred the way to any version of absolute monarchy and made it second nature to talk about government and politics in functional and institutional terms.

More important still was the fact that the foundation of the British view of an acceptable political order is inherently individualistic and utilitarian. A society is not a unity, but consists of numerous individuals each with their own interests and preferences. The purpose of government is to serve the needs of individuals who should be free to do whatever is not prohibited by law. And this objective can only be achieved so long as government – and that has meant specific officeholders who hold office as a trust rather than some entity called 'the state' – is subject to the consent of the governed. It follows that the highest political value is the right of self-government.

This has meant the right to elect representatives to whom the agents of executive government must be accountable. Such in both theory and practice have been the basic essentials of the dominant British view of self-government. The theory was formulated with clarity and subtlety in the writings of the classical English and Scottish political theorists. Its practice was consolidated over a long period in the methods and procedures of parliamentary institutions and in the interplay of competitive party politics.

The practical implications of different concepts of statehood

The issue of the political values in Britain has been put abstractly. Of course, in the day-to-day conduct of public affairs those involved do not as a rule have such considerations in the forefront of their minds. Nevertheless, it is such deeply-rooted values, growing out of shared social and political experience, which shape the way in which many problems are perceived and tackled. And, if at this deeper level of values, there are real differences between the countries engaged in a discussion or debate, then what is likely to follow is either a dialogue of the deaf or what may often be an acrimonious relationship unsatisfactory to both sides. For better or worse, this has frequently been true of Britain's experience within the EU.

It is worth illustrating this by indicating some examples from Britain's relations with the EU. Let us first consider the issue of taxation. Britain objects to surrendering parliamentary control of taxation and, therefore, to granting any tax-raising powers to the EU, whilst many member states do not appear to be worried by such a prospect.[9] Why the difference? Britain gained responsible government through Parliament's assertion of its rights over taxation, an example later echoed in the demand of the American colonies for no taxation without representation. Thus parliamentary control of taxation has been a crucial part of self-definition, and hostility to abandoning any part of it is not merely a bleat about loss of sovereignty. In contrast parliamentary authority over taxation is not such a key component of constitutional conditions within the EU countries. Indeed, in many of them, it is, insofar as it exists, a fairly recent experience.

It follows that proposals to widen the EU's taxing authority, or to diminish the veto rights of member states, are bound to encounter British opposition. Because of this, they immediately present a challenge for British politicians: they have to ask whether the people will put up with it.

A second area in which the differing view of the state affects relations with the EU is environmental regulation. Sometimes the UK is perfectly content to go along with proposals for EU directives. But in many aspects of environmental and consumer protection it would prefer to proceed by persuasion, example, or the setting of standards, an approach followed for long enough in other spheres like working conditions and (at any rate until recently) educational standards. But the European preference for dealing with virtually any problem is to set about establishing formal legal rules. This nearly always means rigidity, at any rate if taken seriously. Thus, Britain runs the risk of too many inappropriate and inflexible sets of regulations spawned by the EU tendency to proceed by formal legally-binding instruments. Sadly, this possibility is sometimes then made worse by British legal traditions which encourage a high degree of precision and detail in domestic legislation and are carried over to the drafting of provisions to implement EU directives. (The looseness of much continental statutory draftsmanship allows in contrast much scope for mitigating what might appear to be over-enthusiasm for formal regulations.)

Another example would be the European preoccupation with formal statements of rights, illustrated by the current convention of representatives of the member states of the EU on the drafting of a European Charter of Fundamental Rights. If the truth were known, the British Government would almost certainly prefer to see this scheme fade away.[10] But we have to go through the motions of taking part and almost certainly will have to accept at the end of the day a declaration of human rights in which we have little faith and which adds next to nothing to the numerous commitments which Britain has undertaken since the end of the Second World War. While adding little, it will spawn yet more costly litigation – litigation that is likely to benefit human rights lawyers more than plaintiffs – and will mean yet more legislative intrusion into our private lives. Rights guaranteed can translate into freedoms curtailed.

Examples like this show that in its approach to the EU as a whole and to the handling of particular policy issues and proposals arising from the work of its institutions, the UK is very often likely to find itself in a minority of one. This often happens because Britain thinks differently about both the whole project and how to tackle particular issues of policy. Britain's historically difficult relationship with the EU is thus not a matter of day-to-day politics or personality: its roots lie far deeper than that. Even though British officials who regularly deal with the EU in one manifestation or another are generally able to adapt to many features of what we may call 'the Brussels way of doing things', there are few grounds for thinking that the British approach as it emanates from London will change significantly in the future.

Of course, some other member states do in varying degrees sympathise with the British approach, for example Ireland (when not inhibited by the feeling that it ought not to do so), the Netherlands, Denmark, Sweden, and occasionally Spain. But these sympathies are generally shifting and uncertain. So far, they have not provided a basis for establishing a strong block of opinion in the EU which might favour a looser, more flexible Union and a greater reliance on methods of informal cooperation in place of binding legal commitments.[11]

Similarly, at any rate in the years before 1997, British Governments have been hesitant about pressing their views on the future development of the EU as in any sense an alternative to the familiar Franco-German calls for ever closer integration. The Blair Government claimed in contrast that it was giving a lead to its partners in the EU, but it is already clear that such a claim lacks substance and carries little weight with most member states.

The Franco-German axis

Alongside these problems, there remains an enduring tension about what should be the objectives of policy in the EU. Basically two states have shaped the evolution of the Community – France and Germany. The former has been far more decisive than the latter. French Governments have pursued over many years and with remarkable consistency a policy of using the French position in Europe to maintain a claim to a large role in the world. There was a time, notably from 1958 to 1969, during the presidency of de Gaulle, when this meant a strong and often aggressive emphasis on national sovereignty. Gradually this gave way to a more subtle approach. France became willing to accept an increasing degree of economic and political integration on the assumption that the loss of freedom of action would be more than compensated for both by the economic benefits of enlarging the European market, and by the greater political influence it might be able to exert in and through the EU. In particular this has meant that leverage was gained over German policy in many spheres. On the German side of the relationship, this bargain – if it can be called such – has remained generally acceptable because Germany is a peculiarly inhibited state when it comes to defining or asserting national interests. Indeed, ideologically, contemporary Germany rejects notions of national interest. In this attitude lies the principal explanation both of its unswerving commitment to the cause of European unification and of its willingness so often to accept the French lead. Only in the later years of Chancellor Kohl's long period in office, and after the reunification of Germany, did he begin in a public way to show that his own policy preferences were often decisive.[12]

In broad terms, so long as the EU was continuing to serve the interests of German industry exporting to EU markets and thereby the prosperity of the German people, the political elites in Germany have been content to let France take the lead. Since this duopoly has for so long represented the unwritten condition of the EU's movement forward and survival, this has meant that on the British side a feeling of resentful exclusion is bound to persist. On the Franco-German side, on the other hand, there is something like self-righteous resignation in the face of what are generally seen as British efforts to hold up the project.

Engineered impotence: the penalties of ever closer union

It is often claimed that the aim of ever closer political union is to enable Europe (or at least that part of it which makes up the EU) 'to speak with one voice' or 'to punch its weight' in the world at large. Such claims have had some force for several years now in international economic negotiations where the EU is required to pursue a single policy on behalf of its members. But even in the sphere of multilateral trade relations, international finance, and the management of world financial organisations the EU is not always successful in sticking to a consistent policy or in concealing internal rifts amongst members.

In the foreign and security policy sectors, the difficulties involved in reaching a common point of view and in acting effectively are far greater. Comparable problems exist in relation to what the French now sometimes call the 'economic government' required for the members of the euro zone – for example agreement on parameters for matters like government borrowing levels, targets for the proportion of GDP to be claimed by taxation, or general principles for facilitating deregulation in the economy. While it may be feasible to set up targets in the area of economic policy, it is much more difficult for all of the member states to achieve such targets and to stick to them in the face of manifold domestic pressures pulling in different directions.

Difficulties of joint decision-making

It is worth paying some attention to the real difficulties of common policy-making in the EU, difficulties which also afflict many other international organisations less closely tied together than the EU. First, it is nearly always difficult to reach any kind of agreement on a policy position. The process of edging towards such an outcome usually lasts a long time and that too implies costs and delay in doing anything. Often enough the only acceptable possibility is something near to the lowest common denominator of agreement. But this is very likely to be an unsatisfactory compromise.

Second, there is the need to pay some attention at least to the claims of the smaller member states who, quite understandably, want to have their say even though they may contribute little in material and practical terms to whatever common policies emerge.

Third, there is the problem of the rivalries and egoisms of the larger member states, all of whom usually have substantial interests at stake. All seek to exploit their bargaining positions, though some do so with greater persistence and regularity than others.

Fourth, notwithstanding the difficulties of reaching agreement on common policies, there is always a powerful urge eventually to agree on something no matter how far it may fall short of dealing with the real problem on hand. This occurs largely because to fail to agree or to decide that nothing should be done is widely held to be contrary to the dynamic of the EU which has always to be moving forward if it is to survive. It is like the fear of someone riding a bicycle who is sure he will fall off if he stops pedalling. This situation of itself tends to confer on obstinate members something like a blackmailing power: they want a particular policy and can secure at least part of it because no significant group of members can be persuaded to say 'No'.

The field of foreign and security policy presents special difficulties. Here effective action may well require something in the nature of a 'unified command structure'. This simply does not exist in the EU and is unlikely soon to do so – and the appointment of officials with high-sounding titles to give the appearance of acting on behalf of the EU will not of itself do anything to solve this problem. The military intervention in Kosovo in 1999 underlined the immense difficulty of conducting an air campaign through committees, and this was action by NATO, the pre-eminent Western military alliance, in which the US played a decisive part. It is perfectly clear that the EU would have been quite incapable of such an intervention, and indeed its record in the aftermath of the peace-keeping operation in Kosovo has not been outstanding.

There is little chance that this situation will change even if current proposals, inspired mainly by France and endorsed by Britain, for establishing a rapid response peace-keeping force with its own command structure are fully accepted and carried through.

Finally, in the spheres just discussed, speed of response is often of the essence. Previous experience indicates that the EU is rarely capable of acting quickly, especially in relation to issues which affect the material and political interests of one or more member states, or involving anything in the nature of military risks. Only when a decision has the character of a more or less costless moral gesture does it appear that it can sometimes be taken quickly. This happened, for example, in the case of the imposition of diplomatic sanctions on Austria after certain member states of the EU, notably France and Belgium, objected early this year to the formation of a coalition which included the Austrian Freedom Party. But it may well be the case that a decision in this instance could be taken rapidly and with little thought about consequences because it was taken more or less informally at a party political gathering and then presented to the world as the spontaneous conclusion of 14 individual governments rather than as a formal decision of the EU.

The wider the remit of the EU becomes, and as it seeks to enter areas of political discretion which have been the preserve of sovereign national governments, the more inadequate will become its decision-making procedures. It is widely believed by staunch defenders of the EU that the underlying weakness of the decision-making process can be remedied by a certain amount of institutional adjustment. This is a constant refrain both from Brussels and from a number of member states concerned by the challenges to existing structures and procedures posed by the prospect of an enlarged membership. But the problem is inherent in the underlying structure of the EU and in the terms on which it has always operated.

The EU constitutes a continuing and unending bargaining process in which decisions can emerge only as a result of trade-offs amongst member states. It is difficult enough to reach sensible decisions in the core economic areas covered by EU treaties and agreements where the exchange of benefits and the trading of interests has usually been practicable. But the EU is now involved in many spheres – for example, social affairs and services, justice and legal systems, foreign and security policy, environmental services – where trade-offs of a material kind are much harder to achieve or are in reality possible only at the price of a sacrifice of deeply-held principles. Inevitably, therefore, movement forward has to be very slow and can occur generally only on the basis of what are often unsatisfactory or messy compromises.

The British perspective

For Britain, the purely political difficulties presented by this situation remain substantial. Policy-making in the EU is a process that cancels out the notion of political accountability. Given that decisions are virtually always the outcome of complex negotiations and bargaining which recall the elusiveness of dealings in a Middle Eastern bazaar, how can it be possible ever to blame a government or a minister for the deal he or she comes home with? If criticised, the answer can always be (and usually is): 'Don't blame me, I got the best deal I could.' It is to guard against having to respond more and more often like this that so far British Governments and especially the British Parliament have resisted further surrender of the right of veto in the EU Council of Ministers. That so many other member states do not appear to be too worried by losing the right of veto reflects, *inter alia*, the far smaller part played by the notion of the political accountability of ministers within their political systems. Unless powerful interests are offended, such as the Länder administrations in Germany or the farming community in France, governments simply do not as a rule have to justify what they commit themselves to in the EU to the same degree and with the same frequency as happens in Britain.[13] Here indeed is the essential political dilemma for the EU: can it ever reconcile the search for 'ever closer union' with the requirements of responsible democratic self-government?

Enlarging the project: the risks of political fantasy

Perhaps the most important consequence of the collapse of the Soviet Union and the reunification of Germany has been the decision to work for enlargement of the EU eastwards.

There was perhaps a kind of fateful inevitability about this. The German Government under Helmut Kohl pressed for it, driven in part by the belief that only in this way could the nations on Germany's eastern borders be reassured that they would never again be exposed to any threat of German domination. But equally the dissolution of the Soviet Union removed the only real obstacle in the way of countries such as Poland or Hungary applying to join the EU: for them, as for others, membership of the EU appeared to offer the prospect of great economic benefits as well as security against both Germany and Russia. So there was hardly any chance that the existing members of the EU would make a cool political appraisal of the problems presented by early enlargement. Instead they signed up to the proposal with hardly a dissenting note to be heard.

Practicalities of enlargement

Nearly all the applicant states have a radically different recent history from the Western European member states. So it does not call for much insight into the practicalities of enlargement to recognise that this commitment constitutes an intimidating challenge. At the very least, all the difficulties about the terms on which the EU has to operate are bound to be compounded if and when enlargement on the scale presently envisaged is achieved. Of the dozen or so potential members only two are states of substantial size and population – Poland and Turkey. And the second of these only has a promise to consider opening negotiations at some unknown date in the future. All the rest are small states, some like Malta very small indeed. Most of them are far behind the bulk of the present membership of the EU in terms of income per head, and indeed of any other economic indicators one chooses to apply.

It follows that the admission of new members will be a slow business and may stretch over more than a decade. What is more, the negotiations already under way with seven of the applicants illustrate the character of the difficulties to be overcome. On the one hand, most of the applicants need a range of derogations from many of the current conditions of EU membership. These might in some cases have to continue for several years. But on the other hand, the present members are for the most part suspicious of such derogations. The Commission has so far bluntly insisted that new members will have to accept with the minimum delay what is familiarly known as the *acquis communautaire*, the existing body of EU law and policies. This stiff-necked approach has already cooled the ardour of some of the applicants who realise that there is little prospect of their adapting within a short period their economic structures and social and environmental protection legislation to meet EU requirements.

In addition to the economic difficulties inherent in accommodating new members, there are political, administrative and legal problems of a formidable kind to be overcome. Most of the applicants have only recently emerged from decades of communist domination and the chaos of its collapse. Inevitably, most applicants therefore face a huge problem of institutional adaptation. Their legal systems are in varying degrees incomplete and inadequate, their administrative structures often backward and underdeveloped, and their political direction in some cases shaky and uncertain.

Problems for the EU

So much for the institutional deficiencies on the side of the applicants. There is also an institutional challenge of a formidable kind facing the EU. This can be summed up in the question: how can an organisation originally designed for six members continue to operate on its current basis if the present membership of 15 is to be expanded to 21 or 22, and later perhaps to 27 or 28?

The orthodox answer offered from within the EU is that there will have to be institutional reform. This would involve taking more decisions by simple or qualified majority vote, abandonment of the veto in all but exceptional circumstances, a revision of the weighting conditions for qualified majority voting in the Council of Ministers, and a Commission that is at least no larger than it is now.[14] But radical changes in procedures and structures would seriously affect the interests of existing members, especially the larger states. For despite the determination of some of them to press on towards 'ever closer union', they are fully aware that they too have vital interests to protect within the EU. Therefore, they may call for the retention of something like a veto in the Council of Ministers or Inter-Governmental Conferences. Yet the more hesitant present member states become about institutional reforms, the more difficult it becomes to meet the challenges presented by the need to accommodate new members within an organisation that was designed for different purposes in a different world.

The preparations now being slowly made for enlargement may well, by the end of 2000, result in minimal institutional changes, leaving the supporters of enlargement to claim that nonetheless the process of negotiation can go ahead. But of course such hesitancy will simply guarantee that the functioning of an enlarged Union will be even more ponderous and difficult.

An alternative

An alternative to reform of the institutional structure and methods of the present EU would be to undertake the far more radical step of considering how to turn the whole organisation into a much looser association. This would probably involve a far smaller central apparatus, a more restricted range of functions chiefly in the economic sphere to discharge, and far more reliance on political cooperation between member states in place of enforceable regulations and uniform policies for all.

In theory at least, such an outcome would have been welcome to every British Government since that headed by Edward Heath. But of course there is at the moment no realistic prospect of any such radical reappraisal of policy even being contemplated. Instead, as already mentioned, new members are expected to be willing and able to take on board the whole body of EU law and to join EMU straightaway. Nor is there evidence from either the European Council or the Commission of a genuine willingness to shed powers rather than extend them.

Heading into an impasse

With hindsight it is clear that it might well have been more rational never to have embarked on enlargement on the scale and at the tempo envisaged. But it is too late for the EU to turn back now without a loss of prestige, even though it remains possible that negotiations with at least some aspirant members may simply run into the sand and so provide a way out of the commitment. Fundamentally the enlargement project bears some resemblance to an attack of *folie de grandeur*. In political terms a Union extending from Lisbon to Riga and from Stockholm to Athens is an implausible prospect. It could not work on the current basis, yet adaptive reform of a sufficiently radical kind appears most unlikely.

Faced with these dilemmas there are, however, still those like the German Foreign Minister who apparently believe that a greatly enlarged and more heterogeneous EU should still be moving ahead to an 'ever closer union', transforming it into some kind of single state with a federal structure. It is a tribute to the honesty and common sense of the Polish Foreign Minister, Mr Geremek, that he lost little time in making it clear that such visions are totally unrealistic. After all, can anyone believe that states which have only recently regained their right to govern would sacrifice their new-found independence to a European federation, no matter how benign it may claim to be?

The component parts of even the present EU are so heterogeneous that those who aspire to see it evolve into a single political unit qualify their hope by accepting that Europe will have to remain in some so far unexplained way an association of nation states. If that is admitted, then how much stronger is the case for recognising that an enlarged EU demands a looser structure if there is to be any chance of achieving it.

Perhaps British policy-makers have, during the last three years, cherished the hope that the process of enlargement would somehow loosen the structures of the EU. Sadly, the evidence suggests that this is an unrealistic hope, at any rate in the absence of any serious British initiative to argue that enlargement should be seen as an opportunity for a radical reappraisal of what the EU stands for and where it is headed.

With or without enlargement, however, the EU seems set to continue on its present course of the gradual and piecemeal transfer of legislative and regulatory powers to its central institutions, once again demonstrating that it is an organisation with very limited learning capacity and hardly any will to adapt to changing conditions in the world. This sort of outcome will leave the long-standing political problems facing Britain untouched. Indeed, an enlarged Union may sharpen these problems through the further dilution of the power of the larger member states to reject policies which they oppose.

The dynamics of the EU and the logic of bureaucracy

The institutions of European economic and political integration have, in their various forms – from the High Authority for Coal and Steel in 1950 down to the recently appointed High Representative for Foreign and Security Policy – grown by accretion. It has proved impossible over the years to stop this process or even to slow it down appreciably. There are many reasons why this is so.

Generalities versus precision

It is necessary to begin by recognising the inherently broad language of the treaties, starting from the initial commitment enshrined in the

Treaty of Rome in 1957 to achieve an 'ever closer union' right down to the open-ended commitments in the Amsterdam treaty 40 years later to extend cooperation in the field of justice, to consolidate the foreign and security policy 'pillar', and to extend EU powers in several other fields already indicated earlier on. But it is unlikely that the looseness of the favoured terminology reflects as a rule some Machiavellian design on the part of those who draft such provisions. Far more important is the fact that it mirrors both the need for a lowest common denominator and the normal style of continental European public law-drafting. Those responsible would generally never think of seeking the precision and certainty sought by legislative draftsmen in Britain. After all they are for the most part people trained in continental public law-thinking and practice, in which a large element of generalisation and discretionary language is normal.

Finalité

Next it has to be remembered that the founding treaties embody a lot of the continental European fondness for '*finalité*', a term very much in fashion at the present time. In relation to legal and political declarations, this means a language that points to ends, aims or objectives. This has allowed the protagonists of continuing integration, and especially during the past ten years or so, to press the case for an on-going commitment to the discovery and elaboration of new aims to which their efforts should be directed.

This approach functions rather like an open invitation to extend the competence of the EU by verbal extrapolation whenever possible. When, as in the Maastricht treaty, there is a provision requiring the Community to: '... contribute to the development of quality education by encouraging co-operation between Member States and, if necessary, by supporting and supplementing their action ...' or for the Community to: '... contribute to the attainment of a high level of consumer protection', the door is opened to any number of new proposals.[15]

Some of these may ultimately lead to directives to be implemented by member states, others just to Commission programmes intended to encourage cooperative action under EU supervision (for example in relation to opportunities for the exchange of students between universities in the EU). This broad and speculative way of formulating obligations and policies remains uncongenial to the British since it tends to suggests that one is buying a ticket for a destination about which one knows next to nothing.

The absence of counterbalancing forces

A third factor is that in relation to the characteristic working methods of the EU just outlined, there is hardly anything in the shape of what we might call doctrinal or institutional counterweights. Some will argue that the doctrine of subsidiarity is precisely such a check on the inherently expansive tendencies of the EU. But this is an illusion. First, there is no evidence that it has in fact during recent years limited the accretion of powers by the EU. Second, the doctrine cannot be relied on to protect the rights and powers of the member states and their institutions. It amounts to little more than a pious wish that those matters which can best be dealt with below the central (i.e. Brussels) level should be so dealt with. If, however, we ask who decides what is subsidiary, there is no satisfactory answer to that question. There is no constitutional definition of what subsidiary is. And it is the central organs themselves – that is, the Council of Ministers and the Commission – which determine what counts as subsidiary according to prevailing political interests and pressures.[16]

It was characteristic of the continental European mindset that when the German Foreign Minister offered the world his thoughts on what might be the 'final shape' of a future European federation – and in that context invoked the ideal of subsidiarity – he failed to offer a single example of how powers might be divided between the institutions of the nation states (which were to continue to exist) and the European central institutions. It is hard to resist the conclusion that all he had in mind was something remarkably like the German federal state in which the predominance of central (i.e. federal) lawmaking is over-whelming.

Politically it can be tempting to resort to sweeping generalities already in the treaties to interpret virtually any new proposal as a natural corollary of some broader pre-existing commitment (such as that great hold-all, the better functioning of the single market).

Nor does judicial interpretation offer much hope of a more restrained view of grand future objectives. The European Court of Justice has usually been only too willing to extract from the language of 'final ends' grounds for taking a generous view of EU powers and their implications for the legal systems of member states. In short there is no coherent doctrinal or institutional counterweight within the EU operating in favour of what from an American perspective would be called a 'states' rights' position. At best there are ad hoc rearguard actions on the part of members of the Council of Ministers.

The ambitions of existing institutions

A further point of great significance is that most of the institutions of the EU have in varying degrees an understandable interest in increasing their powers, undertaking new tasks and, if possible, securing additional resources.

The European Parliament likes to see itself as potentially the seat of democratic legitimacy in the Union. Thus it is not content with a symbolic status and wants to see the powers of co-decision that it recently acquired widened so that it begins to look more like a real legislative body. It aspires also (and cannot be blamed for this) to gain authority over the Commission, and in some degree to call it to account. So there is bound to be continuing pressure from the Parliament for measures which would enhance its role in the decision-making processes of the EU.

The influence of the European Court of Justice has steadily grown as decisions by it have accumulated. There can be no doubt that doctrinally the Court is committed to ensuring that in cases of conflict of laws, Community law prevails. This implies a continuing extension of Community jurisdiction. Against this background, some have argued that the judicialisation of public policy-making represents the shape of constitutionalism in the future both within individual European states and the EU as a whole.[17]

The Commission – the institution that exemplifies more vividly than any other the mixture of bureaucratic methods and political bargaining on which the EU is founded – has inevitably always looked for opportunities to assume new responsibilities and to widen its remit. It is a task for which its strategic role as the body charged with safeguarding the treaties and formulating policies for their implementation renders it well-fitted.

It is, of course, true that the Commission is ultimately dependent on the Council of Ministers, since without their consent, most of its policy initiatives will founder. And the readiness of the Council to accept Commission proposals with or without modifications has varied a great deal over the years. Similarly, the influence of the Commission has varied substantially according to the strength and effectiveness of its members, and the capacity of its President to take a lead. Political patronage dominates the process of appointing commissioners, so that the chances of finding a President with real strength of purpose are usually slender. Thus as a rule the freedom of action of the Commission is likely to be severely limited for most of the time by the very complexity of the immensely wide range of interests and approaches that it has to accommodate.

Apart from the major institutions of the EU there are also others with more limited roles, like the Economic and Social Committee and the more recent Committee of the Regions, which have a similar interest in widening their own scope for interventions. Even the Council of Ministers, nominally the place where national interests are embodied and safeguarded, is subject to the same dynamic of accretion of powers. It has its own substantial administrative back-up organisation under a Secretary-General. There is also the Committee of Permanent Representatives constituted by the ambassadors of the member states to the EU. In addition, there can be pressure from some member states for the EU to embark on some new project, there is the impact of the six-monthly rotating Presidency of the European Council on the hopes of those holding that position to make some kind of mark on EU policy, and there is the ever-present fear in virtually all rounds of negotiation of ending up with no agreement at all.

All these factors come together to ensure that though the Council often hesitates and delays, at the end of the day it is likely to cooperate with the Commission and the Parliament in extending the range of EU activity.

Overall, there can be no doubt that the institutions of the EU reveal the expansionist logic of bureaucracies. There is nothing particularly surprising about this conclusion: it is a common experience the world over. But what is special about the EU – and of crucial importance for Britain's relations with it – is that it has developed in a way which reduces greatly the possibility of any effective countervailing force to this expansionist logic. There is no discipline of market competition and the balance sheet affecting what the EU does and how, and there is no effective control by elected politicians afraid of losing popular support either at the European or the national levels. As a consequence the institutions of the EU inevitably display the familiar pathology of bureaucracy. That is to say, they tend to expand.

This may to some extent involve a claim to more resources such as staff, but equally attractive is the acquisition of further powers and influence. There does not appear to be any realistic prospect of changing this state of affairs significantly. The Commissioners tend to be politically-appointed and politically-motivated bureaucrats – the worst possible combination for those who seek a separation between administration and management on the one hand, and clear lines of political responsibility for policy on the other.[18] The Council is also in practice politically irresponsible since it is only in highly exceptional circumstances that the delegation of a member state might fear that acquiescence in a decision of the Council will provoke the fall of a government. (This was, of course, basically the position of John Major during the negotiations for the Maastricht Treaty and commitment to Economic and Monetary Union: the opt-outs he secured were essential to his political survival.) As for the European Parliament, for structural and political reasons it too is in a strict sense irresponsible: it has no government to sustain or remove and the electorate cannot call it to account.

It has often been argued that the initial institutional formula for the construction of the institutions of European integration – a policy proposing executive agency in the Commission, a policy and legislation deciding agency in the Council, a consultative and advisory body in the Parliament, and a Court to see that Community law is upheld – was an inspired solution to the challenge of making a start on economic integration and of carrying that process forward. For many years this was no doubt a fair judgement on what the founding fathers had set up. But the question now has to be faced whether this formula is any longer appropriate to the future of the EU.

The EU has gained and claims very extensive policy-making responsibilities, but it has no effective democratic legitimation for the exercise of such powers. Its *modus operandi* flies in the face of the principles of popular consent and responsible government. Its structure has acquired an almost Kafkaesque degree of complexity which renders it incomprehensible and impenetrable to virtually all the citizens of the EU. The system is, in short, plainly incompatible with notions of democratic self-government. It may well not be reformable without the creation of something like a European state with a responsible government and representative institutions. But even the protagonists of 'ever closer union' recognise that this is certainly not going to happen within the foreseeable future. In any event there are perfectly reasonable grounds for challenging both the desirability and the feasibility of such an outcome. This leaves a very large and worrying question – what is to be done? After one further piece of the critical jigsaw has been sketched out, we shall turn to this question.

Some ideological dimensions of the EU

Some might hold that as the EU is still primarily an association dedicated to economic growth and prosperity, it must be more or less indifferent to ideological commitments other than that of wealth maximisation through the market. Moreover, there can be little doubt that in the contemporary Western world, the ideological differences associated with particular political parties have been substantially eroded; nearly all parties have become highly pragmatic in outlook and tend to be reluctant to profess support in public life for sharply-defined principles which might limit their freedom of action.

Yet this view of ideology underestimates the extent to which there are attitudes and beliefs at work in both the EU and its member states which deserve the name of ideological preferences. They express values and aspirations that influence public perceptions of what politicians are or should be doing, and they similarly find expression in the behaviour of politicians and officeholders. The ideological preferences of the EU that can be detected are for the most part not congenial to most people in the UK, even though it is possible to rub along with them for much of the time without too much overt tension or trouble.

Tendencies to anti-Americanism

First, there is an undercurrent of anti-Americanism hardly ever encountered in Britain. This has become more overt in recent years. Such sentiments have been present in France ever since the end of World War II, reflecting in part the difficulty many people in France still have in acknowledging American economic and scientific achievements and the dominant influence of the US. But there are signs that anti-Americanism has begun to gain sympathy elsewhere – notably in Germany where the collapse of Soviet communism has diminished the sense of reliance on the protective defence shield provided by American commitment to NATO. While this trend probably does not add up to much in terms of a firm foundation for policy decisions by a German government, it does encourage support in Germany (and at any rate in Blairite circles in Britain too) for the pretensions to an EU foreign and security policy. This, it is hoped, might one day counterbalance American predominance in the world. The French Government, needless to say, loses few opportunities to press the benefits of a European foreign policy and defence capability on its partners in the EU.

The profession of human rights

Second, there is another development which has the potential for providing a bit of ideological ballast, both in the European search for a political identity and in the shaping of a stance in foreign affairs. There have been increasing signs of the growing attractions of a loosely defined theory of universal human rights as the emergent core of the EU's self-image of itself both in relation to the world beyond its borders and to the standards expected of its own members. It is clear that there is little foundation for a common sense of national identity or patriotism in the EU as a whole, and neither is a basis for shared loyalties to be found in religious belief or in any deeply-held political ideology. Thus it is not surprising that a rather nebulous universalism in relation to human rights becomes something like a rallying cry for those who hope to differentiate the EU's special characteristics and role in the world. It is easy to point to the weaknesses of this line of thought, most obviously the fact that as the US tends to profess support for a remarkably similar set of moral values, it is hard to see how in this regard the EU and the US can be distinguished from each other. Nevertheless, this universalism is beginning to have effects on EU policies and on the reactions of member states to certain developments within the EU.

The most striking example of this was the EU reaction to the formation of the present coalition government in Austria. The diplomatic sanctions imposed (and only very recently suspended) were justified in part at least by the alleged threat to the protection of human rights in Austria following the entry of the Austrian Freedom Party, then led by Jorg Haider, into the coalition. It was asserted that this development called into question Austrian fidelity to the values for which the EU claimed to stand. Leaving on one side the rights and wrongs of this particular case, it is clear that the EU's actions imply a claim that the EU is entitled to override the consequences of free elections in a member state, and to do so on a purely precautionary basis rather than as a consequence of any actions by the member state in breach of its EU obligations.

Quite apart from the mystery of how the universalism of human rights doctrine is reconciled with a parallel EU commitment to the rule of law, this kind of claim is authoritarian in its thrust. It exposes a strange desire to stifle change and to ensure that existing party political constellations are preserved at all costs. Sadly, the universalism expressed in the profession of human rights as the highest good offers no firm promise of an open and tolerant EU. Instead it may point to a self-righteous 'Fortress Europe' mentality.

The European social model

Third and quite closely linked with the preceding issues is the concept of the 'European social model' which many wish to see as a vital ingredient in the European ideological cocktail. This social model does not receive support everywhere in the EU: despite the Blair Government's shift towards accepting the Social Chapter and a range of protective social measures stemming from it, there is considerable opposition to the idea in Britain, and plenty of reservations in Scandinavia too. In many respects there is nothing original about this 'social model': it is little more than a new way of talking about what used to be called the welfare state in Britain. But in the search for distinguishing ideological positions, a European social model has emerged which is intended to contrast virtuously with hard-nosed American capitalism. This supposedly prevents governments from pursuing policies offering social support and protection to those in need, leaving people exposed to the rigours of market competition and unregulated employment conditions. This is, of course, a travesty of the situation in relation to social policy in the US, but it is a refrain that continues to be repeated by many of the advocates of both the European social model and what in Britain has been called 'the third way'.

In general, the appeal to the social model serves to buttress particular privileged relationships rooted in the past. This is neatly illustrated, for example, by a reference in the proposed EU directive on race discrimination in employment recently approved by the British Government. Member states are obliged to '... promote social dialogue between the social partners to address different forms of discrimination'. Such language vividly underlines the desire in so many parts of continental Europe to perpetuate the social and economic environment of the 1970s into the future.[19]

Overall there is little doubt that the principal impact of the social model lies in the high costs it generates: it bolsters extensive social welfare expenditures, especially in respect of state-funded pensions, the continued regulation of labour markets, and the imposition of detailed public regulation in many other fields of social protection. Inevitably this approach entails high levels of taxation and works on the whole against reliance on the market and the achievement of a flexible economy. It does nothing to sharpen individual responsibility for contributing to one's own social security and that of one's family.

Many of the above comments imply an undercurrent of hostility to the market economy and the social and moral conditions which underpin it. At first sight, there is something puzzling about this tendency. After all, the European Community was originally set up precisely in order to develop a 'common market' and to demonstrate the benefits of the free market. It cannot be denied, for example, that the EU remains in principle strongly committed to competition and to equal market conditions for all. But there is a growing squeamishness about using the language of market economics and competition. In its wake is a revival of the ingrained sympathy on the part of many continental European politicians and intellectuals for some form of *dirigisme*.

Yet even this preference is almost certainly the expression of something much simpler and more basic. Politicians and officials often dislike the market and to some extent even many features of contemporary information technology: for so many of them who were brought up in the traditions of the state, allowing markets to operate freely threatens a loss of control. It is this outlook which goes a long way towards explaining why the preference for solving problems by the drafting of binding regulations persists on the part of the EU institutions. The standard reaction to a problem in the economic sphere as in most others is to say: 'We must prepare regulations which can then be used to enforce behaviour in conformity with their terms.' Sometimes indeed this may be an appropriate course of action, but often it is not. There would be alternatives to regulation to harmonise standards and practices, most notably in the habits of cooperation and consultation which have been a favoured British method of achieving progress in the pursuit of policies involving public and private agencies. Instead it is thought to be far better to apply the force of the law to hold everything in place. Once again, this is a wide-ranging sphere in which a change of attitudes within the EU, and especially in those states where legal formalism remains very strong, can occur only slowly. In the meantime, the gap between British *laissez-faire* preferences and continental European reservations about the market and what it will do to and for people, remains wide.

Where do we go from here?

This analysis suggests that the difficulties in the British relationship with the EU stem principally from deep-seated disharmonies between the EU and its methods on the one hand, and Britain on the other. In the current jargon, Britain is simply not 'comfortable' in the EU. Moreover, given the nature of the difficulties, it should now be reasonably clear that after nearly 30 years of trying to become 'comfortable' in and with Europe, the situation is not going to change radically in the future.

The problems which generate this awkward and uncomfortable relationship are fundamentally political, not economic. That is what renders them so intractable.

The widespread reluctance to acknowledge what should be obvious is perhaps to some extent a consequence of the fact that joining the process of European integration was presented to the British people very much as an economic project. We were going into a common market, something like a large free trade area, offering the promise of faster growth and prosperity.[20] This was something that most people were prepared to welcome. Though membership has had its costs, it has also without doubt brought economic benefits, though as always it remains hard to quantify these. Therefore it is difficult to present a reliable balance sheet.

The belief that membership of the EU is primarily a matter of economic self-interest and benefit continues to be in the forefront of public attention whenever arguments about the pros and cons of the EU take place. Yet the overall economic context has changed in recent years – and this in turn significantly affects the equation. The EU certainly provides a large single market for the exchange of goods and services. But we now live in an increasingly open and mobile world market in which transactions of all kinds have been globalised in range and effects. For historical reasons, Britain has always been oriented towards the wider world market outside Europe. This bias of interest and attention has grown more marked in recent years as economic recovery has proceeded, and as the shift from manufacturing to services, especially of a financial nature, has continued.

Despite British involvement in the EU, it is the links with the economy of the US and opportunities in the American market which have grown relatively more important in recent years. A question mark therefore hangs over the argument that the future prosperity of Britain depends in some unique and special way on continued membership of the EU. There are, of course, advantages in the EU association, especially for trade in manufactured goods. But continuing in it on current terms is almost certainly not a matter of economic life and death. Instead it is a question of more or less, of balancing advantages of one kind off against disadvantages of another kind.

The persistent concentration on the EU as a mainly economic undertaking has made it difficult to ask whether the political costs of membership might not in fact outweigh the economic benefits derived from belonging to an organisation operating like the EU. To some extent, this difficulty stems from the character of contemporary democracy in Britain, and indeed in other countries too. Economic gains and losses can always be presented in simplified form – most people see them in terms of more jobs or fewer, rising or falling incomes, more goods in the shops at lower prices or less choice and variety, and so on. In contrast, there is something abstract and certainly unquantifiable about political gains and losses. It is simply not possible to put a price on the values of self-government: ultimately it is a matter of people deciding what their overriding values are and what sacrifices they might be ready to make in order to preserve them.

But the diagnosis of difficulties is not enough, and indeed by itself can easily turn out to be a somewhat sterile exercise. We have to ask the questions: what can be done? what are the options available for the future? These questions have to be set within both the short-term context and the longer time span of the evolution of the EU so far and the shape it seems likely to have in the future.

The immediate future

The immediate and present-day context is defined by the experience of the British Government in dealing with the EU and the negotiations scheduled for the second half of 2000 under the French presidency. These negotiations are intended to lead to a new treaty preparing for the adaptation of internal EU procedures to enlargement. Despite highly exaggerated claims made by the Blair Government for its success in changing Britain's standing within the EU, and despite a variety of British support for positions strongly supported by France and Germany, there is no reason to believe that a fundamental change in the British position has occurred. There have been few if any practical innovative proposals for dealing with the future development of the EU from this Government. Nor is there any sign that Britain is any more comfortably lodged inside the inner circle of EU policy-making than it was five or even ten years ago.

As so often in the past, Britain finds itself generally in the role of a restraining force, a brake on both the Commission and those partners who are anxious to endorse some fresh EU directive or initiative in one field or another. In relation to the institutional adaptations called for by enlargement, Britain has been cautiously reactive, with the British Government responding to proposals from others rather than putting forward its own ideas. The readiness of the French Government in particular to press ahead with grand schemes for majority voting and a sacrifice of influence by the larger member states should not, however, be exaggerated. Though still plainly determined to push the EU in a direction reflecting the French belief in the desirability of reducing American influence both in Europe and the world at large, statements by both the French Prime Minister and the President leave no room for doubt about French circumspection in the pursuit of something like an EU political identity. The commitment remains, but is one to be fulfilled gradually and with due regard to the traditional interests of France as the leading nation state in continental Europe.

Three options for Britain

The policy options available to Britain amount to three possibilities. The first is to continue more or less as at the present time. This means working inside the EU framework as best we can, contributing more or less positively to proposals against which we have no serious objections, but putting a brake on schemes thought damaging to British interests or generally unsatisfactory. This policy requires retention of a veto on major questions if it is to be credible.

The second option is to take the lead in demanding that the EU should seriously rethink its strategy for the future. This involves a direct challenge to the commitment to 'ever closer union'. In particular, an approach of this kind would seek to confine the EU to core economic functions associated with a single market whilst leaving participation by member states in most other spheres optional. This option is sometimes referred to as 'variable geometry', or 'flexibility'.

The third and most drastic option is an orderly withdrawal from membership into a situation analogous to that now enjoyed by Norway and, following recent agreements, Switzerland. It is, of course, widely regarded as unacceptable to mention withdrawal even as a remote possibility. But the logic of that position must be acceptance of the inevitability and desirability of the loss of the rights of self-government to an 'ever closer union' which is bound in some form or another to assume the character of a state.

Option one: 'business as usual'

The first option is essentially the policy of both the present and recent British Governments. It involves doing the best we can for British interests within the EU as it is and showing benevolence at least towards a process of continuing and widening integration. But this policy of continued cooperation in the EU venture is qualified by opposition to some of the consequences of closer integration.

Despite the expression of support 'in principle' for joining the common currency 'when the conditions are right', there is hardly any sign that Britain is closer to doing that than it was two, three or even five years ago. Meanwhile, the obstacles in the way of joining remain formidable and are, to a large degree, not even within the control or influence of either the Blair Government or any successor. There is too the additional uncertainty stemming from the promise of a referendum on any recommendation to join the euro zone.

It is, therefore, hardly surprising that many representatives of the states now in the euro zone show increasing impatience in the face of the British Government's touchiness about any efforts they may make to establish an 'economic government' for the euro zone. After all, no historical example can be found of a successful common currency which has not been backed up by coherent supportive policies on the part of the relevant government(s).

The weakness of the euro since its launch in January 1999 is in part due to the absence of such a context of congruent and effective economic policies applied by all the members of the monetary union. It is surely, therefore, somewhat perverse of the British Government to object to Euroland governments which are trying to put in place arrangements intended to make a success of this hazardous experiment.

On the broader issues raised by continuing EU membership, it is not yet clear that the alternative offered so far by the Conservative party leadership differs in essentials from the policy pursued by the present administration. The slogans describing it refer to 'in Europe, but not run by Europe' and 'a flexible Europe'. In particular, flexibility, it has been suggested, should leave member states free to decide whether or not they will apply EU directives and policies. This approach could amount to a shift to the second policy option detailed below. So far it remains uncertain whether this is so. Moreover, the call for greater flexibility may well be an unrealistic position to adopt.

For, if flexibility simply means something like a purely á la carte EU, then it is unlikely to be workable. Nor would it be acceptable to many or most member states. In short, the term calls for a degree of definition that it has not so far received. In general terms, flexibility must point to a policy of both defining and limiting the functions and role of the EU, and it would appear to entail acceptance of the prospect of a two-tier or two-speed Europe. After all, if a number of states seriously wish to join in establishing some kind of federal construction, why should they be prevented from doing that, provided they undertake to avoid discriminatory measures against those partners who prefer to remain outside such developments?

To keep on with present policies, even though they might be expressed rather differently by a Conservative Government, is the option most likely to be taken in practice. Alter all, everything else seems to be fraught with great risks and uncertainty. There is nothing politicians and their senior officials dislike more than that.

Yet to keep going on down this road will have two consequences, both of which are unattractive. In the first place, it guarantees that the uncomfortable and often tetchy relationship with the EU and many of our partners in it will continue. It will remain something like a running sore in British political life, consuming energies and abilities that could better be applied to many other problems of concern to the people of this country.

In the second place, however, it has to be recognised that the EU has already evolved to a situation in which the scope for effective democratic self-government in its member states is seriously limited. When the point of no return will be reached, no one can be sure. It could come very soon, but the more likely prospect is for a continued and inescapable erosion of the capacity of the political institutions of the member states to offer to their citizens either self-government or genuine democracy. For all member states the prospect is not that of a genuine democratically governed federation such as the US exemplifies, but instead of becoming a province within a sprawling, slow-moving bureaucratically governed quasi-state.

If there is an historical parallel for such a phenomenon, then it might after all be the Holy Roman Empire: in his reactions to Joschka Fischer's dreams of a future federation of Europe, the former French Interior Minister may have been nearer the mark than his critics were willing to admit. Be that as it may, there can be no doubt that a political outcome of the kind just sketched out is not one that a majority of people in Britain would be ready to accept.

Option two: changing direction

The second option presents a straightforward challenge to our partners in the EU about the ultimate objectives of the course on which the organisation is set. It means the abandonment of the language of *finalité* and a reversion to a much more pragmatic and limited understanding of what the EU should be doing and how it should continue to develop. Another way of describing such a policy is to put it in terms of trying to find a resting place for the EU, a point at which its members no longer feel obliged to press on to conferment on the central institutions of ever wider powers and objectives. Certainty about what the EU can do and what it stays clear of entirely would be established.

It is not easy to provide a crisp and persuasive formula for the option now under discussion. Essentially it involves the pursuit of policies explicitly directed to achieving and maintaining something like an area of free trade and close economic cooperation. This is, of course, suspiciously close to the remit of the European Economic Community before it was superseded by the notion of a European Union. Perhaps it would be more honest to give up the search for a catching slogan with which to sell such a policy and to concentrate instead on setting out the implications it might have for existing policies, for the structure and operations of the EU, for the prospects of enlargement, and for acceptance in the EU of variations in obligations and commitments. A few examples might help to illustrate what is being suggested.

Competition policy should continue to be applied vigorously. But many of the harmonisation of standards measures applied so far could be modified or abandoned since they tend to diminish, rather than strengthen, competition and narrow the range of choice for consumers.

In relation to structure and methods of work inside the EU, it might well be desirable to press for a formal specification of some of the implications of subsidiarity – that is, in what sectors the Community may be expected to take initiatives and where it is specifically excluded by the rights of the member states to manage their own affairs. Similarly, it is possible to envisage the Commission being placed under a formal duty to provide a statement justifying any new proposals it makes by reference to the remit of the EU under the treaties. Such a duty might be subject too to a formal right on the part of member states to object to such proposals and to propose in the European Council that the measures envisaged should not be proceeded with.

As far as the admission of new members is concerned, there can be little doubt that a policy directed to limiting the wider social and political competences of the EU, and accepting a more variable pattern of obligations within it, would be welcome. Certainly it would render the entry of many of the applicants a more realistic prospect. The applicant states would have to accept that their entry would be subject to numerous and lengthy derogations. As a result, they could not expect to assume immediately on entry all the rights of existing members in the decision-making procedures of the Union.

Acceptance of variable conditions for membership and variable obligations on the part of member states is apparently what is envisaged in the call for flexibility contained in the recent Conservative draft manifesto, *Believing in Britain*. But such an approach does require a serious effort to specify the sectors to which flexibility might apply and under what conditions. This policy, if implemented, would inevitably for a time make the running of the EU more difficult. It would also call for a degree of tolerance of differences not always shown by many member states or by the Commission.

Yet it need not be dismissed as wholly impractical. For we should remember that there are societies in which diversity of conditions in the political and public law spheres are accepted with a fair degree of good will. The United Kingdom has itself for the best part of three centuries been a 'variable geometry' union in which nothing like the uniformity of continental administrative states was ever contemplated. This tolerance of difference – some might say of oddity and quirkiness – continues and is fully reflected in the various measures of devolution recently put into operation. Spain accepts measures of devolution too. These do not require every regional government to assume exactly the same responsibilities and powers. Switzerland attaches great importance to the autonomy and individuality of its cantons, whilst a relatively uniform institutional structure in the American federal union nonetheless does not result in the complete standardisation of laws, policies or patterns of social life across the whole of the US.

The fundamental problem with the notion of variable conditions – including provisions allowing some countries to bind themselves together in more sectors of public policy than others – lies surely in the continental European mindset. And that has undoubtedly expressed the French tradition's preference for uniformity, reinforced by the legal formalism which became so strong in post-war German public life. It is this outlook that finds great difficulty in adapting to the prospect of a world that is not only increasingly messy, but less easily controlled.

The chances of persuading members of the EU to accept a substantial change in direction – towards greater flexibility, less uniformity of regulation and a recognition that diversity is generally beneficial in a competitive market – are not good. Indeed, it would be argued by some member states that such an approach simply amounts to putting back the clock and that this is clearly impossible. If this proves to be the response, then it can only sharpen the choice facing any member state unhappy about the direction taken by the EU: either its citizens have to put up with gradually drifting into a bureaucratically organised semi-state which inevitably reduces their effective political rights; or they must withdraw from the association in order to regain their full rights of self-government.

This option offers no hope of making an impact unless Britain can mobilise and maintain support for such a line. Unfortunately it has been a persistent weakness of British tactics within the Community and the Union that it has never put enough effort into finding and maintaining allies and friends. It is so often assumed that France and Germany have only to lay down the guidelines for some stage of future development for others then to accept them. But there are member states with governments sympathetic to many of the British reservations about 'ever closer union'. Some are certainly ready to agree with British objections to specific policies and draft regulations. Denmark, Sweden and Finland come into this group; the Netherlands will often see the point of British scepticism about more action by the EU; and Spain is by no means always ready to accept what France or Germany propose. Enlargement would bring in new sympathisers simply because it would embrace countries which have recently regained their independence from Soviet dominance.[21]

Whatever the circumstances may be, there would be a far better chance of making progress with British policy initiatives if they were to secure and hold the support of a reasonable number of other member states. To find oneself continually in a minority of one is not a good basis for exerting influence on outcomes in an organisation like the EU.

Option three: withdrawal

The possibility of withdrawal is presented as one to be considered only if the EU and most of its members obdurately refuse to contemplate policies allowing for a looser Community for those members who would prefer that way forward. It would be the choice of last resort. Withdrawal is usually dismissed as a doomsday scenario, leading to catastrophe for the British economy. But there is no reason to assume that an orderly withdrawal negotiated with due regard to both British interests and those of the EU states would have such dire consequences. Indeed, the dire effects of withdrawal as they are sometimes painted by protagonists of British membership at all costs could only occur if it is assumed that the EU would refuse to negotiate something like an association agreement such as is enjoyed by Norway. Furthermore, it is assumed that the EU would seek to impose trade sanctions that are almost certainly illegal under international trade agreements. As for investment flows, there are interests on both sides. In any event, experience shows that inward investment from world capital markets nearly always goes where the prospects of profit are best.

Nevertheless, withdrawal would not be an easy option to take. It would upset many people in continental Europe and for a while would produce political turbulence, not least within the political, business and administrative elites in Britain. In particular, withdrawal should not be seen as a 'little Englander' option and nor should it be confused with the xenophobic resentments so often expressed in the populist press in Britain. It makes sense only as a rational and considered response to the intractable difficulties of an unsatisfactory relationship.

In terms of practical politics, there is no doubt that a policy of seeking a complete renegotiation of Britain's association with the EU has to be treated as a position of last resort. Instead, some version of the second version is to be preferred. A serious attempt to develop a cluster of policies in support of this way forward – a looser and more 'economic' community, at any rate for those members who prefer that option – might just operate as healthy shock therapy inside the EU itself. It would compel all member states (some more than others) to think again about what kind of association they want the EU to be. It is at least possible that some would decide that the time has come to transform it by reverting to an association focused on a reasonably well-defined range of functions, to be performed by simpler and less pretentious institutions. The realisation of such a possibility would, of course, require those member states wishing to press ahead with the 'ever closer union' agenda to accept with tolerance an EU with variable geometry. It would certainly be necessary to envisage a two- or even three-tier Community allowing one group of states to go for closer political integration, another to stop short at a stage of well-developed economic integration, and perhaps yet another group remaining content with some form of association. Above all, it would have to be accepted that for many members 'political union' would simply not be on the agenda.

Putting the choice to the people

Despite the dismissive criticisms to which it has been exposed in recent years, only the nation state has so far provided a tolerably satisfactory and successful framework within which the requirements of democratic self-government can be met. And it is only the nation state that has so far been able to nurture the institutions of freedom and to act as a focus for the loyalty of its citizens. The fact that in the past some nation states have gone off the rails and that today many are still unstable and exposed to all kinds of internal strains should not, however, mislead us into concluding that we can or should try to dispense with them.

Notwithstanding their many failings, nation states have so far provided the only enduring framework within which democratic self-government has been possible. It is this simple fact of political experience that still justifies the retention of sovereignty by the nation state, even though there are so many forces at work in the contemporary world restricting and qualifying the exercise of that sovereignty in various ways. Indeed, a number of political leaders in various EU member states have recently affirmed their belief in the survival of nation states. Yet experience teaches us that those who drive the project along – and they are tiny and privileged minorities – do see *finalité* as supplanting nation states and replacing them with some kind of pan-European government.

The road to this goal no doubt stretches a long way ahead and nobody yet knows what this European government or state would be like – benign or malign. But there can be no doubt that the final state would not be a meaningful political democracy; nor can it be doubted that the rights and opportunities for self-government within the familiar and manageable units of the nation states of Europe would be steadily subverted and diminished. No matter how great might be the material economic benefits of such an evolution, the political price for them would be paid in the loss of democratic self-determination.

This is the political challenge that faces all members of the European Union, whether they recognise it or not. In the light of British political experience, it is one which cannot be swept under the carpet here. Any recommendation by the British Government to go into the euro zone will have to be put to the British people in accordance with the promise of a referendum on this issue. Already it has proved impossible to conceal the wide-ranging political consequences of such a step, and doubtless these would receive yet more attention in any referendum campaign.

No matter where they stand on Britain and Europe, the primary duty of politicians is to be honest about the consequences of what they recommend. If they believe that there is no turning back and that Britain should cooperate wholeheartedly with its EU partners in working towards full political and economic integration in Europe, then they should say so openly. They should acknowledge its consequences for the prospects of meaningful self-government. But if they see such an outcome as unacceptable, then similarly they have a duty to be frank about the difficulties and even the penalties of taking such a stand. It is only on such a basis that the seriousness of the matters at stake can be understood and decisions reached that may then be both legitimate and conclusive.

Notes

1. The preamble to the Treaty of Rome 1957 setting up the European Economic Community opens by referring to 'an ever closer union among the European peoples'. Article 2 then refers to 'closer relations between its Member States'. It is an interesting question of conceivable judicial interpretation of which condition should take precedence.
2. Some of the ground covered in this chapter was admirably and lucidly surveyed by Crispin Blunt MP in his pamphlet *Britain's Place in the World – Time to Decide*, published by the Centre for Policy Studies in 1998. His emphasis was, however, more on the broader foreign policy aspects of Britain's Position in the EU than on the structural reasons for the difficulties inherent in membership.
3. Letter to *The Daily Telegraph*, 27 May 2000.
4. The enabling legislation was contained in the European Communities Act 1972. Whilst in constitutional theory at least, repeal of this act would end Britain's membership of the Communities, in reality withdrawal would be a much more complicated matter than that.
5. This passage foreshortens considerably the emergence of a commitment to a common currency. The scheme has forerunners in the early 1970s and in the setting-up of a rudimentary European Monetary System in 1978. The gestation period for major EU policy changes is nearly always extremely long.
6. Strictly speaking the European Communities still survive alongside the EU, so that for some purposes Community action is required, for others EU action.
7. Mrs Thatcher's speech at Bruges in 1988 was her most notable effort to present her vision of a Community focused on economic functions and firmly based on the cooperation of independent nation states.
8. For a thorough historical examination of this subject see K. Dyson, *The State Tradition in Western Europe*, Martin Robertson, Oxford 1980.
9. Not surprisingly the area of taxation is extraordinarily complex and harmonisation has made only limited progress. But the discretion of member states to vary or impose taxes is already limited in various ways by EU measures.
10. This has been denied by Government ministers who have presented the proposed Charter of Fundamental Rights as no more than an effort to give a higher profile to existing rights. For such a view see a letter from Keith Vaz, a Foreign Office minister, in the *Daily Telegraph*, 3 June 2000.
11. It should be added that successive British Governments do not appear to have put much effort into the construction of alliances within the EU.
12. This was particularly clear in the case of the slow march towards monetary union, a goal to which Chancellor Kohl was totally committed.
13. Apart from Britain only Denmark and the Netherlands have made serious efforts to allow their Parliaments to engage in the examination of EU proposals before they are finally approved.
14. It will only be possible to prevent the Commission growing to an unwieldy size (and some would say that it has reached that condition already) if the larger member states are reduced to one Commissioner each. The smaller members may also be required to take turns in providing Commissioners. Such changes would have grave implications for the quality and internal dynamics of the Commission.

15. These two examples are taken from Title VIII and Title XI respectively of the Maastricht Treaty, as published in the white paper containing the Treaty and presented to Parliament as Cm 1934, HMSO, May 1992.
16. The Amsterdam treaty includes a protocol on subsidiarity, but this fails to provide any answers to the questions posed here.
17. For a vigorous presentation of this view of the future constitutional development in Europe, see Alec Stone Sweet, *Governing with Judges: Constitutional politics in Europe*, Oxford University Press 2000.
18. For an analysis of this confusion of roles, see Tom King, *The European Commission: Administration or government?*, Centre for Policy Studies, 1999.
19. The text of the directive is to be found in the material published by the House of Lords Select Committee on the European Union along with its report on EU Proposals to combat Discrimination, HL Paper 68, May 2000, p. 50.
20. Some people, including Sir Edward Heath, have tried to argue that at the time of entry into the Communities it was made clear to the British people that far more than a 'common market' was at stake. None of this is at all convincing, however. The term 'European Communities' meant little to most people and the ballot paper for the 1975 referendum referred explicitly to staying in the 'Common Market'. The same reference can even be found in the Explanatory Notes issued with the Political Parties, Elections and Referendums Bill after it was sent to the House of Lords in March 2000 (p. 47, note on Clause 103).
21. However, it must not be forgotten that these new entrants (like some others in the past) will also be keen to gain maximum benefits from membership even if this involves agreeing to policies they do not like.

11
Separate Ways*

Peter Shore

To tell the story of Britain's evolving relationships with its continental neighbours – and hopefully, to make that account intelligible – I have found it necessary to cover more than half a century's history of events. This has not been confined to just Britain and the European Community but has had to include major events in the other five continents in whose affairs the United Kingdom is also involved.

What conclusions are we entitled to draw? Some have already been stated in the different chapters devoted to major specific issues, such as the single currency and defence commitments. But a number have been left implicit, or only half explicit – and certainly they are scattered around the text. It may help therefore to draw them together here, and summarise briefly what those conclusions are – together with the global institutional framework best suited to meet our existing and emerging needs.

I have seven major findings. *First*, on the relationship with the EU. Nearly 30 years of membership have demonstrated the essential truth about Britain and its continental neighbours: we are good friends and allies and happy to cooperate in many joint endeavours. But the British people simply do not share the widespread desire, among the governments and peoples of their neighbouring European states, to develop an 'ever closer union' to the point where national decision-making has been largely replaced by either majority votes in the Council of Ministers or by supranational authorities in Europe. These include the unelected European Central Bank, the unelected Brussels Commission, the unelected European Court of Justice and the elected, but impotent, European Parliament. We did not experience, during

* Originally published by Duckworth, 2000.

those traumatic years of World War II, that common destiny of defeat, ruin, occupation and liberation that our continental neighbours were forced to endure. The curious bonding that arose from that shared humiliation and defeat was an experience that we could not and did not share. Nor have we endured the experience, repeated more than once since 1870, of German conquest or invasion of its neighbours – that scarring experience that has inspired successive French governments to construct an ever stronger constitutional cage to contain their over-powerful neighbour.

In all this, our approach has been shaped neither by prejudice nor by ignorance nor by old hatreds; we have simply reflected our island geography and the separate history that that geography, particularly the Channel and the Atlantic – the sheltering seas – have enabled us to shape.

Second – and linked closely to the first – we conspicuously lack any strong sense of European identity. In recent years, there has been much discussion about identity and, in particular, whether the sense of identity within Britain itself is strong enough to continue to keep subordinate the parallel sense of identity that people in geographical England, Wales, Scotland and Northern Ireland undoubtedly feel.

I think it is. But the crucial point is that *unless* such a strong identity continues to exist, there can be no possibility of maintaining long term our commonly accepted sovereignty.

Clearly, that strong and necessary sense of identity does not exist between Britain and Europe. The evidence for this statement is overwhelming. Some five years ago, to mark the twentieth anniversary of Britain's 1975 referendum, the BBC asked Mori to report on the British people's attitudes to Europe.

A substantial sample of 2000 electors were asked these most salient questions: first, how European do you feel; and second, with which of a list of six countries (France, Germany, Spain, the United States, Canada and Australia) do you feel you have most in common?

The conclusions – and there was virtually no difference between the figures for different age groups – made quite plain that the bond of sentiment, of a special relationship or of identity with our main European Union neighbours was weak indeed. To the first question, how European do you feel etc., 8 per cent said a 'great deal' and 15 per cent a 'fair amount' while 49 per cent said: 'not at all'. And on the countries with whom people felt they had 'most in common', 9 per cent said France, 7 per cent Germany and 5 per cent Spain. In contrast, for the English-speaking countries, the figures were 23 per cent for the United States, 15 per cent Australia and 14 per cent Canada. In short, while 21 per cent felt they had 'most in common' with three of our principal European neighbours, no less than 52 per cent chose the three English-speaking nations, separated as they are by several thousand miles of ocean from the United Kingdom.

The European Union, through the Information Department of the Brussels Commission, itself polls opinion in the member states. Every six months, the europoll records the state of feeling towards the European Community–European Union of the peoples of its now 15 members states. And year after year, poll after poll, places the United Kingdom as the least enthusiastic, the least committed of them.

The British people cannot be frog-marched to the altar, a pistol at their heads, and told to take out the vows of eternal love and commitment to a European bride for whom they have only friendly feelings.

My *third* conclusion follows, inexorably, from the above: from the gulf that separates European aspirations from British realities. British governments, Labour or Tory, one after another, are forced to live a kind of lie about their relationships with Europe. They tell our European partners that Britain wishes to be 'at the heart of Europe'. But they tell the British people that the European Union is only about cooperating with neighbour states to do things more effectively than we can do on our own. Doubletalk, deception and self-deception do not make for healthy politics or honest debate. But there is a further and potentially much more damaging consequence for our democracy. In signing up to successive European Treaties, with their very special supranational features, we are entering into commitments that allow the European institutions to make, more and more, the laws in our land – without the specific consent of our electors or our Parliament. Inevitably, such laws lack the legitimacy of consent and sooner or later will lead those adversely affected to open defiance or worse. As it is, governments are constantly engaged in the task of hiding from the British people the fact that unpopular decisions are being made not by the Westminster Parliament but by one or other of the unelected bodies in Europe. For those who respect, with all their imperfections, our democracy and our Westminster Parliament, this is an intolerable situation – and it is one that is bound to get worse.

The *fourth* major conclusion of this study is that there is really no limit, no frontier, to the encroachment of European institutions on our national affairs. While the public gaze, understandably, has been focused on the crucial issue of the pound and the single currency, the European integrationists have made a substantial and dangerous inroad into the control of our own foreign and defence policies. Unless it is halted, the European Union's present drive to establish a common European foreign and defence policy will increasingly absorb and engulf the UK's own foreign policy. The control over our own foreign policy – including our ability to articulate the issues and causes we support, to use our resources to disadvantage enemies and reward friends and to determine our own defence and security arrangements – is essential to our continued independence as a sovereign state.

These European initiatives in foreign and defence matters are relatively new developments. The country has not yet begun to understand what is taking place. It is a process that the Blair government has not just accepted but actively encouraged – and it will make a fundamental change in the very nature of the European Union. What has been primarily an economic and social Union is now being developed into a quasi state, with its own foreign policy and a military capacity to project European power outside its own frontiers.

The priorities of our continental neighbours are not necessarily the same as our own. The UK has not just a European role – which it played to the full in the difficult years of the Cold War – but it has connections and responsibilities elsewhere and a role to play as a permanent member of the Security Council of the United Nations. It cannot play those roles if its armed forces are virtually absorbed within the 'rapid reaction' forces and command structures of the European Union and made available for their priority use.

Moreover with every further advance towards European Union, the voice and vote of a member state becomes absorbed within the European Union. I do not believe, that for Britain to have a voice in formulating the European Union's external policies and then accepting that the European Union (whether in the person of the Commissioner for External Affairs or the new High Representative of the European Council) thereafter is empowered to speak for Britain, is an adequate exchange for the loss of the right to speak and vote in the wider councils of the world.

My *fifth* conclusion follows logically from the first four. We need to establish a new treaty relationship with the European Union, one that recognises and accepts the differences of purpose and history that separate the UK from many of its European neighbours, one which accepts a necessary repatriation of powers from the institutions of the Union to the UK.

This will not be easy. But past experience shows that it is far from impossible to arrange a UK exemption from new European Union laws, directives, judgements etc.: all that is required now is agreement on an opt-out protocol for the UK from *all* future treaties and domestically, an amendment to the 1972 European Communities Act under which for any future European Union enactment to be effective, it will need to have the authority of an affirmative order in the UK Parliament.

However, to sift through the accumulated laws and treaty commitments already entered into, to agree what needs to be discarded and what powers should be repatriated to the UK – and over a realistic time scale – is much more difficult, perhaps impossible. But it is a task worth essaying. It is worth pursuing because, as already explained, a virtually unique opportunity for such change has arisen. There is the Helsinki commitment by the European Union states – as recent as December 1999 – to admit a further 12 applicant members. They will bring with them problems of such a magnitude and require such major adjustments of existing EU policies that accommodation within a single treaty is virtually impossible. A two-speed, or multi-speed Europe is not enough. A two-tier or multi-tier Europe is inevitable. And the projected entry of the 12 applicant states almost certainly rules out any possibility of achieving with all 27 participating members that still deeper integration that the Founding Six and their closest allies are urgently seeking.

The French government for one has clearly woken up to the implications. In an interview with the newspaper *La Croix* on 3 April 2000, M. Pierre Moscovici, French Minister for European Affairs, made the point: 'It's clear that the new Europe will no longer be as homogeneous as the old one, that enlargement modifies the nature of European Union and that, in this context, elements of flexibility become essential.'

That 'flexibility' is the provisions in the 1997 Amsterdam Treaty which specifically allow for so-called 'enhanced cooperation' whereby if a majority of states in the Union wish to deepen their immersion with each other and carry forward still further the project of ever-closer union, they can do so – provided only that at least eight are involved and that they have the consent of those who are left outside.

In other words, the states that do not wish for 'enhanced cooperation' have been given a treaty veto. Not surprisingly, M. Moscovici in his interview of 3 April indicated both that France wished to make use of 'the enhanced cooperation' procedures but also that they 'were keen to remove the clause, on the need for the Council's authorisation which gives every member state a virtual veto on initiatives its partners might wish to take'.

Subsequent statements made by Prime Minister Jospin and President Chirac make it clear that the abolition of this veto will be among the changes pursued in the IGC that is to report to the Nice Summit.

Here indeed is a situation that a determined and competent British government, with some understanding of the wishes and interests of its own people, their institutions and their history, should grasp and through it establish a long-lasting, mutually agreeable and far more honest relationship with its continental neighbours.

The basic bargain is this: the UK will only agree to abolish the veto it possesses on moves towards 'enhanced cooperation' – or further integration – if at the same time the European Union Treaties are amended to allow for a tier of members, including both existing members and applicants, that can confine its obligations to those of a trade and economic treaty and, for political cooperation purposes, to a council of Europe.

If that genuinely 'fundamental renegotiation' were to fail, then of course the UK would be free to consider whether a different non-membership relationship would be preferred. The European Economic Zone Treaty, that includes Norway and Switzerland in an apparently perfectly satisfactory economic relationship with the European Union, may well be a model to be pursued.

But the point is this: we are free to choose. We do not have to belong to any trade grouping – other than the World Trade Organisation that establishes trading rules across the globe. When the British establishment lost its nerve in the early 1960s and desperately sought UK membership of the then Common Market, there was at least the case that the common external tariff that the Six were busily erecting imposed a duty of 12 per cent on foreign, including British, industrial goods. Successive negotiating rounds – the Kennedy Round, the Uruguay Round – have brought down that common external tariff to 3–4 per cent. And no doubt, the forthcoming Millennium Round will achieve still further global tariff reductions.

But, already, a tariff that was once a high fence has become no more than a low garden wall. And when non-membership would relieve the United Kingdom of the obligations to buy high-cost Community food and re-establish connections with low-cost agriculture producers in Australasia, South America, Canada and the US, the overall effect will certainly not be to our trading disadvantage. In addition, if we were to become non-members, we would cease to go on adding to that £40 billion plus net contribution to the funds of the European Union which we have paid so far since 1973 and which continues to cost us, net, at least £2 billion a year.

And that brings me to my *sixth* and penultimate conclusion. In resisting its integration within the emerging European Union state and maintaining its separate political identity, the UK is marching with, not against, the great movements of our time. In the same 50 years that have passed since Robert Schuman launched his European Coal and Steel Community idea, the world has been reshaped and convulsed by the triumph everywhere of the emergent nation state – and indeed the mini-state as well. The United Nations that was launched in 1946 with 52 members, has now 188.

Here is one of the great dynamic forces that has shaped and is continuing to shape our contemporary world: the wish, the passion, of people for self-government: to be ruled by those with whom they feel strong bonds of identity, culture, language – and equally, *not* to be ruled, however enlightened that rule may be, by those with whom they do not feel a close identity.

The great tide of sentiment that is backing the almost universal demand for self-government is itself being massively reinforced by a tide within that tide – the demand for democracy, for the rights of the peoples in self-governing states to be directly involved in the appointment and dismissal of their rulers.

This commitment to democracy is now the declared main external political objective – apart from resistance to armed aggression – not just of the United States, the United Kingdom, the old British Dominions and a handful of Scandinavian states, but of the whole Commonwealth, of the whole continent of South and Central America, of the countries of the European Union – and of many more.

In some countries, the process has yet to begin. In many more it is still imperfect and insecure. But there can be no doubt that the democratic process has been both extended and accelerated by the end of the Cold War. Oppressive and dictatorial regimes can no longer expect to be supported or indeed tolerated because they were reliable allies of either side in that struggle.

So, the twin doctrines of the nation state, self-government and democracy – and with democracy increasing respect for minorities and the rule of law – are becoming in this twenty-first century the general rule and experience of the majority of mankind.

So far so good. But the second great requirement of our time is the further development of a rule of law, not just within states, but between states and their dealings with each other; and the further need of all, in a global economy, for effective means for maintaining and promoting prosperity; defending the environment from its many threats and catering for our still soaring human population.

And that brings me to my *seventh and last conclusion*. This new world of nation states requires global arrangements and institutions: their needs cannot, and will not, be met by regional organisations with their inevitably limited interests and perspectives, even by so powerful a body as the European Union.

The basic framework for a better and saner world and for the necessary international cooperation was laid down, not in the Rome Treaty, but in the Charter of the United Nations in 1945. And the main institutions, the specialised agencies for developing such cooperation in different sectors of human affairs, were also established, along with the main political institutions, the General Assembly and the Security Council and the International Court of Justice, that were empowered to establish and develop, and where necessary to enforce, the rule of international law.

That framework has endured and while its functioning was greatly limited by the near global rivalry of the old Soviet Union and the Western democracies, even then some considerable successes were achieved. In the post-Cold War world, no longer divided and frustrated by the superpower rivalry of the Soviet Union and the US, the role of the United Nations, and its effectiveness, can be and should be powerfully increased. Britain and its fellow Commonwealth members, 54 no less, have an obviously important part to play in the General Assembly and in other international forums. And the United Kingdom itself has the particular strength and influence that goes with permanent membership of the Security Council and with the right of veto and of initiative that the permanent five possess.

This UN system clearly needs further development and strengthening – and the United Kingdom should certainly now bend its efforts, in cooperation with its partners and allies in the European Union, the Commonwealth and the English-speaking world, to that end.

And the first requirement is the vital need to safeguard peace and security against the threat and the reality of armed attack. We need both the reaffirmation of the doctrine of collective security, of the commitment to resist aggression, and the mobilisation of forces internationally to give these central undertakings the credibility they need. The world community of approaching 200 sovereign states that has developed over recent decades and which will certainly continue in the future, includes many militarily weak, vulnerable but resource-rich states. Some (e.g. Singapore and the Gulf States) are well within reach of much more powerful neighbours. Their independence in the last resort needs the guarantee of the world community, a world community committed to enforcing the basic principles of the UN charter.

Today, in spite of some post-Cold War successes, the forces available for UN peace enforcement missions have proved to be slow to mobilise, inadequate in fire power and, in some recent missions in parts of Africa, a failure.

The US, the power best equipped to organise, lead and finance UN-sanctioned armed force is, unhappily, reluctant, even hostile, to perform that leadership role. It does not want to be the world policeman – particularly when other nations contribute so marginally to collective enforcement measures. It is necessary therefore for those who believe in international order and, where necessary, its enforcement by military means, to make manifest their commitment to collective action.

The earmarking of 'rapid reaction' forces, dedicated to assist in Security Council-approved military expeditions – as negotiated by the UK with the UN in the 1999 Memorandum of Understanding – is just the sort of undertaking that is required. But there are limits to what Britain itself can, or should, do. Our diplomacy should be focused on persuading other nations to make arrangements similar to those that we have ourselves agreed. Success here would have a significant effect on US public opinion – for the US, providing it is sufficiently supported by its allies, has shown both in the NATO and European Areas – as well as the Gulf – a notable, if reluctant willingness to undertake military tasks: in the case of Kosovo, at the very margin of its own, narrowly conceived, national interest.

The other main development needed in this world of the twenty-first century is the development of a new Economic and Financial Council, with a worldwide brief to identify and help combat the main threats to economic progress. Global institutions have now long existed with expertise, authority and resources to tackle aspects of the world economy: the World Bank, the International Monetary Fund, the Food and Agriculture Organisation, the International Labour Organisation, the World Trade Organisation and the World Environment Forum are among those that spring to mind. But, as has already been noted, what is clearly missing is an over-arching Council, with an inclusive economic/social/environmental remit. The Group of Seven – or Eight – has done some of the necessary work. But it needs developing to the point where it would become the focal point of reference, of guidance and coordinated action for dealing with problems that are simply too large for lesser, even large regional bodies, to tackle. A world economy based overwhelmingly on free markets in capital and trade and with giant multinational corporations does need at the minimum, organised counter-capitalist, inter-governmental pressures – better still the discipline of some effective regulatory power with a global reach.

Finally, both the Security Council of the United Nations and the Group of Seven – or Eight – need additional members to bring in those new power centres that have emerged since their own formation.

The only alternative and challenge to the development of such an *international* order, is the creation of a small number of powerful *regional* blocs, to defend and promote the collective interests of their members. That of course is the old, largely out-of-date vision of the European federalists, of those who shared Prime Minister Heath's belief that the future belonged to a 'world of giants' in which nation states would become redundant and international organisations and treaties would be largely replaced by a new balance of power between a handful of superstates.

Such a development is now highly unlikely – as well as being highly undesirable. It is highly unlikely because, in the world picture of the Euro federalists and Ted Heath, the future belonged to great power blocks including the then Soviet Union, the United States, Japan and later, China and India and – they hoped – a United Europe to sit by their side. The dissolution of the Soviet Union in 1991 and the clearly stronger tendency to dismember existing states rather than to merge states into still larger aggregates, is self-evident. That is simply not the way the world is going. As for the desirability of regional superblocs, if such a choice existed, there is a genuine danger that rivalry between them, competition for markets and resources, inadequate contact and understanding with areas outside their own, could lead to unnecessary divisions and estrangements between power blocs.

There is indeed a particular value to be attached to genuinely international, rather than continental or regional associations and organisations, of which the United Nations itself and the Commonwealth are the world's leading examples – if for no other reason than that they do bring together different cultures, different interests, different continents and different problems of security.

But there is a vitally important additional factor that argues against regionalism of the kind exemplified by the European Union. For its member states, it provides not just the defined constraints, rights and obligations that all treaties impose upon their signatories, but, in addition, it demonstrates acceptance of the authority of its specially created supranational institutions. These appointed, not elected, bodies are vested not just with the power to enforce treaty provisions but the right to develop and enlarge them as well. The powers of the nation states, the right of accountability and redress that democracy affords their people, is thus transferred to non-elected institutions. Thus has been established a new independent legal order and treaty-making power in the European Union, superior to the laws passed and decisions made in member states by their elected members of Parliament and their Ministers responsible to them.

Inevitably, the price paid for the benefits that supranational treaty arrangements confer, is the progressive loss of self-government: a growing democratic deficit is thus built into arrangements of this kind.

It is a heavy price to pay. Fortunately it does not have to be paid in order to achieve necessary inter-state agreements. The alternative is of course the normal bilateral, multilateral or international treaty which also involves defined constraints, obligations, rights and benefits. And no one can doubt the need for an increasing density and coverage of agreements between nation states in the more integrated world in which we live.

But such international treaties do *not* involve the transfer of law-making power and treaty-making power to external authorities. The rights of the democratic state and the parliaments and people within them are preserved.

Through their supranational treaties and institutions, the countries of the European Union have been driven into a non-democratic cul-de-sac.

Its only way out – but only for those to whom the existing relationships of peoples and governments is so close that there is no longer any serious sense of 'us' and 'them', but of near total identity – is to elect parliamentary institutions whose majority decisions can be accepted by minority peoples and states without any sense of being imposed upon.

In the years ahead, the Founding Six and some other European Union states may well, with the help of 'enhanced cooperation', sufficiently strengthen that new European identity that makes 'ever closer union' and a European state achievable.

It will not be easy, even for them. For the great bulk of mankind living in nation states both in the other continents of the world and indeed in Europe itself – many of whom are now achieving for the first time the goals of democracy and the rule of law together with self-government – it is an unattractive, even a repellent prospect.

For the United Kingdom and its people it is not merely unwanted: it is deeply repugnant and offensive. We don't want it. We don't need it. The goals that really matter – independence, democracy, security, relative prosperity and effective international cooperation – are well within our grasp. They are not even under threat.

To surrender such assets for an uncertain place inside the European state that is now so clearly emerging, would be an act not far short of madness and betrayal.

12
Nice and Beyond: The Parting of the Ways

Christopher Booker

Introduction

The decision of the people of Denmark on 28 September 2000 to reject their country's entry into the euro set off a shock wave across the European Union. But what escaped general notice was just why, at this particularly crucial moment in the EU's history, that shock should have run so deep.

This is because the Danish vote has brought to a head a fundamental debate already raging at the heart of the EU as to which way the 'European project' should develop.

It is remarkable how little attention has so far been paid on this side of the Channel to the way in which, in recent months, the terms of the debate over the future of the European Union and Britain's involvement in it have been dramatically transformed.

Even many close followers of the debate, Europhiles and Eurosceptics alike, seem to have missed the significance of a startling new initiative on the continent, one which raises a huge question mark over where the EU is now heading. Just when political attention was beginning to focus on the next EU treaty, due to be signed in Nice between 7 and 9 December 2000, the leaders of Germany and France have thrown down a challenge which in some respects makes Nice seem almost like a side-show.

In a series of major speeches between May and July 2000, Germany's Foreign Minister Joschka Fischer, France's Prime Minister Lionel Jospin and French President Jacques Chirac – supported by such elder statesmen as Jacques Delors, Helmut Schmidt and Valéry Giscard d'Estaing – proposed not only that the EU must now drive ahead to full political integration, but that this should be led by a 'pioneer group' or 'avant-garde' of nations, prepared to move ahead of the rest.[1]

This is a departure from anything previously on the agenda. Now, for the first time, continental leaders are openly envisaging a division of the EU into two groups: a 'hard core' or inner club of countries, probably based on the euro zone, determined to move to political federation as soon as possible, if necessary with their own treaty and their own collective institutions; and a second wider grouping, including applicant countries from Eastern Europe, which would no longer be part of the EU's central core.

The declared purpose of this initiative is to overcome two obstacles to maintaining the EU's momentum towards political union: firstly, how to accommodate the applicant countries without the difficulties which have arisen in granting them full membership; and, secondly, how to get round the problem of those reluctantly integrationist members, like Britain, Denmark and Sweden, which have not even yet joined the euro.

Indeed, as Mr Blair and his colleagues are uncomfortably aware, no nation has been more obviously put on the spot by this Franco-German initiative than Britain. This is because an inescapable condition of admission to the inner club is membership of the single currency. Yet in the immediate future the chances of the British people being persuaded to accept the euro are so problematical it seems inevitable that, as this next decisive phase of EU integration takes shape, Britain must remain excluded.

The implications of all this for Britain's future involvement with the European Union run so deep that they can scarcely be exaggerated.

If the countries of euroland now intend to move rapidly forward to forming a full political federation, this must reopen the question of just what Britain's future relationship with the EU should be. It may seem hard at present to imagine circumstances in which our politicians could talk the British people into accepting all the steps necessary to join that inner core. But what if the only alternative is to remain, with Denmark, Sweden, Poland, Hungary and Slovenia, on the outer fringes of a new two-tier Europe?

As the Nice Treaty approaches, the parameters of Britain's involvement in the European Union have suddenly altered, in a way which even a few months ago might have seemed unthinkable. It is a matter of highest priority that we should now engage in a full and open debate as to where our nation's interests should lie.

But a first precondition of such a debate must be a proper understanding of what our EU partners are now proposing, and where the European Union is now heading: issues on which, as so often before on matters concerning our relations with 'Europe', the British Government is being remarkably secretive. This pamphlet brings out some of the background which is necessary to that understanding. Its aim is to show how the EU's drive to political integration has unexpectedly brought us to what, both for our continental partners and for our own continuing relationship with them, is a moment of truth.

Approaching Niagara

For 40 years, the United Kingdom's involvement with the economic and political entity gradually taking shape on the continent of Europe has presented the British with one of the most perplexing challenges of their history.

The heart of the problem is that there has always been a fundamental difference of perception between Britain and its continental partners as to the real nature of this project. British politicians consistently portrayed it to their fellow-citizens as little more than a means of increasing trade and sharing prosperity: a common or single market, through which, as a bonus, it might live in greater political amity with its neighbours.

On the continent, however, from the time of its original inspiration in the vision of its founders, Jean Monnet and Robert Schuman, it was always seen as something much more ambitious than that. It was viewed as a long-term project to lead Western Europe eventually, step by step, to complete economic and political integration; towards what Winston Churchill, in a series of historic speeches in the immediate post-war years, called a 'United States of Europe', comparable with the United States of America. Except that, as Churchill made explicitly clear in those speeches in Zurich, London and Strasbourg between 1946 and 1949, he did not foresee any part for Britain in that new Western European state, since Britain and its English-speaking Commonwealth had their own separate destiny in the world.

Even when Britain decided in the 1960s and 1970s, for reasons related to its loss of empire and economic decline, to make a dramatic change of course and to join this great continental adventure, for a long time it still remained possible for its political leaders to maintain their separate, insular view of its nature. But gradually, as the 'European Economic Community' evolved in the 1980s into the 'European Community', then in the early 1990s into the 'European Union', it came ever more clearly out into the open where the whole project was heading.

In the Council of Ministers and the European Commission it already had its own embryonic government and executive. It had its own parliament and its own supreme court. In the 1980s it adopted its own flag; in 1986 its own anthem; in the early 1990s its own citizenship, passport and driving licence. At Maastricht, it laid the foundations for its own currency and its own foreign and defence policy. Piece by piece, it was taking on all the attributes of a sovereign state. And this inevitably imposed increasing strain on the determination of Britain's politicians to insist that this was not the project's real intention; and that, however far Europe's nations might develop new means of working together, the last thing anyone intended was that they should be irrevocably welded together into a political federation, 'a country called Europe'.

It was this sense of strain, from being torn between two incompatible views of what 'Europe' was about, which underlay all the difficulties bedevilling Britain's relations with the EU during the years of John Major's premiership; and which, after an unreal honeymoon period, soon resurfaced when he was succeeded in 1997 by Tony Blair. It was this sense of irresolution which, at a conference in London in March 1999, provoked Lord Jenkins of Hillhead, one of the most committed British supporters of 'the European project', to an unusually frank speech, warning his fellow-countrymen that the time had come when they must make a fundamental choice as to which way they wanted their country to go:

> My central belief is that there are only two coherent British attitudes to Europe. One is to participate fully ... and to endeavour to exercise as much influence and gain as much benefit as possible from the inside. The other is to recognise that Britain's history, national psychology and political culture may be such that we can never be other than a foot-dragging and constantly complaining member; and that it would be better, and certainly would produce less friction, to accept this and move towards an orderly and, if possible, reasonably amicable withdrawal.[2]

Between these two views, insisted the former President of the European Commission, there could be no half way house:

> Both in the national interest and in the interests of national politicians, Mr Blair included, [Britain must take] a firm, clear, unequivocal approach in favour of being fully in or out.

The one course the British could no longer afford was to

> hang about in the middle of the road, where you are merely asking to be run down.

Nothing had perhaps made it easier for the British to think they could still afford to wander on uncommitted down the middle of that road than the fact that even on the continent there had long been an engrained reluctance to come out into the open as to where 'the European project' was heading. But by the time Lord Jenkins spoke, as we shall see, decisive moves were already in train which were to bring that long period of reticence to an end. Within little more than a year, the degree of Britain's commitment to a 'European' future was at last to be put to the test as at no time since she had first thrown in her destiny with the 'Common Market' nearly three decades earlier.

Enter the Germans

The story of how 'political union' moved to the centre of the European Union agenda really began in one extraordinary week at the end of November 1998.

For some time there had been a comparative lull in coverage of the EU in Britain. Only recently had the EU states completed the ratification of the Amsterdam Treaty, signed in June 1997, the fourth European treaty since Rome in 1957. There were no immediate plans for another. Such coverage as there was tended to focus on preparations for the launch of the EU's single currency, the euro, on 1 January the following year. This was due to coincide with Germany taking over the EU's six-monthly presidency under its new Social Democrat-Green Government, elected just seven weeks earlier on 30 September 1998.

Then, suddenly, the EU erupted onto Britain's front pages and stayed there for six days. Attention centred on two issues. The first had been grumbling along in the background for some time, but only now became the top news of the day, set off by the launching in Brussels on 22 November of a manifesto by 11 EU left-of-centre finance ministers entitled *The New European Way: Economic reform in a framework for monetary union*. With the approach of the euro, it was a clarion call for the harmonising of EU taxes, to provide, as Austria's Finance Minister Rudolf Edlinger put it, 'a common economic roof' for our 'common house of Europe'.[3]

Behind the scenes, the thorny issue of tax harmonisation had already for some months been pushing Britain into the position of the EU's odd man out. In December 1997, seven months after the election of Tony Blair's New Labour Government, EU finance ministers had agreed a resolution on the need 'to tackle harmful tax competition'. This specifically included the intention to introduce a 'withholding tax' on 'cross border savings'.[4]

Even at the time, Britain's Chancellor of the Exchequer Gordon Brown had insisted that this must not be allowed to damage the City of London's position as the world's leading capital market, not least through its role as easily the largest issuer of Eurobonds (75 per cent of the total). For a long time, the Chancellor remained curiously reluctant to pledge publicly that, if necessary, he would veto such a tax. Yet, by the autumn of 1998 it was clear that both the proposed directive on a withholding tax, and tax harmonisation generally, had become a major bone of contention between Britain and its partners. And although Mr Brown signed the manifesto, *The New European Way*, he immediately caused a storm by stating publicly for the first time that Britain would be prepared to use its veto to block any moves towards tax harmonisation.[5]

Over the next few days, the temperature was raised by statements from three European Commissioners. Commission President Jacques Santer challenged Mr Brown's threat that he would use Britain's veto, by claiming the UK had already signed up in principle to greater tax harmonisation the previous December.[6] Mario Monti, the single market Commissioner, insisted that the EU would proceed with plans to harmonise rates of VAT, energy taxes and excise duties.[7] Yves-Thibault de Silguy, the Commissioner for economic and monetary union, suggested in London that tax harmonisation could ultimately lead to EU-wide rates of income tax.[8] This was reinforced by a promise from Germany's Finance Minister Oskar Lafontaine that tax harmonisation would be a top priority for the forthcoming German presidency, which provoked the *Sun* in a famous front page on 25 November to dub him 'the most dangerous man in Europe'.

But the temperature was raised still further when two of Lafontaine's colleagues took the debate into a new dimension. On 26 November, the *Daily Telegraph* reported on its front page an interview with Germany's new Foreign Minister Joschka Fischer, under the headline 'Germany prepares to push for a single European state'.

Interviewed by a Frankfurt newspaper, Fischer had promised that 'deeper integration' would be the priority of the German presidency in more than just tax matters. He said:

> Just as we worked on the first real transfer of sovereignty in the field of currencies, we ought to work on a common constitution to turn the European Union into an entity under international law.

Asked whether he wanted a European army, Mr Fischer replied: 'If it is going to turn into a full union, then one day foreign and defence policy will also have to become community tasks.'[9]

The next day in Brussels, Gerhard Schroeder, Helmut Kohl's successor as Chancellor, tried to downplay his Foreign Minister's enthusiasm, as he spoke of the need to proceed carefully on the EU's plans for eastward enlargement. But he did reaffirm that the vision of a 'united' and 'ever more integrated Europe' was an idea which 'unites all German politicians'.[10]

This only inspired still more media frenzy, despite efforts by 'British officials', according to the *Daily Telegraph*, 'to play down the extent to which the public would be scared away by such comments from supporting a more pro-European stance and entry into monetary union'. 'The British press', a Downing Street spokesman explained, 'has reacted in an entirely predictable way. But people are sensible. In the end they will realise there are a lot of scare stories around.'[11]

By the end of the week all these excitements were enough to provoke the *Telegraph* into summing up: 'the danger of Britain being subsumed into a not very democratic European superstate suddenly seems more alive than ever before'.[12] But before the story could develop further, the 'European Project' was about to hit the front pages for a quite different reason.

The Commission in crisis

Over the next few months coverage of the EU was dominated by the extraordinary crisis set off when, on 9 December 1998, Paul van Buitenen, a Dutch accountant, sent MEPs a 34-page letter, with 600 pages of supporting documents, describing instances of corruption and fraud he had identified in his work as an assistant auditor in the European Commission.[13] These included cases directly involving two Commissioners.

His charges came as no great surprise. Reports and rumours of wholesale corruption and mismanagement in the Commission had been building up for a long time; and in November, for the fourth year running, the EU Court of Auditors had refused to approve the Commission's accounts on the grounds that at least 5 per cent of its spending – £3 billion – had been fraudulent or mismanaged.

In January 1999 the Commission enjoyed a reprieve when the European Parliament withdrew a censure motion on all 20 Commissioners, after the promise of an investigation by a committee of five 'Wise Men'. But the respite was only temporary. In March, the 'Comité des Sages' confirmed van Buitinen's allegations, reporting that it had been 'hard to find anyone in the Commission who was prepared to take responsibility for anything'. On 16 March the scandal reached its climax when President Santer and all his 19 fellow Commissioners resigned.

Optimism about the future of 'the Project' had been briefly rekindled at the start of the year by the launch of the single currency, easily the most ambitious step so far in bringing the EU into 'ever closer union'. But heady boasts that the euro would rival the dollar as one of the strongest, most stable currencies in the world soon died away as the new currency began a headlong slide which in little more than a year was to see it losing a quarter of its value.

It had not been an auspicious start for the German presidency. This was not helped when, on 11 March, its most fervent integrationist, the Finance Minister, Oskar Lafontaine, resigned, only two months after proclaiming 'we want to see the EU develop into a political union'.[14] The first summit of the German presidency, held in Berlin in March, was also marred by the failure of German efforts to reform the EU's finances, not least through Britain's refusal to give up the rebate on its budget payments negotiated by Mrs Thatcher in 1984.

But what had been hailed as 'the most serious crisis in the EU's history' turned out to be only a temporary hiccup. It was not long before the momentum towards 'closer integration' was resumed. On 24 March, the EU heads of government in Berlin announced that they had chosen the former Italian Prime Minister, Romano Prodi, as the new President of the European Commission. Despite being himself dogged at home by persistent suspicions of corruption, for which he had twice been formally investigated by local prosecutors, Prodi was universally acclaimed by the EU's leaders – not least by Mr Blair, who rather oddly described him as 'a high-quality person'. And his integrationist credentials were impeccable, as he demonstrated when he made his first public appearance before the European Parliament on 13 April. The challenge now, he told applauding MEPs, was to move the EU towards 'a single economy, a single political unity'.[15] The task of building 'the Project' seemed to be firmly back on track.

Mr Prodi takes centre stage

One thing which soon became obvious about the former economics professor suddenly plucked from the murky maelstrom of Italian politics to be President-designate of the European Commission was that he was determined to play an absolutely central role in turning the EU into a politically unified state, capable of acting as a major power on the world stage. At the heart of that state, he made clear in interviews after his appointment, would be the Brussels Commission, acting as what he liked to describe as 'the Government of Europe' or even 'my Government'.

In his first speech to the European Parliament, on 13 April 1999, he declared his intention that the President of the Commission should be given greater power to appointment his fellow Commissioners; and that to play its new collective role in foreign affairs, the EU needed a new treaty 'that will give us our own defence capabilities'.[16]

In an interview with the *Financial Times* on 12 April 1999, he said his 'real goal' as President was to build on 'the consequences of the single currency and create a political Europe'. He hoped that, under his Presidency, the EU would begin to develop 'a common European soul', for which 'you need a very high, top-level Commission, not in terms of bureaucracy, but in terms of common feeling and understanding of what is happening'.

On 23 April, interviewed on the BBC's *On the Record*, Prodi reiterated his view that 'the Commissioners have a political responsibility. They will be the Government for the power that is given to Europe.' He also confirmed his view that Europe risked being 'marginalised' unless it forged its own defence capability independent of the United States, and that the 'logical next step' in the integration of EU foreign policy was the creation of 'a European army'.[17]

By July, when he had been established in Brussels for three months and had just announced the names of his 19 Commissioners-designate, the *Sunday Telegraph* (11 July) reported, under the headline 'Prodi lays foundations for "United States of Europe"', that he was 'planning the biggest centralisation of power in the history of Brussels politics'. Julian Coman wrote:

> Mr Prodi is to model his administration on a national government, giving himself an unprecedented prime ministerial role at the heart

of Europe, making Brussels a power to rival London, Paris and Berlin ... Mr Prodi, a convinced federalist, has abandoned the collegiate idea and aims to create a European government ... set to become an aggressive promoter of causes such as tax harmonisation and a European army.

In the same article, a former associate of Prodi at Bologna University, Stefano Zamagni, was quoted as saying:

What Prodi is doing is putting in place the structures and aides he needs to become the first European premier ... he wants his tenure to help accelerate the move to a United States of Europe.

Only towards the end of the report was there any hint that this ambitious new President might not have things entirely his own way, when Coman added 'the most serious opposition to Mr Prodi's plans is likely to come from ... France and Germany, who have already tussled with the President over nominations to the new Commission'.

It was to prove a prescient comment. But for the moment, the Brussels' new broom seemed to be sweeping all before him. And whatever difficulties might eventually emerge, there was certainly no difference of opinion on the overall goal, as was made clear in a speech given in Frankfurt the following month by Gerhard Schroeder.

Addressing Professor Hans Tietmeyer on his retirement as president of the Bundesbank, the German Chancellor said on 30 August 1999:

You were always conscious that the European monetary union would have to be based on a closer political integration within Europe ... It was an original political act to hand over sovereignty over one of the most important areas of national authority, namely monetary policy, to a European authority. For this reason alone monetary union requires of us Europeans decisive advances in the field of political integration.[18]

Even President-elect Prodi could not have stated more plainly where the goal of 'the Project' now lay.

The rocky road to Nice

One of the most respected sources in Brussels is Agence Europe, a press agency which issues a daily briefing on everything going on at the heart of the European Union. Early in 2000 its keenly Europhile editor, Ferdinando Riccardi, issued an almost breathlessly excited bulletin.[19]

> All is moving faster than expected. The landscape surrounding the forthcoming institutional reform of the EU is no longer what it was on the eve of the Helsinki summit, at a time of great disenchantment, when things seemed to favour a mini-reform that for a Europe with 28 members or more would have meant disintegration towards a Union without ambition or ability to act.

But then had come 'many indications', Riccardi revealed, that 'certain heads of government had become aware of the dangers surrounding European construction'. Behind the scenes, significant shifts of opinion had taken place. 'The discussions on Europe's future have finally entered the debating chamber at the highest level. Following years of silence and evasion, nothing may now prevent the real issues being raised, and answers provided.'

What had excited Mr Riccardi's enthusiasm was the startling headway being made by the idea floated in the Dehaene–Weiszacker–Simon report that a group of nations should be permitted to engage in 'closer cooperation', allowing them to move towards fuller integration ahead of the rest.

This proposal had been picked up in a speech in Berlin to the Aspen Institute on 14 November 1999 by that tireless champion of European unification, Jacques Delors, former Commission President and shaper of the Maastricht treaty. Faced with the threat that enlargement might dilute the original vision of a united Europe, Delors suggested, 'the new treaty should allow' an 'avant-garde' of nations to move ahead 'further and faster', to achieve full 'confederation' ahead of the others. Furthermore, to avoid any confusion, 'this avant-garde should have its own institutions'. This was the only way to stay 'faithful to the ideals and political thinking of Fathers of Europe, Monnet, Schuman, Adenauer, de Gasperi and Spaak'.[20]

At Helsinki, where publicly the agenda had still been limited only to the 'Amsterdam leftovers', the same idea had been forcefully taken up by Jean-Claude Juncker, Prime Minister of Luxembourg. The prospect of enlargement, he warned his colleagues, raised 'the disastrous spectre' of Europe disintegrating into nothing more than 'a free trade area'. This could only be avoided by allowing 'enhanced co-operation' between 'member states prepared to go further in integration'. 'Eight States,' he suggested, 'or whatever the total number, should be able to form an avant-garde of integration, without the others being able to prevent them through a vote'.[21]

Furthermore, on 13 December 1999, two days after Helsinki, the same thought had been echoed by President Chirac, previously one of those who had argued for 'a limited agenda for the forthcoming IGC', to ensure its conclusion by the end of the year. Referring to that 'flexibility' which had allowed certain countries to move ahead in signing up to monetary union and the Schengen agreement dismantling border controls, Chirac had mused, might not the same principle be applied to moves towards fuller political integration?

Other leaders, Riccardi reported, had so far been 'less explicit and precise'. But some, including Mr Schroeder and Prime Minister Massimo D'Alema of Italy, had not ruled out the idea of widening the Nice agenda. And President Prodi himself, who had previously said the 'door was closed' to anything but the 'Amsterdam leftovers', had now let it be known the agenda was open.

Suddenly, it seemed, the pressure was building up to widen the new treaty to allow a 'hard core' of countries to move forward to political union, not just ahead of new members but, 'should the need arise', as Mr Riccardi emphasised, 'without one or two of the current ones'. And lest anyone should miss to whom he was referring, he added that 'at least two heads of government' still remained firmly opposed to extending the agenda in such a controversial direction. These were Jose-Maria Aznar of Spain and Britain's Tony Blair.[22]

The Commission's treaty proposals

On 26 January 2000, President Prodi appeared before the European Parliament in Brussels to present the 'Commission Opinion' on what the Nice agenda should contain. Headed 'Adapting the institutions to make a success of enlargement', it was a good deal more radical than anything agreed so far.[23]

Emphasising that enlargement must not be allowed to create a Union 'weakened and diluted by its mere size', Prodi began with the three core items:

1. On the number of Commissioners, he suggested, there were two options. The Commission could remain limited to its present size of 20 members. But if so, in a Union expanded to more than 20 countries, this would mean that each country no longer had the automatic right to a Commissioner. This could only work if 'a rotating system' ensured that member states took it in turns to be excluded,

regardless of size. Thus eventually there would come a time when even countries as large as Germany, France or Britain were not represented. If, on the other hand, it was insisted that every country must retain the right to a Commissioner, this would make the Commission so unwieldy that it would have to be divided into 'two tiers'. This would inevitably mean 'a stronger President', while an inner ring of his senior colleagues 'co-ordinated' the work of lesser Commissioners.

2. On voting, the Commission recommended that the existing QMV system requiring a minimum of 62 votes out of 87, should be replaced with one based on a 'double simple majority'. To be carried, any decision would only now need the support of a majority of member states, so long as these also represented more than 50 per cent of the EU's population.

3. On the vexed issue of where national vetoes should be retained, Mr Prodi was adamant that 'majority voting should be the general rule'. The veto should only remain in five areas, four of which related to treaty changes or major international agreements. In addition he reluctantly agreed that the veto would still also have to remain for decisions on 'taxation and social security'. But here the significant rider was added that this should not apply to those relating to 'the operation of the single market'. If a tax proposal could be presented as necessary for the single market, such as the harmonisation of VAT (which the Commission had proposed as a single market measure in 1996), it could go through under QMV, and no country would have the right to a veto.

Having dealt with the three essential issues, however, Mr Prodi went on to suggest that the treaty should also include considerably more than just these 'Amsterdam leftovers'.

For a start, it should 'add a judicial dimension to the action to combat fraud against the Community budget'. This was shorthand for the so-called *corpus juris* project to allow an EU prosecution office to operate in member states above the jurisdiction of national courts, widely looked on as a first step towards creating a common EU legal system.

Mr Prodi then reminded his audience how 'several parallel debates' were taking place on other important issues, which would also 'ultimately converge on the conference table'. These included 'the debate on security and defence', which meant the moves towards a fully integrated EU defence capability including the EU's own armed forces; the 'remarkable work which has now begun on a Charter of Fundamental

Rights'; and 'our idea of re-organising the Treaty', to create an EU constitution.

The Commission also suggested that a greater role should be given to the European Parliament, by making it the rule that Parliament should be involved by 'co-decision' in the making of all EU laws; and that some seats in the Parliament should be reserved for MEPs representing 'Europe-wide' parties, elected by voters from all the member states, on EU-wide lists.

The Commission's last crucial proposal, taking up the idea which had recently been winning such significant support, was that a change should be made to the 'closer co-operation' rules introduced in the Amsterdam Treaty. This would reduce to only a third the number of countries needed to sanction any move allowing a group of member states to integrate more closely on chosen issues and would remove the emergency brake. If a 'core group' wanted to forge ahead of the rest, this would eliminate the power of the others to stop them.

The IGC opens

Certainly the Commission and Parliament had set out a much more far-reaching shopping list for the Nice Treaty than anything so far agreed by the Council of Ministers. But the moment had now come for the member states themselves to get involved, as they began the process known as the Inter-Governmental Conference to hammer out the final agenda.

When ministers gathered in Brussels on 14 February 2000 for the formal start of the IGC process, President Prodi appeared before them to 'remind' them of what he described as 'a few simple points'.[24]

The first was that 'the question before us is enlargement', and how this must 'concentrate our minds on the absolute need for institutional change'.

The second was that 'we must not think, even for a moment, that this is just the beginning of reform' and that there would be other opportunities in the future.

Everything would have to be settled in one go. 'I see no room for a second IGC', said Prodi; 'we cannot countenance any leftovers from Nice'.

Most important of all, if the EU was to continue to work, was that there would have to be an end to national vetoes:

> I genuinely believe that, with 28 members, any areas that are still decided by unanimity will be condemned to stagnation.

But Mr Prodi then reminded them that 'we are still discovering the problems we face'; and that the Nice agenda would inevitably have to be extended from those Amsterdam leftovers. The Commission had already put forward its own suggestions. For example, the new treaty would have to take into account:

> ... the consolidation of the common foreign and security policy into a European security and defence policy;

and it would also need to review:

> the 'closer co-operation' arrangements which must be looked at again if a 28-member Union is to work.

With these brief points Mr Prodi left the ministers to begin their ten months of negotiation.

The British response

One Government which declared its hand right from the start was Britain's. On the day the IGC began, it issued a White Paper, *IGC: Reform for Enlargement*. This opened with a foreword by Tony Blair proclaiming that 'unlike its predecessors, this Government is unwaveringly pro-European'.[25]

After the usual platitudes about how 'the Government's approach to the IGC is part of a wider policy of getting more out of Europe by working within the European Union, rather than against it', the document explained the Government's position. This was largely focused on those three original core issues, the 'Amsterdam leftovers'.

The section on the make-up of the Commission recognised the logic of both the Commission's own proposals, without choosing between them. The same applied to the proposals on re-weighting votes. 'Whichever approach' was adopted, 'the right balance needs to be struck between the ease with which legislation can be passed or blocked'.

On reducing national veto powers, the Government similarly concluded that it would agree to an extension of qualified majority voting where this was 'in Britain's interests. But in areas of key national concern, we will insist on retaining unanimity.'

What was bizarre about this document was how little it contained in its glossy 38 pages. A succession of bland 'on the one hand, on the other' paragraphs revealed almost nothing of Britain's negotiating position, with the one exception of a firm commitment that Britain would 'insist on retaining unanimity' for 'key issues of national interest' including 'taxation, border controls, social security, defence and Own Resources' (i.e. payments into the EU budget).

There was a brief reference to the proposed 'restructuring of the treaties' (code for giving the EU its own constitution). Here the White Paper stated that 'a majority of Member States, including the UK, has made clear that this issue should not be discussed at this IGC'.

But the drafting skills of the officials were nowhere more in evidence than in the page devoted to downplaying what they explained was sometimes referred to as 'closer co-operation', although the FCO preferred the term 'flexibility'. This was defined as the suggestion that 'a core of Member States' might on occasion wish 'to move ahead with an activity while others stay out'. The White Paper loftily observed that:

> The Government feels that a stronger case will have to be made in order to justify procedures that were agreed only in 1997 and which have not yet been put to the test, or indeed used at all. The conditions governing the use of closer co-operation were intended to ensure that too much flexibility did not undermine the Single Market, or could not be used against the interests of a minority of Member States. These remain important objectives.

Not for a moment did the Government admit openly how alarmed it was becoming about the interest continental countries were now showing in the possibility of a 'core group' being permitted to 'move ahead'. But for insiders this careful wording plainly flagged up concern at the way things were moving. On this, as on other proposals, it was clear that, for the Blair Government at least, the road to Nice was suddenly threatening to become strewn with some rather large rocks.

Enter the 'avant-garde'

The next treaty was to be signed in December 2000. This meant it would come at the end of the six months when France held the EU presidency, giving the French Government the maximum chance to influence its contents. But no one, when the date was fixed, could have foreseen how important to the leaders of France and Germany such an opportunity would be.

The idea about to take centre stage in the debate over the future of the EU was the one put forward by Jacques Delors in his November speech to the Aspen Institute in Berlin, 'Our Historic Challenge: the Reunification of Europe'. In this speech, Delors proposed that an 'avant-garde' of EU countries should lead the way forward to full political integration ahead of the rest. The glory of this strategy was that, in one bold stroke, it could provide an answer to all the three major problems now giving such concern.

If the 'core group' were permitted to forge ahead on its own, this would create a 'two-tier Europe', an inner and an outer ring. The awkward British, with their refusal to join the euro, could be left in the outer ring. It would also enable the applicant countries from the East to be admitted to the outer ring, without having to give them full membership. And if the 'core group' could set up its own institutions, this might equally help resolve the third problem: it could sideline the Prodi Commission.

The new initiative first began to emerge in a speech given to the French Parliament by Lionel Jospin on 9 May 2000, to mark the fiftieth anniversary of the launching of the embryonic European Union by the French Foreign Minister Robert Schuman on 9 May 1950.[26] Jospin observed that 'Europe had established itself a model of integration unparalleled anywhere in the world.' He then sketched out how this process might be continued under the French presidency due to start at the end of the following month.

The first half of Jospin's speech was concerned with general points. 'Our first priority' he said, 'will be the adoption of a social agenda'. Economic modernisation in Europe was 'inseparable from the strengthening of the social model'. He then paid tribute to the 'success' of the euro, which had 'played the role of "shield" expected of it, thereby sheltering Europe from monetary turbulence' (an interesting point, since it had by now lost 25 per cent of its value against the dollar).

In a direct sideswipe at Britain, he went on to promise:

> We will also endeavour, despite some well known reluctance, to make headway on the tax harmonisation necessary for the proper functioning of the single market and the fight against unfair competition.

Mr Jospin outlined various steps towards bringing 'Europe closer to its citizens', such as setting up 'an independent European food authority'; 'real advances in the harmonisation of working hours in the transport sector'; and 'tightening up measures to prevent illegal immigration' (it was to be only a few weeks later that 58 Chinese immigrants were found dead at Dover, after having had no difficulty in boarding a lorry in Calais).

France's Prime Minister then came to the subject of the forthcoming treaty. He would not dwell in detail on the negotiations still in progress, but he did wish to underline how, to 'avoid paralysis' from the use of national vetoes, it would be essential to extend qualified majority voting in EU decision-making. France would also insist that the treaty included the Charter of Fundamental Rights, strongly favoured by Germany.

The real point he wished to make, however, went rather wider:

How can we make sure that the European Union, in enlarging, does not merely become a free trade area but continues to be a genuine community?

Mr Jospin referred to the ideas which had been floated about the setting-up of 'a federation' by 'a vanguard' or 'hard core of a few more closely integrated countries', and 'the drawing up of a European constitution'. 'Such thinking', Mr Jospin insisted, was 'legitimate and must be actively pursued', although 'it must also be realistic enough to be shared'.

He was unequivocal on one thing. 'To promote the process of European integration' it would be necessary to 'improve an institutional mechanism already existing in the European Union, reinforced co-operation'. 'This approach' would allow 'a few states to move faster and further' towards the goal; and 'we are all aware that this mechanism is vital'.

Mr Jospin's speech met with enthusiasm from other French politicians, and it was Daniel Cohn-Bendit, leader of the rebellious Parisian students in 1968 and now leader of the French Green Party in the European Parliament, who underlined an important sub-text. 'Tony Blair', he said, 'must be put on the spot. He is being depicted as a leader of Europe. In fact he is a brake on Europe.'[27]

Three days later, on 12 May, the new initiative was given much more powerful and unambiguous voice in a speech by Joschka Fischer, the German Foreign Minister, at Humboldt University in Berlin. Under the title 'From Confederacy to Federation: Thoughts on the Finality of European Integration', he declared that if the EU was to meet the historic challenge of enlargement without losing its capacity for action, 'we must put into place the last brick in the building of European integration, namely political integration'.[28]

This process, Fischer pointed out, had already begun:

The introduction of the euro was not only the crowning point of economic integration, it was also a profoundly political act; because a currency is not just an economic factor but also symbolises the power of the sovereign who guarantees it.

Similar advances, Fischer went on, had begun to be made in other areas. The European Council in Tampere had

> marked the beginning of a new far-reaching integration project, namely the development of a common area of justice and internal security, making the Europe of the citizens a tangible reality. But there is even more in this new integration project: common laws can be a highly integrative force.

Again, in the wake of the Kosovo War, the Cologne and Helsinki Councils had agreed on 'a new goal: the development of a Common Security and Defence Policy'. This was all quite logical. After all how could it be

> justified that countries inextricably linked by monetary union and by economic and political realities do not face up together to external threats and together maintain their security?

All this had so far been achieved by the 'Monnet method' of cooperation between sovereign governments. But now, with the prospect of enlargement to 30 members, it was a matter of highest urgency to recognise that, unless the most radical changes were made, the EU would become completely unworkable. These must be so far-reaching that, although 'the first step towards reform' might be taken in the forthcoming treaty at Nice, this would 'not in the long term be sufficient' for the integration that was needed.

There could only be one very simple answer:

> The transition from a union of states to full parliamentarisation as a European Federation, something Robert Schuman demanded 50 years ago. And that means nothing less than a European Parliament and a European Government which really do exercise legislative and executive power within the Federation.

Such a Federation would have to be based on 'a constituent treaty', creating a 'European constitution'.

Mr Fischer was tactfully keen to emphasise that such a Federation would not mean the complete 'abolition of the nation state':

I say this not least with an eye to our friends in the United Kingdom, because I know that the term 'federation' irritates many Britons. But to date I have been unable to come up with another word.

The treaty would have to draw a clear distinction between those areas which were to remain the responsibility of each nation state and those to be taken over by the new federal government. This could, for instance, be reflected in giving the European Parliament 'two chambers': one 'for elected members who are also members of their national parliaments', the other perhaps modelled on the American Senate, with 'directly elected senators from the member states'.

But even then, Mr Fischer went on, it might be difficult for 'all EU members to move ahead' at the same time. And in this case, it might be necessary to draw on the precedents of monetary union and Schengen, to look to a process of 'enhanced co-operation' allowing some states to move on ahead of the rest.

Fischer cited Jacques Delors, Helmut Schmidt and Valéry Giscard d'Estaing as having

> recently tried to find new answers to this dilemma. Delors' idea is that 'a federation of nation states' comprising the six founding states of the European Community should conclude 'a treaty within a treaty' with a view to making far-reaching reforms in the European institutions. Schmidt and Giscard's ideas are in similar vein, although they place the Euro-11 states at the centre.

But if the alternative facing the EU was 'either erosion or integration', and if it proved impossible to win the agreement of 'a majority of member states to take the leap into full integration', was not the only way forward then for 'a smaller group of member states' to 'take this route as an avant-garde?'

Should not 'a few member states which are staunchly committed to the European ideal, and are in a position to push ahead with integration' form a new 'centre of gravity'? 'Such a group of states would conclude a new European framework treaty', on the basis of which 'the Federation would develop its own institutions, establish a Government … a strong parliament and a directly elected president'.

Fischer was quick to point out that:

> Mechanisms would have to be developed which permit the members of the centre of gravity to co-operate smoothly with others in the larger EU.

But 'the steps towards such a constituent treaty' required 'a deliberate political act to re-establish Europe'. And if Europe's development was to continue 'far beyond the coming decade', 'one thing at least' was certain:

> No European project will succeed in future without the closest Franco-German co-operation.

As it happened, on the same day that Mr Fischer made his remarkable speech, the Italian Government published its official position on the Nice Treaty.[29] This showed complete support for the direction in which France and Germany were moving. Italy agreed the treaty should include a 'revision of enhanced cooperation mechanisms', by lowering the required threshold of votes needed to permit a smaller group of countries to integrate ahead of the rest:

> The recent history of the Union shows that, if enhanced co-operation mechanisms cannot be achieved within the institutional framework, they will come into play anyhow, but outside this framework.

Italy added that the need for qualified majority voting to be the general rule was another 'politically defining aspect' of the negotiations; that the treaty must include the 'Common Defence Policy'; and that the Charter on Fundamental Rights should be included 'as an annexed protocol which could become the core of the future European constitution'.

No one was happier about all these developments than the man who in a sense had set them in train with his Aspen Institute speech six months before. As the *éminence grise* of European integration, Jacques Delors gave a significant interview to *Libération* on 17 June 2000, in which he set out more clearly than ever just what the overall strategy might be.[30]

What he proposed was that, at Nice, the EU should set a December 2001 deadline for negotiations with all would-be member states whose discussions with the EU had 'reached an advanced stage'. In the meantime 'Europeans should have a frank discussion about what they want to achieve together.' Since complete agreement between all EU states was unlikely, 'we will have to create an avant-garde', open to all those countries who wished to join it and were in a position to do so. This 'Federation' was 'the only way to reconcile enlargement and deepening'.

The essence of Delors' proposal was that the EU would divide into two tiers. The 'avant-garde' would make up the 'Federation', with 'its own institutions', including 'its own Council of Ministers and its own Parliament'. The remaining countries, including the new members from the East, would be part of the wider Union.

The Commission 'would remain unchanged' since its responsibilities would still cover both Union and Federation, and the Federation would have its 'own institutions' to look after its particular interests. But in general so different would the status of the two tiers be that it might one day even be possible for the 'avant-garde countries' to send only 'a single representative' to meetings of the European Council; armed of course 'with the appropriate number of votes'.

One enormous advantage of this strategy, Mr Delors pointed out, was that it would get round the problem of the 'applicant countries'; 'particularly', he added in a tart reference to Poland, 'when we hear one of them demanding to benefit immediately from the entire Common Agricultural Policy and the free movement of people'. Under his proposals, such applicant states could be offered 'a place in the European fold without delay', because they would only be joining the wider Union, without having to be given all the benefits of full membership.

But in the same outer ring, of course, they would also be joining any of the existing member states which could not or did not wish to join the avant-garde. The most obvious candidate for that status, it was becoming clear in the summer of 2000, was Britain.

Fog in channel: continent isolated

It was somehow apt that, on the very day when Italy publicly joined Germany and France in insisting that a high priority for the Nice treaty should be the Charter of Fundamental Rights, the *Guardian* should report on its front page that the British Government was planning to 'block ambitious plans for a new European Charter of Fundamental Rights'.[31]

The specific point at issue here, as had emerged in the discussions of the 62-strong body which had been drafting the proposed Charter since the previous December, was the British Government's insistence that any such Charter should not be included in the treaty, and that it should only be 'a simple confirmation of existing rights' rather than setting out new ones.

This was not how it was seen by most continental governments, who saw the Charter as a crucial building block in European integration, laying out more than 50 'fundamental rights', including 'economic and social rights', to be enshrined in the treaty as EU law overriding all national laws, and ultimately enforceable by the European Court of Justice with power to overrule any national court.[32]

Britain's isolation on the Charter was merely another item to be added to that list of major issues on which she was now at odds with all or most of the other member states, from the harmonising of taxes to the elimination of almost all national vetoes.

But easily the most alarming of these, from the British Government's point of view, was this suddenly dawning prospect of a clause in the new treaty allowing an 'avant-garde' group of member states to move ahead towards political integration on their own. The reason why Mr Blair and his Ministers were so alarmed was that they were just beginning to grasp what an impossible position this would leave them in.

As supporters of Britain's membership of the European Union, the last thing they would want was for Britain to be left out in the cold, excluded from the top table, consigned to some kind of second-class status along with Poland and Slovenia. But they could also now see that the one absolutely essential condition which would have to be met if they were to remain in the inner club, which was most likely to be based on the euro zone, was that Britain must join the final stage of economic and monetary union, the single currency.

They further knew, of course, that, for that to happen, they would first have to win the support of the British people in a referendum. And not only did that already look for the foreseeable future highly problematical, with polls showing opposition to the euro rising above 70 per cent. If the British people came to realise that the real purpose of joining the single currency was to qualify Britain to join in the final moves towards the EU's political integration, any remaining chances of winning that referendum were likely to vanish in a puff of smoke.

By the end of May, Mr Blair and his colleagues could see how profoundly these latest manoeuvres on the continent had put them on the spot. Their first response was for senior ministers – including Robin Cook, Peter Mandelson and Stephen Byers – to make a series of somewhat agitated speeches in a desperate effort to reactivate the flagging campaign for Britain to join the euro. But this forlorn effort soon petered out, as it became apparent just how far the debate and general opinion in Britain had moved against them. This left Mr Blair the rest of the summer to puzzle over what had suddenly reared up at him as the most insoluble riddle of his premiership.

The only advantage he had in his travails was that, so far, few people in Britain had yet woken up to the extraordinary significance of what was going on across the Channel. But the determination of continental politicians to forge ahead with their new initiative was now hardening by the day. It scarcely held out much hope for Mr Blair that he might somehow be miraculously let off the hook.

Britain and Europe: the moment of truth

As the autumn of 2000 began, it was clear that not all was well in the European Union. As the euro plumbed new lows against the dollar, having lost more than a quarter of its original value, there were reports of doubts from various countries in the euro zone as to whether the experiment should be allowed to continue; most notably in Germany, where polls showed a two-to-one popular majority now hostile to the new currency, even before the psychologically crucial moment where it would take physical shape in notes and coins.

With world oil prices hitting their highest levels for nearly ten years, there were widespread popular protests, notably in France and Britain, against the record levels of fuel taxation. This was scarcely helped when it emerged that EU finance ministers had agreed at an Ecofin meeting in Versailles on 9 September not to lower their taxes on environmental grounds.

But on 28 September all this was overshadowed by the result of Denmark's referendum on the euro, when the news came through that the Danish people had snubbed their country's political, big business and media establishment in rejecting the euro by 53 per cent to 47 per cent.

What was interesting about the general response to the Danish vote was how widely it was interpreted across Europe as a popular revolt against the EU's relentless advance towards ever more political and economic integration. But the response of the EU's political elite, as *The Times* reported under the headline 'Europe's leaders shrug and carry on regardless', seemed only a determination to ignore the 'wider political message sent by the only nation that has been able to vote on this latest step towards ever closer union'.[33]

The European Commission's chief spokesman Jonathan Faule, according to *The Times*:

> ... denied that there was 'a yawning chasm' between Europe's political leaders and its people. He did not believe that the Danish vote amounted to 'a resounding rejection of the EU or of anything', or that 'the Commission got anything wrong whatever'.

In Berlin, Germany's Finance Minister Hans Eichel said that, while Denmark's decision was 'regrettable', 'European integration is an historic process which is irreversible. The sooner you join the better.' In Brussels, *The Times* reported:

> Commission officials privately predicted a new drive from countries such as Germany and France for a two-speed Europe in which more sceptical countries such as Britain are left behind. 'It bolsters the view of those who already believe they have a consensus among themselves to press ahead. It's another crack in the taboo about a two-speed Europe', one said.

In Paris, according to *The Times*:

> The 'no' was welcomed by pro-EU politicians and the media because it would reinforce the development of a two-tier Union, with the single currency bloc at its heart and non-members outside.

In Italy, *The Times* went on, *La Stampa* had pronounced in a front-page comment that it was

> a tragedy that 'a few thousand Hamlets' had been able to weaken not only the euro but the wider process of European integration. Coupled with British and Swedish hostility to the euro, this would lead to 'internal fracturing' of the European Union. The Danes had 'irresponsibly and selfishly' voted for reasons that were 'both irrational and foolish' without any thought for the damage to the European Union as a whole.

All this was taking place less than three months before the Nice Treaty; and already attention had been further focusing behind the scenes on the question of that crucial amendment on 'enhanced co-operation', which could allow the French and the Germans to proceed with the plan to set up a 'pioneer group' free of any threat of veto.

When the ministers making up the Inter-Governmental Conference had reconvened in Brussels after the summer holiday on 4 September, 'enhanced co-operation' had been top of their agenda. According to Agence Europe, the earlier opposition of some delegations, including Spain, had been 'smoothed away'. According to a source within the talks, 'the camp of total opponents' to the proposals allowing a 'core group' to forge ahead to form their own 'Federation' had now diminished to just four countries: Denmark, Sweden, Ireland and the United Kingdom.[34]

Despite its commitment to Denmark joining the euro, the Danish Government had thus expressed opposition to this proposal even before it knew the result of the referendum 24 days later. As for Sweden, ever since it joined the EU in 1995 the opinion polls had shown a consistent majority in favour of reversing the narrow 1994 referendum vote in favour of entry, and it was regarded as even less likely to join the euro than its Scandinavian neighbour.

Ireland, as the only one of the four already in the euro, was a peculiar case. Despite the Eurobarometer finding as late as July that Ireland registered the highest level of popular support for EU membership of any country in the Union, there was now a rising tide of scepticism. With a soaring inflation rate, Ireland was set to become the first victim of the euro zone's one-size-fits-all interest rate. Within a year or two, ahead of enlargement, the tidal wave of EU funding was expected to shrink drastically. Now the prospect of finding themselves isolated, without the UK, in a political federation dominated by France and Germany, was for the first time provoking even Europhile Irish ministers to express serious doubts about the EU's drive to political integration.[35]

As for the people of Britain, they were scarcely as yet aware that the prospect of 'enhanced co-operation' leading to a two-tier Europe existed. Nor were they aware, since their Government had never bothered to tell them, on just what a range of other key issues to be covered in the forthcoming Nice Treaty Britain was now in a minority of opposition to most or all of her partners. These included:

- extension of majority voting and an end to national vetoes
- tax harmonisation
- the Charter of Fundamental Rights
- a 'constitution' for the EU.

But the most important issue of all, it now seemed, was 'enhanced co-operation' and the abolition of that 'emergency brake' which would allow Britain to veto any move to set up a 'pioneer group' moving ahead to political integration. And once the most Eurosceptical people in the EU realised they might soon have to share second-class status on the Union's outer fringes with applicant countries from the East, like Cyprus, Slovenia and the Czech Republic, it was hardly likely this would increase their enthusiasm for remaining in the European Union at all.

So familiar has this development become that we do not really appreciate just how debilitating it is to our political life; all because we never face up openly to what the project is about and that its real agenda is the ceaseless drive to integration, brick added to brick: Single Market, single currency, single economy, single foreign policy, single defence policy, single legal space, until unification is complete.

In fact it was all there right from the beginning in October 1962, when a much younger Edward Heath was first trying to negotiate our entry into the Common Market, and the two party leaders of the time made speeches to their party conferences on what had suddenly become the biggest political issue of the day and the source of the most fundamental divide in British politics.

On the one hand was Hugh Gaitskell, warning the Labour Party of the dangers of going into 'Europe', using his famous phrase about 'the end of a thousand years of history'.[36] What people often forget is the context in which he used that phrase. The point he asked his audience to consider was the question:

> What does federalism mean? It means that powers are taken from national governments and handed over to federal governments. It means – and I repeat it – that if we go into this we are no more than a state in the United States of Europe, such as Texas and California ... we must be clear about this: it does mean, if this is the idea, the end of Britain as an independent European state. It means the end of a thousand years of history.[37]

On the other hand, a week after Gaitskell's speech, as Harold Macmillan was trying to woo the Tory faithful in Llandudno into supporting Britain's entry into the Common Market, he quoted the words of an old music hall song:

> She wouldn't say 'yes', she wouldn't say 'no'
> She wouldn't say 'stay', she wouldn't say 'go';
> She wanted to climb, but she dreaded to fall,
> So she bided her time, and clung to the wall.

Macmillan used this song to ridicule all those like Gaitskell who were fearful of what Britain was letting herself in for by cutting loose from her history and throwing in her destiny with this new continental experiment. But how telling his words were later to become, in summing up the position to which the issue of 'Europe' has reduced almost every British Prime Minister since: with the exception of Heath, whose determination to get us in was so total that it could not admit any shadow of a doubt.

Nice and Mr Blair

The heart of the problem, as the Nice Treaty approaches, is that, after 27 years of being the most conspicuously reluctant member of the club, Britain has in effect been confronted by its partners with an ultimatum. If the EU splits into two camps, the avant-garde and the outer ring, Mr Blair knows the one essential admission ticket to the inner club is membership of the single currency. But he cannot take Britain into the euro without winning a referendum, which he knows, in the immediate future, would be all but impossible. He therefore faces the prospect of being frozen out of the core group as it moves on to political union, with Britain consigned to second-class status.

If Britain is to remain as part of that 'wider Union' outlined by Jacques Delors, we obviously do not know precisely what such a status might involve because no one has yet given it any thought. All the intellectual energy of Mr Delors and his allies has been concentrated on thinking about the nature of the new 'Federation', which would rule the roost at the heart of the Union.

No doubt the 'fringe' members of the new EU such as Britain would continue to enjoy access to the Single Market, so long as they complied with the mountain of directives and regulations which are the required rules of membership. But of course that in itself does not necessitate membership of the EU, as Norway, Switzerland and Mexico among other non-EU countries have demonstrated.

More questionable would be whether we could continue as part of the CAP, since one of the triggers for the idea of an inner core has been the impracticability of admitting the new Eastern European members to all the supposed benefits of the CAP. Unless there is to be a three-tier membership, Britain could hardly remain in the CAP if other fringe members were excluded.

There would, of course, be huge pressure on Britain to remain in the Common Fisheries Policy, since Britain's fishing waters contain up to 80 per cent of Western Europe's fish; yet more than 80 per cent in value of the fish caught in those waters are allocated under the quota system to other EU states.

Other highly questionable areas would include the Common Foreign Policy and the new Common Defence Policy, since so many of the decisions shaping these would inevitably be taken by the new

Federation, with its own policy-making institutions and procedures. And since a large part of the purpose of these was to further political integration, it might seem odd for Britain to remain bound by their rules and requirements when it has been excluded from that process of further political integration.

Most questionable of all, perhaps, would be Britain's relationship with the Federation's economic policy, since another key element in forming the inner core is that it should make it much easier to integrate its members' economies according to the aims of Economic and Monetary Union. Yet it is little appreciated that, despite not having signed up to stage three of EMU, the single currency, Britain is nevertheless fully signed up to stages one and two, which already place very considerable constraints on its freedom to run its own fiscal and budgetary policies. Again, since a Federation based on the euro zone would be centrally concerned with integrating its own economic and monetary policies, it might seem strange for Britain to remain part of a system over which, by definition, it would have even less influence than if it had joined the euro.

The truth is that, although it may at least in theory be possible to see how the proposed new Federation might work, it is extraordinarily hard to see how in practice Mr Delors' proposed 'wider Union' could possibly work at all. The fact is that no one has yet given any thought to it, because all the concerns of those who support the idea of a Federation are focused elsewhere.

One might observe how odd it is that all the thinking on issues so hugely important to Britain's future has so far been coming from France and Germany, and that no one in Britain itself seems to have given much thought as to how this country's interests might best be served under the kind of arrangement now being so actively discussed on the continent. But one might also observe that possibly one of the central intentions of the 'core group' initiative is precisely that our continental partners no longer wish to be troubled by having to think about Britain's concerns.

It may even just be that, to solve their own problems as much as ours, they hope the British will take Lord Jenkins' advice, and 'move towards an orderly and, if possible, reasonably amicable withdrawal' from the whole project. But if this is to be the end of the story, then of course it will not be taking place as a result of any initiative by the British themselves. It will only happen because, after 30 years of tolerating Britain's fractious, semi-detached participation in a project to which it came late and always remained an outsider, its partners could put up with it no longer.

The prospect which has come into view through the events of the year 2000 is not that Britain may decide as an act of its own will to leave the European Union. It is that the European Union may have set itself on a course which makes it impossible for Britain to remain within it. It will be 'Europe' which leaves Britain, rather that the other way round. What a curious reflection it would be on the state of dependence to which those 30 years have reduced Britain's political class if the impetus for such an outcome should have had to come from our continental partners rather than from any decision of the British people themselves.

Notes

1. Fischer speech of 12 May 2000 at Humboldt University reported in British Management Data Foundation (BMDF), 7 June 2000. Although Fischer had been keen to emphasise that he was only offering a 'personal view' which did not represent his Government's policy, it was to become clear as the summer progressed that this reflected the informal discussions going on between German, French and other EU leaders (as when Fischer's thinking was later echoed by President Chirac) and that it represented the beginning of a concerted initiative between the various governments involved.
2. Lord Jenkins of Hillhead, former President of the European Commission, conference speech, 22 March 1999.
3. *The Times*, 23 November 1998.
4. Conclusions of the Ecofin Council Meeting concerning taxation policy, 98/C 2/01, 1 December 1997, *Official Journal of the European Communities*, 6 January 1998.
5. *Daily Mail*, 25 November 1998.
6. Ibid.
7. Ibid., 26 November 1998; *Guardian*, 27 November 1998.
8. *Daily Telegraph*, 27 November 1998.
9. Ibid., 26 November 1998.
10. *Financial Times*, *The Times*, 27 November 1998.
11. *Daily Telegraph*, 27 November 1998.
12. Ibid., 28 November 1998.
13. Paul van Buitenen, *Blowing the Whistle: One man's fight against fraud in the European Commission*, Politico's, 2000.
14. *The Times*, 19 January 1999.
15. Prodi speech, as reported in the *Daily Telegraph*, 14 April 1999.
16. *Daily Telegraph*, 14 April 1999.
17. *The Times*, 24 April 1999.
18. Speech by Gerhard Schroeder, Frankfurt, translated by BMDF, 8 September 1999.
19. Agence Europe, 10/11 January 2000.
20. Speech to the Aspen Institute, Berlin by Jacques Delors, 'Our Historic Challenge: the Reunification of Europe', 14 November 1999.

21. Agence Europe, 10/11 January 2000.
22. Ibid.
23. Commission Opinion on the reform of the institutions of the European Union, 26 January 2000 and Prodi speech to European Parliament on the same day.
24. Prodi speech to IGC, General Affairs Council, 24 February 2000.
25. *IGC, Reform for Enlargement: The British approach to the EU Inter-Governmental Conference*, FCO, Com 4595, 14 February 2000.
26. Jospin's speech to the French Parliament, BMDF translation, 9 June 2000.
27. *The Times*, 10 May 2000.
28. See note 1.
29. Agence Europe, 13 May 2000.
30. *Libération*, 17 June 2000; Agence Europe 23 June 2000.
31. *Guardian*, 13 May 2000.
32. The Charter of Fundamental Rights (not to be confused with the European Convention on Human Rights, incorporated into UK law on 1 October 2000) was being drawn up by a 62-strong convention deliberately modelled on the Philadelphia convention which drafted the US constitution in 1787. Its members came from the European Commission, the European Parliament and national Parliaments. The draft contained 54 articles, under the headings 'Dignity', 'Freedoms', 'Equality', 'Solidarity', 'Justice' and 'General Provisions'.
33. This and the quotes which follow come from *The Times*, 30 September 2000.
34. Agence Europe, 6 September, 2000.
35. On 18 September, Sile de Valera, Ireland's Minister for Arts and Culture and former President de Valera's grand-daughter, broke ranks by making a speech in which she warned that 'while the Irish Government is promoting policies of decentralisation, in the European Union the opposite is taking place, with the push towards closer integration. It is a move I would not personally favour. It is not necessarily in our interests.' In calling on her country 'to express a more vigilant, more questioning attitude to the European Union', Ms de Valera was supported by Ireland's Deputy Prime Minister, Mary Harney, who said 'Ireland favours a Europe of nation states, not a centralised superstate or United States of Europe.' Despite calls for the Irish Prime Minister Bertie Ahern to 'repudiate the speech in its entirety', he declined to comment (Press Association report, 19 September 2000).
36. Hugh Gaitskell's Brighton speech 1962, reprinted in M. Holmes (ed.), *The Eurosceptic Reader*, Macmillan, now Palgrave, 1996.
37. It was interesting that, nearly 40 years later, a Labour Foreign Secretary, Robin Cook, should use the same analogy, of becoming no more than a 'Texas or California' in a federal Europe, to make exactly the reverse point, by dismissing as absurd that anyone could want such a thing to happen.

13
Aiming for the Heart of Europe: A Misguided Venture

John Bercow

Conflicting views of the aim of the European Economic Community

The founding fathers of the Treaty of Rome had three objectives. First, to achieve peace in Western Europe and the reconciliation of France and Germany. Structures were to be created that would render impossible a repetition of the wars of the 1780s, 1870, 1914 and 1939. Secondly, to form a customs union, and importantly not a free trade area, with high external tariffs, facilitating the emergence of a strong trade block in Western Europe. Thirdly, to build an alternative superpower to rival the United States and the Soviet Union.

The Treaty of Rome called for 'an ever closer union among the peoples of Europe' but, beyond the goal of a Common Market, it provided for common domestic policies only in the spheres of agriculture and transport. However, the reference to ever closer union, and the stated wishes of European leaders, meant that you did not have to be Sherlock Holmes to sense what was in store for us. The Schuman Plan, devised by Monnet and Schuman, aimed

> to place the French and German production of coal and steel as a whole under a common 'higher authority' within the framework of an organisation open to the participation of the other countries of Europe ... by pooling basic production and by instituting a new high authority whose decisions will bind France, Germany and other member countries.

It added 'This proposal will lead to the realisation of the first concrete foundations of a European federation.' Interestingly, in his memoirs, Monnet recalls remarking at a dinner that 'the British will not find their future role by themselves: only outside pressure will force them to change'.

Initially, Conservative statesmen perceived the federal or centralised Europe that was in prospect and wanted no part of it. Churchill, in his 1947 Temple of World Peace Speech, emphasised that the Temple would have four pillars: the United States of America, the Soviet Union, a United Europe and the British Empire and Commonwealth. He radiated goodwill towards the idea of a United States of Europe but saw the future of Britain as being outside it.

In 1962, Anthony Eden foresaw the direction in which the EEC was intent on travelling. He said:

> The experiment of the Six cannot succeed without federation and I think it most probable that if we join the six we shall be faced with that decision in a few years time. I am sure that it must be federation in the sense of one parliament, one foreign policy, one currency etc. So far as I can judge events in the continent of Europe, I do not want to become a part of such a federation.

Despite Eden's prescience, Conservative Prime Ministers from Macmillan onwards sought to place Britain at the heart of this process. Variously, they either believed, or simply conveyed the impression, that they could halt the process of European integration and instead replace continental ideas with an Anglo-Saxon model for the new Europe.

Harold Macmillan personified a generation of Conservatives who accepted the inevitability of the end of empire and realised that Britain could no longer afford an imperial role. To Macmillan, and like-minded fellows, a new role for Britain would be found in the European Economic Community. We could provide the Europeans with political leadership due to our diplomatic experience, special relationship with the United States and skills in negotiation. Britain would have a new Empire on her doorstep.

Macmillan misjudged the determination of the founding fathers of the European Communities to achieve their federal goal. That goal was incompatible with the British vision of a Europe of sovereign nations dedicated to free trade and cooperation. There could be only one winner in the battle over the future of Europe and it would not be Britain. The first rebuttal came with De Gaulle's veto over Macmillan's application for British membership of the EEC. De Gaulle said:

> England, in effect, is insular. She is maritime. She is linked through her exchanges, her markets, her supply lines to the most distant countries. She pursues essentially industrial and commercial activi-

ties and only slightly agricultural ones. She has, in all her doings, very marked and very original habits and traditions. In short, England's nature, England's structure, England's very situation differs profoundly from those of the Continentals.

The agenda and tactics of Edward Heath were different. He simply misled the British public until he achieved British membership of the EEC. The 1971 White Paper, proposing Britain's entry to the Community, a copy of which was sent to every household in Britain, emphasised that there was 'no question of Britain losing essential sovereignty'. Heath dismissed fears of a loss of independence as 'completely unjustified' and was at pains to reassure the doubters that Britain would keep control of her own affairs. 'No nation' in the Community would be able to 'over-ride another', the vital interests of Britain would be guaranteed and, above all, she would keep her own Parliament, courts and legal systems. On the strength of this propaganda blitz, you may think that Mr Peter Mandelson and Mr Alastair Campbell have been wrongly credited as the inventors of 'spin' and that Edward Heath had mastered the technique some 25 years earlier. I could not possibly comment.

Of course, Heath was not acting alone. In 1972, his Solicitor General, Sir Geoffrey Howe, said that a common market was at the heart of the Community, and added: 'The impact of the Community law is, by definition, confined to essentially economic matters.'

In practice, Community law has extended far beyond such matters but it is only fair to record that in order to secure Britain's entry to the EEC, Heath gave in on the 'essentially economic matter' of Britain's fishing rights, notwithstanding repeated pledges by his chief negotiator, Geoffrey Rippon, that the Government would not do so.

Given Heath's pre-entry assurances, and the remarks of Geoffrey Howe, it is interesting to note that in 1990, when asked by interviewer Peter Sissons whether, when he took Britain into Europe, he really had in mind 'a united states of Europe, with a single currency', Heath replied 'of course, yes.' Whether Heath confided in Sir Geoffrey at the time, we do not know. I think we should be told.

The impact of the European treaties on Britain

The Single European Act (1986)

As we have seen, signing the Treaty of Rome committed Britain to a common market, common agricultural and transport policies and the significant but unelaborated goal of 'ever closer union amongst the peoples of Europe'. Accession to the European Communities also entailed the primacy of Community law over our own. Despite the professed aim to create a common market, the Community concluded that it had not been achieved. Hence the need for the next major milestone in the development of the Community, the Single European Act of 1986. Margaret Thatcher was herself a driving force behind the Act and some of her Ministers positively fizzed with enthusiasm about the Single Market which it spawned. She and they believed that the Act achieved the Thatcherisation of Europe through the furtherance of free trade. Perhaps the fact that the then Commission President, Jacques Delors, an avowed socialist, was a passionate advocate of the Act and the Single Market should have sounded the alarm bells to British Conservative leaders, but it did not.

The Act provided for a major extension of qualified majority voting. There are 87 votes in the Council of Ministers, weighted loosely according to size of population; 62 are required to pass a proposal and 26 to block it. The UK has 10. The Act also reduces the use of the national veto and substantially increases the number of European Union competences, notably in environmental and social policies. It also conferred new powers upon the European Assembly, now the European Parliament. The European Commission ruthlessly used the Single Market programme to push through a determined harmonisation programme. This entailed no fewer than 1,368 directives, and a mass of attendant regulations, that were binding upon Britain. As a result, a uniform, heavily regulated Europe emerged, instead of what Britain had envisaged: a diverse, freely trading Community in which products would be mutually recognised. Ludicrous examples included carrots being defined as a fruit when applied to jam made from the vegetable and laws being proposed on the noise made by lawn mowers. British industries were hit particularly hard when having to comply with the harmonisation legislation. All firms had to comply with the Single Market legislation even if they had no intention of exporting their products. Yet only about 30 per cent of our output is sold abroad, under half of which goes to the European Union. Despite this we had to suffer the triple torture of more red tape; the burden of harmonisation on businesses, making it harder for many of them to export; and the fact that many countries ignored the rules of the Single Market, continuing to protect and subsidise their own industries. While the Market may now be functioning effectively in some industries and parts of Europe, it is a disservice to the debate to pretend that it is an unqualified success. It is not.

Examples abound of the damage done to our businesses by a number of directives: 400 smaller abattoirs, half the total number of slaughterhouses in the UK, have been forced to close because they could not afford the cost of compliance with new EC export standards – which they had to satisfy even if they did not export. The Recreational Craft Directive, which came into force on 16 June 1999, requires thousands of small boat builders to comply with 50 new safety standards. It is expected to raise the price of yachts, motor cruisers and other pleasure craft by up to 15 per cent, forcing many small boat builders out of business. The Taxation of Savings Directive, imposing a withholding tax, will raise costs, and plans to compel the payment of royalties on all sales and resales of works by artists still alive and for up to 70 years after their deaths have already dealt a swingeing blow to the London art market which hitherto yielded Britain £2 billion per annum in foreign earnings. These effects are a far cry from the rhetoric of removing barriers, boosting trade and increasing opportunity which accompanied the launch of the Single Market.

The Treaty of Maastricht (1992)

If the Single European Act was significant, the Maastricht Treaty was if anything still more so. Sadly, the tendency of successive Prime Ministers to claim that they were winning the argument in Europe, and that Britain was punching above her weight, applied to John Major. He was the master of this genre and returned from the Maastricht Summit to proclaim that Britain had won game, set and match in the negotiations. Scrutiny of the Treaty, and events since, show that in fact he suffered a straight sets defeat.

It confers on Community institutions a breathtaking raft of new powers in respect of a range of subjects from roads to consumer protection, from training to the environment. The number of areas in which the European Commission has the sole right of legislative initiative increased from 11 to 20 and the Treaty provided for 111 increases in qualified majority voting. There are more powers for the European Parliament too.

You might question whether there is enough common ground between the member states to facilitate a common foreign and security policy but moves towards it were made. The policy allows 'joint actions' which, we are told, 'shall commit the member states in the positions they adopt and in the conduct of their activity'.

John Major did win consolation prizes of 'opt outs' from the Social Chapter and the single currency. With a cavalier disregard for the potential costs to British industry, the present Government has thrown away the first concession and signed the wretched Chapter. The second opt out is valuable, but it is only from the single currency itself. Britain is still committed to the first two stages of economic and monetary union.

The Treaty of Amsterdam (1997)

The Amsterdam Treaty continues the onward march of the federalists. The Treaty extends qualified majority voting to 16 new policy areas. Few of them relate directly to trade or competition which were the original pretexts for QMV in the Single European Act. Employment, equal opportunities, research and development, public health, 'social exclusion' and statistics all form part of the EU's agenda.

The European Parliament also received a significant boost at Amsterdam. This is no cause for good cheer amongst Conservatives or other supporters of British national sovereignty. For many federalists hanker after a more powerful European Parliament as the basis for a supposedly democratic European state. That is why they have consistently pressed for the extension of 'co-decision', the one form of European legislation which, instead of giving the balance of power to the Council of Ministers, accords the Parliament and the Council equal status. The Amsterdam Treaty extends co-decision to 27 new areas of policy including employment, equal opportunities, social policy and transport. This will do nothing to enhance competitiveness and could well be used in such a way as to undermine it. Yet the Prime Minister, far from being a bulldog on the subject, has been a poodle of our European partners, uttering not a word of protest.

The Treaty establishes a new Employment Chapter, which gives Brussels a role in coordinating the employment policies of the member states.

Health and safety at work, working conditions, information to, and consultation of workers, the 'integration of persons excluded from the labour market' and policies on sexual equality will all be determinable by qualified majority voting. Furthermore, the Treaty moves further to a common foreign and security policy and a common defence policy.

The Amsterdam Treaty is not a recipe for diversity but a menu of uniformity. Centralising power, reducing the veto and deepening integration, it flies in the face of the Conservative vision of European cooperation. It is clear enough now why Jacques Delors, speaking to the European Parliament in July 1988, predicted that by 1998 the European Community would be the source of 80 per cent of our economic legislation and perhaps even our fiscal and social legislation as well. He was not merely celebrating the 1986 Single European Act but planning the next moves on the chessboard of Community politics.

What is the effect of successive Governments' quest to be at the heart of Europe? We are now signed up to a European Union which has a Parliament, a passport, a citizenship, a flag and an anthem and which wants a single currency, a single army and a single foreign policy. Of these, a single currency is the most imminent prospect.

The political motivation for the single currency

This is not the occasion for a detailed study of the arguments for or against Britain's entry to a single currency. However, as support for entry is high on the agenda of most of those who advocate that this country should be at the heart of Europe, it is as well to look at some of the economic and, in particular, the political considerations.

Economic

British membership of a single European currency is not an obviously sensible economic proposition. Our business cycle has long been out of step with that of continental Europe and there is no evidence that convergence, if it happens, will be more than a meeting of ships which pass in the night. The start-up costs for business will be enormous, hitting small firms and retailers the hardest. We could no longer use the exchange rate to absorb shocks, be they rises in prices or the impact of natural disasters. Moreover, membership of a single currency will prevent member states taking policy decisions to react to asymmetric shocks, e.g. the collapse in confidence in the Russian economy. The UK's pattern of trade is global, not continental, and that pattern is set to continue. Sterling does not move with the European currencies but is influenced also by the US dollar. Changes in the European interest rate would affect this nation of homeowners far more directly than those of other EU member states. This country has funded its pension arrangements – others have not funded theirs. A single monetary policy will need to be accompanied by a single fiscal, i.e. tax policy, as the President of the Bundesbank has freely acknowledged. Unlike the United States, the European Union does not have the labour mobility that is a prerequisite of a successful currency union. The unemployed of Lewisham will not shift to Luxembourg to get a job. As the Governor of the Bank of England, Eddie George, has observed 'it's less likely that people will be able to move to where the work is because of language and cultural differences'. Above all, the single currency entails a 'one-size-fits-all' policy. A single interest rate would apply to every member of EMU whatever its economic situation. That rate would usually be either too high or too low. The single currency would be the permanent form of the Exchange Rate Mechanism of which Britain was a member from October 1990 until September 1992. In barely 23 months, unemployment went up from 1.67 million to 2.85 million, interest rates were artificially high for too long and rose briefly to 15 per cent, thousands of people saw their homes repossessed and many others were driven into bankruptcy.

I hope the ten economic considerations cited above give cause for thought.

Political

For me, the political objections to British entry to a single currency are the most compelling. Yet I was reminded recently that the political implications are not always recognised. An intelligent woman, whom I like and respect, came up to me and advanced the most common economic argument for the single currency. 'I would like such a currency', she said, 'because I wouldn't have to change money when I go abroad in Europe.' I said that if that was all the single currency were about, I would agree with her. 'Isn't it?', she replied.

Let us be clear. We are not talking about a common currency, but about a single currency. Whilst some opinion polls have been seemingly ambiguous on the subject of the single currency, these polls, without exception, have not mentioned that Britain's joining the single currency will entail the abolition of the pound and the recalculation of everything into euros, from shop prices to pension entitlements. Those polls that have mentioned the obligation to abolish the pound have all recorded a significant majority against Britain joining a single currency. The most recent Gallup poll, for example, showed that 65 per cent of respondents were against British entry to a single currency on this basis and only 33 per cent in favour. Amongst Conservatives, the figures were 76 per cent and 23 per cent respectively.

The legal framework is clear. Under the single currency, the European Central Bank will be responsible for monetary policy. It is prohibited by Article 108 of the Treaty of Amsterdam from seeking or taking instructions from any other body, even a democratically elected body, about its conduct of monetary policy. Equally, member states undertake not to seek to influence the Bank. So the Bank, comprising people whom we will not elect and cannot remove, will be empowered to make decisions affecting millions of British people. Yet their elected representatives have foresworn any attempt to influence those decisions. Stripped of the verbiage, that is the brutal reality of the single currency project. It will be no use electors complaining to the Government, let alone their local MP, about the effect of the ECB's policies. We should be mindful too that the Bank intends to regulate member states' borrowing and deficit levels and to bring about economic, as well as monetary, union. In short, a single currency means a single monetary policy, a single budgetary policy, a single fiscal policy, a single economy, a single Government and a single state. This is the federal European state which many member states want, which has long been developing by stealth but which virtually every British democratic politician except Sir Edward Heath and the Liberal Democrats claims to oppose. Politics has long been the driving force of the architects of the single currency. That is why the convergence criteria have been fudged – economics plays second fiddle to politics.

Let the politicians speak for themselves. Chancellor Kohl, speaking in the Bundestag on 13 March 1991, said pithily; 'However important the completion of economic and monetary union, it would remain mere patchwork unless political union were established simultaneously. These two undertakings are, in our opinion, inseparable.'

Yet the prize for candour must surely go to the former Prime Minister of Spain, Felipe Gonzalez, who wrote in May 1998:

> The single currency is the greatest abandonment of sovereignty since the foundation of the European Community ... It is a decision of an essentially political nature ... We need this united Europe ... we must never forget that the euro is an instrument for this project.

The application of subsidiarity

Article 3B

Even without a single currency, the powers of the European Union over member states have increased exponentially over the last decade or so. John Major understood the growing public anxiety that Community dictat was becoming ever more widespread. In an apparent effort to allay concern, the Maastricht negotiators produced the so-called 'subsidiarity' principle. Actually, it was not novel and had been espoused by the Vatican in Rome when Mussolini was in power. However, Community leaders enshrined the concept in Article 3B of the Maastricht Treaty and said it meant that decisions should be taken at the lowest possible level. What does the article say and what does it really mean?

> In areas which do not fall within its exclusive competence, the Community shall take action, in accordance with the principle of subsidiarity, only if and in so far as the objectives of the proposed action cannot be sufficiently achieved by the member states and can, therefore, by reason of the scale or effects of the proposed action be better achieved by the Community.

Two objections to this immediately arise. First, the article is not saying that action will be taken at the lowest level, as its supporters claim, but rather that the Community shall act if it judges it necessary to do so.

Secondly, if there is a dispute between the European Union and a member state as to which should be empowered to act, it is justiciable by the European Court of Justice. It is not an impartial arbiter but a body which is committed to European integration and which prides itself on a 'dynamic' approach to EU law. In the Court's hands, application of the law has often been replaced by its invention. This hardly inspires confidence in the likely robustness of subsidiarity. Moreover, it can be argued that the notion of subsidiarity, far from being a tool of decentralisation, is in fact an admission that powers rest with the European state and that it will decide which of them it delegates. Suffice it to say that the wording of the article fully warranted the description of it by Lord Mackenzie Stuart, a former President of the European Court of Justice, as a 'prime example of gobbledygook'. He averred that to regard it as a constitutional safeguard showed 'great optimism'.

A crucial test of the robustness of the provision came on 12th March 1996 when the Advocate General gave his opinion on the Working Time Directive. He said 'in view of the fact that the objective provided for in article 118a is harmonisation, there is no doubt that the aim of the contested directive can be better achieved by action at Community level than by action at national level'. So those who hoped that we could preserve sovereignty over our domestic working practices were to be disappointed. Subsidiary had been hyped and John Major had suggested that it could serve to scrap 25 per cent of European regulations but Article 3b has not brought about the repeal of a single directive or regulation. If anything, it has been a cloak for further centralisation.

Protocol on subsidiarity and proportionality

The Treaty of Amsterdam makes a bad situation worse. It contains a protocol on subsidiarity and proportionality. It states:

> The application of the principles of subsidiarity and proportionality shall respect the general provisions and objectives of the Treaty, particularly as regards the maintaining in full of the acquis communautaire and the institutional balance; it shall not affect the principles developed by the Court of Justice regarding the relationship between national and Community law, and it should take into account Article F4 of the Treaty on European Union, according to which the Union shall provide itself with the means necessary to attain its objectives and carry through its policies.

In other words, where the Union already has power, it will not relinquish it. No net decentralisation can be expected. Moreover, Section 3 of the protocol states that 'Community action within the limits of its powers' may 'be expanded where circumstances so require'.

The protocol does specify criteria which should be met before Community action can be taken. First, an issue should be 'transnational' in character. Many would contend that the regulation of working hours is not a matter of transnational concern. The Community, backed by the Court of Justice, insisted otherwise. In truth, there is no agreed definition of 'transnational' for this purpose. Secondly, for Community action to be taken, it should be necessary for the requirements of the Treaty to be fulfilled. This is no protection. Those who want maximum Community action need only draft clauses that either require or allow it. Thirdly, there should be benefits in scale or effect to justify Community action. The disbenefits in scale and effect of the Working Time Directive across the EU should have prevented its adoption but they did not. The truth is that the Community has only to invoke the 'general provisions and objectives' of the Treaty to proceed as it wishes.

At the last count, in 1995, there were reported to be 24,000 regulations having immediate effect and 1,700 directives to which member countries must give effect through their domestic legislatures. Subsidiarity, which had been claimed as a benefit from the heart of Europe approach pursued at Maastricht, proved irrelevant as regulations increased by over 1500 and directives by 120 in 1994 alone. This panoply of measures is part of the tidal wave of European law long lamented by our most celebrated judge, Lord Denning.

The cost of British membership of the European Union

It is estimated that the annual cost of Britain's membership of the European Union is £10 billion in gross budgetary contributions. Of that sum, a little over half is returned in EU spending. The tendency of euro partisans to cite a lower figure as the 'net' or 'real' cost of membership is a trifle cheeky, however, as it erroneously assumes that EU monies are spent in Britain just as we would choose. This point has been powerfully made by Norman Lamont.

The Common Agricultural Policy jacks up our food prices to the tune of £6 billion per annum, though about half of that sum is rebated directly to our farmers. At a conservative estimate, therefore, our membership costs a minimum of £8 billion per annum, or 1 per cent of GDP, and probably rather more than that. This bald figure takes no account either of the costs of regulation or of the loss of sovereignty we experience, though both are considerable. Those costs and that loss are incurred in the name of under 15 per cent of our output.

Despite these costs, those who insist on continued British membership cite our trade with the EU as a benefit which alone outweighs the undoubted costs. This thesis ignores a number of inconvenient facts. First, as Conrad Black has reminded us, if we include exports which are shipped on through Rotterdam and other European ports outside the EU and overseas investment earnings are included, the EU takes about 40 per cent of our total exports. As a proportion of our total output, sales to the EU amount to less than 15 per cent of our GDP. Secondly, we currently have an annual trade deficit of £3 billion with the EU. Thirdly, over the last ten years, direct net investment in the UK from the US and Canada has been half as much again as we have received from the European Union. Similarly, our net investment in North America has been more than double UK investment in the EU. In view of these numbers, the knee-jerk reaction of Euro fanatics that life for Britain outside the EU would yield untold economic devastation seems misplaced. The EU needs us for trade at least as much as we need it. Under the auspices of the World Trade Organisation, the Uruguay Round of trade liberalisation agreements has cut the EU's common external tariff from 5.7 per cent to 3.6 per cent and the drive for freer world trade should bring about further reductions. At least as important, both commercially and psychologically, is the evidence that other European countries outside of the EU happily trade with it. For example, Swiss exports to the EU have grown faster than those of Britain. Norway can tell a similar story. Outside of Europe, both Japan and the United States enjoyed faster export growth to the EU than Britain in the ten years from 1983 to 1993. Moreover, the proportion of Canadian output exported to the US is four times that of Britain but Canada sees no need to share a court, a parliament or a currency with the Americans.

The reality is that Britain is a global trading nation. We sell our wares wherever we can and our success, especially since our economy was restored to health under Conservative Governments, has been conspicuous. That success is not contingent upon the EU. Our trade surplus until recently with every other continent bar Europe is testimony to the fact that we provide goods and services of a quality people want and at prices they can pay. That is why in telecommunications, in oil, in civil engineering, and in financial services, to name but a few, our trade is soaring. Politics forms no part of the equation save in so far as it creates a framework of open markets.

Two further reasons are adduced as to why we must stay in the European Union at all costs. First, we are reminded of the huge inward investment that we receive, notably from North America and Japan. Indeed, Britain attracts approximately 40 per cent of the total, more than any other member state. Europhiles present a doomsday scenario in which there would be an exodus of this investment if we were outside the EU. Access to the European market may be important to those inward investors but trade liberalisation agreements mean that access is not at risk. Surveys of foreign direct investors into the UK suggest that several other factors are uppermost in their minds when they choose Britain. Our costs and taxes are lower. Our labour market is more flexible. Our industrial relations are better. Our inflation is low. Our language has global reach. Our public administration is honest and we enjoy political and social stability.

The political argument for our EU membership is that we carry more weight as part of a block of countries than if we act alone. This is what might be described as a political economy of scale. Yet it is persuasive only if and in so far as club members share a common goal. In the recent round of trade negotiations Britain had to play along with the French line which was much more protectionist than our own. A prime example is trade in the audio-visual sector in which French brinkmanship put up barriers to United States products. Given a free hand, and taking account of our strong trade relationship with the United States, it is doubtful that we would have pursued such a course. We were, in other words, obliged to uphold a position directly in conflict with our own national interest. This is an inevitable consequence of being jammed into a common position – a consequence met especially often by Britain, whose interests tend to diverge from the continental mean far more than do those of other states.

Conflict situations do not make a cogent case for the EU's indispensability to us either. In the Falklands, we gained practical help from the United States and much vacillation from a number of our European partners. In the Gulf, the meeting of minds with our American allies was palpable and the prevarication of the EU equally so. As for the imbroglio in Bosnia, the less said about how the EU acquitted itself, the better.

De Gaulle long ago pinpointed the Franco-German relationship as the key fact in European politics. He said: 'there is an inter dependence between Germany and France. On that inter dependence depends the immediate security of the two peoples. One has only to look at a map to see this. On that inter dependence depends the destiny of Europe as a whole.' The partnership between France and Germany is akin to what is known as an open marriage. The partners row and are sometimes even unfaithful but they always return to each other because they need each other.

It is a rarely observed fact that some of the most fervent advocates of closer European integration pride themselves on being traditional Conservatives or, as they often prefer to be called, Tories. A hallmark of a traditional Tory is an innate suspicion of grand schemes, overarching theories and elaborate constructions of any kind. He is more comfortable with institutions and power that are rooted closer to home. He is a pragmatist who wants to see that an idea works. His is a natural scepticism which befits a Tory but there is sometimes scant evidence of it in the attitude of a number of my euro-enthusiastic colleagues. The mantra that 'there is no alternative' to the ratchet of euro integration will not wash. Neither will the attempt to induce the public to sleepwalk to federalism by telling them that it is 'inevitable'. Such an approach is disingenuous and a counsel of despair. There are alternatives. Parliamentarians owe it to their constituents honestly to address them.

Before doing so, let us remind ourselves of the situation we have reached. Continental leaders have long shared a federal or centralising agenda which British leaders either disbelieved or denied. The succession of European treaties has increased the powers of EU bodies and steadily reduced the spheres in which nation states can act alone. Our partners do not view a single currency as merely an economic device but as either a handmaiden or a tool of political union. Subsidiarity has proved at best an empty gesture and, at worst, a cloak for legislative expansion. Our EU membership imposes heavy costs on taxpayers and the Union's ambition to be a growing world power makes it a safe bet that those costs will rise. What can Britain do? We should seek a renegotiation of our relationship with the EU. That renegotiation should start from the premise that we will stay in the EU if we can strike a deal that is in our interests and pull out if we cannot. It is in that spirit that we should look at the alternatives to the status quo.

The alternatives

The European Economic Area

We could opt out of the EU, but remain within the European Economic Area. It comprises the 15 members of the EU as well as Iceland, Liechtenstein and Norway. It offers four freedoms of the Single Market – of goods, services, capital and people. Its members must adopt single market legislation but they are free of the CAP, the CFP, the fiscal and monetary policy, home affairs policy and foreign and security policy of the EU.

Its advantage is that Britain would not join in further political integration but would maintain access to the Single Market. However, we would have only a right to be consulted about future Single Market directives, and in disputes about the interpretation of such legislation we would be bound by the jurisprudence of the ECJ. We would also have to pay into a number of cohesion and structural funds. There are merits in the EEA option but given the jurisprudential ambition of the ECJ and the ballooning budgets of the EU there would be significant burdens too. There are probably better deals on offer.

The Swiss option

There is the Swiss option of a free trade agreement with the EU. Access to the Single Market entails more paperwork but the obstacles are not insuperable. Swiss exports to the EU constitute 63 per cent of its total exports and 15 per cent of Swiss GDP – much higher figures than ours. Growing trade for the Swiss has not required political integration and, importantly, they are not bound by single market legislation. What are the debits on the balance sheet? There are two. In trading with the EU, the Swiss have to adhere to preferential rules of origin to distinguish products sourced from the free trade area and those which originate outside it. In practice, these can be complex and burdensome. Secondly, the Swiss option provides only for free movement of goods – not of services, capital or people. This would jar with many British people and businesses. As an existing EU member, we could well obtain a different and better agreement.

NAFTA

A third option would be to seek to join the North American Free Trade Association. It is already negotiating with the European Free Trade Association and with Chile. Its culture, distinctively Thatcherite, fits more neatly with Britain's experience than the corporatist dirigisme of the EU. The combination of low taxes, restrained public spending and labour flexibility in the United States and Canada has created 2 million more jobs per year than the European Union for 15 years. Moreover, measured over the last 25 years and allowing for German unification, the US has created almost five times as many jobs as the EU. Newt Gingrich has signalled enthusiasm for British involvement in NAFTA, and as US anxieties about a fudged single currency and EU protectionism grow, the link becomes daily a more serious proposition.

No agreement

The other alternative is not to confine ourselves to one agreement but to use our position in the EU and our influence outside it to secure our interests. They are served by the widest possible free trade and international engagement. We have nothing to fear from global free trade, towards which the world is gradually moving, and everything to gain from it. William Hague has been right to challenge the EU to stop addressing the problems of the 1940s and to start addressing the challenges of the next millennium. The most central of those challenges for Britain is to build its trade relationships with North America, Asia Pacific and China.

Allied to a crusading internationalism in trade and diplomacy is the self-confidence to preserve our own institutions. Where other countries have suffered dictatorship, civil war or foreign occupation the British experience has fortunately been different. What some see as insularity by Britain is a justified attachment to the way in which we run our affairs. Napoleon said that a nation's policy is determined by its geography. If that is so we do well to remember that Britain is not at the heart of Europe but on its western edge.

Policy needs also to be determined by successful history and present need. In the spirit of liberty, democracy and the pursuit of prosperity, we need for the second time since 1945 to reverse a ratchet. Keith Joseph and Margaret Thatcher identified the socialist ratchet that undermined our prosperity at home, lowered our esteem abroad and sapped our faith in ourselves. They set out to reverse that ratchet and they succeeded. Today the task is to recognise that there is a ratchet for European integration. As the federalist juggernaut speeds ahead, ever more power is taken from the peoples of Europe and handed to unelected bankers, bureaucrats and judges.

The people of Britain will never knowingly consent to be governed by those who do not speak their language, live in their country or depend upon their votes. The power of self-government, the right to hire and fire our rulers and the capacity to chart our own destiny are inalienable birthrights. They should not be traded in for a mess of pottage otherwise known as a back-row seat at a show called 'The Heart of Europe'. Our destiny is surely as a self-governing nation which trades freely with the world. The future is bright; the future is global. Our success in it is dependent upon the vision, self-confidence and calibre of our leaders, our businesses and our workforce.

Index